SEDONA
HIKES

EIGHTH EDITION

By
Richard K. Mangum
and Sherry G. Mangum

PRESS

Look for Our Other Publications

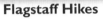

Flagstaff Hikes   **Flagstaff Historic Walk**

Route 66 Across Arizona

NONLIABILITY STATEMENT

While we have expended considerable effort to guarantee accuracy and have personally taken every one of these hikes, errors in field notes, transcription and typesetting can occur. Changes also occur on the land and some descriptions that were accurate when written may be inaccurate when you read this book. One storm, for example, can block a road, or the Forest Service can change a trail. In addition to the problems of accuracy, there is the problem of injury. It is always possible that hikers may sustain harm while on a hike. The authors, publishers and all those associated with this book, directly or indirectly, disclaim any liability for accidents, injuries, damages or losses whatsoever that may occur to anyone using this book. The responsibility for good health and safety while hiking is that of the user.

Produced by Santamaria Design Group
Cover Design by Joan Carstensen Design, Flagstaff
Cover Photo by Sherry G. Mangum:
Cathedral Rock

First Edition 1992   Fifth Edition 2000
Second Edition 1994   Sixth Edition 2001
Third Edition 1997 ·   Seventh Edition 2003
Fourth Edition 1998   Eighth Edition 2004

Table of Contents

About the Authors

Dick was born in Flagstaff and has lived there all his life. When his family acquired a second home in Back O' Beyond, south of Sedona, in 1951, he began his love affair with the redrock area. He learned that by driving 25 miles (the distance between Flagstaff and Sedona) the hiking enthusiast can hike year around: in cool Flagstaff in the summer and warm Sedona in the winter—and in either place in between.

After graduating from Flagstaff High School in 1954, he became a lawyer. He practiced law in Flagstaff for 15 years, then became a Superior Court Judge for Coconino County in 1976, retiring in 1993 to devote full time to hiking and writing.

Sherry has lived in Flagstaff since she was seven years old. The daughter of hiking parents, she has enjoyed getting into the outdoors from the time she was a toddler. She loves the scenic beauties of Sedona.

She also inherited a love of photography from her parents, both professional photographers. Adept at all aspects of photography, she prefers landscapes. Her work has been published in books and periodicals locally, nationally, and internationally, since 1978. Sherry has gone digital with this edition (images were taken with her Nikon D100) and has become a master of Adobe Photoshop™ which she uses to adjust her images for the best effect. She had to convert all of them from color to black and white for this edition.

Tips on Sedona Hiking

Access

Many of these hikes can be reached on paved roads. For hikes reached on unpaved roads, you need to pay attention to conditions. Some of the roads become slippery and impassable when they are wet. Some, such as the upper part of Schnebly Hill Road, are closed during the winter by locked gates. The table on page 11 shows which hikes require driving high clearance vehicles to the trailhead.

Rock Climbing

We do not provide any rock climbing information in this book. If you want to go rock climbing, you are on your own. Much of the rock around Sedona is sandstone, a notoriously unstable substance.

Thorns

It seems sometimes that every plant along the hiking paths in the Sedona area has thorns, spines or sharp-edged leaves. Pay attention. Learn to identify the fanged plants and avoid them.

Varmints

Sedona is in a life zone favorable to rattlesnakes. Even so, we have only seen a couple on all our hikes and received a warning buzz from several feet away. There are also some scorpions and black widow spiders in the area, though we have never seen either. Pests like mosquitoes are scarce. There are no chiggers nor swarming insects like black flies. Our advice about varmints is: be watchful but not paranoid.

Water

Do not count on finding drinking water on any of these trails. Take your water with you. In Sedona's hot dry climate you will need plenty of it.

Weather

Sedona is in a high desert location, at an elevation of about 4,500 feet. Its finest weather is from October to May. During the summer it can be quite hot, with many days over 100 degrees F. Some of the strenuous hikes can be exhausting in this kind of heat, so be forewarned. Wise hikers who want to get out in the summer will drive up Oak Creek Canyon and take one of the high altitude hikes that are available there.

How to Use This Book

Alphabetical arrangement. The 130 hikes in this book are arranged from A-Z.

Index. The index starts at page 255.

Layout. The text describing a hike is on the left-hand page, while a photo and the map of the hike are on the right-hand page so that you can take in everything at once without thumbing back and forth.

Maps. The maps are not to scale but their proportions are generally correct. The main purpose of the maps is to get you to the trailhead. The maps show mileage point-to-point. The text gives cumulative mileage.

Larger scale maps. For the big picture, the Forest Service provides maps and there are commercially produced maps as well.

Bold type. When you see a trail name in bold type it means that the hike is described in this book.

Ratings. We show hikes rated as easy, moderate and hard. We are middle-aged hikers in normal condition, not highly conditioned athletes who never tire. Hikers should adjust our ratings for their own fitness level. The hike-in-a-box on each map may best show how hard a hike is.

Mileage. Driving distances were measured from the **Sedona Y**, the junction of Highways 89A and 179. It doesn't look like a Y any more, as a road up the hill to the north was created in 2003, making it look like a +. Maybe Sedonans will stop calling the intersection the Y in the future, but for now we will still use the term. All hikes start from this point. Milepost locations are also shown on the maps (as MP) on highways that have mileposts.

Access roads. To reach many of these hikes, you will have to travel unpaved roads, some of them rough. Our vehicles have 4-wheel drive but we seldom have to use it if the roads are dry. Our access ratings were based on how well our cars handled the roads. Some drives require a high-clearance vehicle.

Safety. We avoid taking risks on our hikes. None of these hikes requires technical climbing.

Wilderness Areas. The Sedona area is blessed by having many of its hiking places included within federally designated Wilderness Areas. This is great for the hiker, as Wilderness areas are open to foot traffic, while being closed to bikes and motor vehicles.

Cairns. These are stacks of rocks used as trail markers. Some are officially placed and wrapped with wire, while others are made by hikers.

Mileposts. Major Arizona highways are marked every mile by an oval green sign with white lettering—size about three feet high—on the right side of the road on most paved highways. These are handy markers.

Crowds. We show how crowded a trail is likely to be by the number of hiker symbols there are on the trail map, on the line depicting the trail itself. The scale is 1-5, with 1 being the least crowded. Weekends produce the biggest crowds, especially holiday weekends.

Handy Charts and Data

Hours of Daylight

	JAN	FEB	MAR	APR	MAY	JUN	JUL	AUG	SEP	OCT	NOV	DEC
SUNRISE	7:35	7:26	6:57	6:14	5:36	5:14	5:16	5:35	5:59	6:21	6:48	7:16
SUNSET	5:26	5:55	6:22	6:48	7:12	7:35	7:45	7:30	6:54	6:11	5:33	5:15

Normal Precipitation—Inches

JAN	FEB	MAR	APR	MAY	JUN	JUL	AUG	SEP	OCT	NOV	DEC
1.70	1.54	1.67	1.17	0.56	0.49	1.89	2.42	1.51	1.16	1.32	1.73

Normal Temperatures F—High and Low

JAN	FEB	MAR	APR	MAY	JUN	JUL	AUG	SEP	OCT	NOV	DEC
55	59	63	72	81	90	95	92	88	78	65	56
30	32	35	42	49	57	65	64	58	48	37	30

Converting Feet to Meters

Meters	910	1212	1515	1818	2121	2424	2727	3030	3333	3636
Feet	3000	4000	5000	6000	7000	8000	9000	10000	11000	12000

Average Walking Rates

Time	1 Hour	30 Min.	15 Min.	7.5 Min.
Miles	2.0	1.0	0.5	0.25
KM	3.2	1.6	0.8	0.4

Our Personal Favorite Hikes Are Marked With This Symbol

Hike Locator

Hike Locator Map

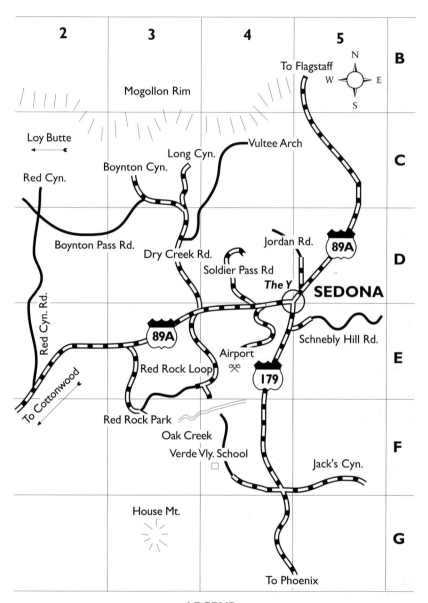

LEGEND

Paved Road ▬▬▬▬

Unpaved Road ▬▬▬

The map starts with Row B and Column 2 so that places beyond the map can be indicated in the articles

Hikes Rated by Difficulty

Length in miles is shown, but other factors enter into our ratings, such as steepness, etc.

Easy
Allen's Bend—0.5
Boynton Vista—0.75
Carruth— 0.9 Loop
Cibola Pass—2.25
Coffee Pot—1.0
Cow Pies—1.5
Crescent Moon—1.0
Honanki—0.25
H. T. Trail—1.25
Jail Trail—0.5
Lower Chimney Rock Loop—1.5
Mystic—1.0
Overlook—0.7
Palatki—0.6/0.3
Red Rock State Park Mixed
Robbers' Roost—1.5
Sedona Cent.—0.5
Slide Rock—Mixed
Submarine Rock—1.0
Sunrise—1.2
Thunder Mtn.—2.0
Two Fences—2.1
Van Deren Cabin—0.5
V-Bar-V—1.1 Loop
West Clear Creek—1.5

Moderate
Airport Loop—3.6
Arizona Cypress—2.7
Baldwin—1.75
Bandit—0.9
Bear Sign—3.2
Bell Rock—0.5/0.7
Bell Rock Pathway—3.7
Big Park Loop—2.6
Boynton Canyon—3.75
Brewer—1.0

Brins Mesa—4.3
Broken Arrow—1.5
Carroll Canyon—4.3 Loop
Chapel—2.4
Chimney Rock Pass—2.25
Cockscomb Butte—0.75
Cockscomb Trail—3.0
Courthouse Butte—4.3 Loop
Dawa—2.5 Loop
Dead Horse Ranch—mix
Deadman Pass—1.4
Devil's Bridge—1.0
Doe Mountain—1.8
Dry Creek—2.0
Fay Canyon—1.2
Herkenham—2.0
HS Canyon—2.0
Jim Thompson—3.0
Jordan—1.5
Kel Fox—2.0
Lime Kiln—2.8
Little Horse—2.2
Llama—2.75 Loop
Long Canyon #122—3.0
Lost Canyon—2.2
Margs Draw—1.4/2.0
Mescal Mtn.—2.5
Mitten Ridge—2.5
Old Post—3.0
Parsons—3.7
Pumphouse Wash—1.5
Rabbit Ears—2.75
Raptor Hill—2.8
Rattlesnake Cyn.—1.0
Red Rock Loop—1.8
Rupp Trail—2.0
Sacred Mt.—0.5
Schuerman Mtn.—1.1
Soldier Pass Arches—1.5
Soldier Pass Trail—2.2
Sugarloaf Loop—2.2

Summit Route—0.7
Table Top—1.9
Tavasci Marsh—1.0
Teacup—1.6
Templeton—3.5
Verde River Greenway—1.0
Twin Pillars—1.0
Vultee Arch—1.6
Weir Trail—3.0
West Fork—3.0
Wilson Canyon—1.5
Woods Canyon—3.25

Hard
A. B. Young—1.6
Apache Maid—4.2
Bear Mountain—2.4
Beaverhead—2.0
Bell Trail—6.8
Casner Canyon—3.0
Casner Mtn. South—2.0
Cathedral Rock—0.7
Cookstove—0.75
David Miller—7.3 Loop
Dogie—5.4
Girdner—5.0
Harding Spring—0.8
Hot Loop—3.0
Huckaby—3.0
Jack's Canyon—5.0
Long Canyon #63—2.5
Loy Canyon—4.0
Mooney—4.5
Munds Mtn.—2.9
Munds Wagon—4.5
Purtymun—1.0
Ridge—2.3
Schnebly Hill—2.4
Secret Canyon—5.5
Sterling Pass—1.65
Telephone—1.25
Thomas Point—1.5
Turkey Creek—3.5
White Mesa—2.4
Wilson Mtn. North—4.3
Wilson Mtn. South—5.3

Driving Distance to Trailhead

Bold Type=High Clearance vehicle recommended

5 Miles or Less
Airport Loop—1.5
Allen's Bend—2.3
Bandit—2.6
Brewer—1.5
Brins Mesa—1.9
Broken Arrow—2.1
Carroll Cyn.—2.6
Carruth—2.1
Cathedral Rock—4.1
Chapel—3.6
Chimney Rock—4.3
Cibola Pass—1.9
Coffee Pot—2.85
Cow Pies—3.8
Girdner—4.4
H. T. Trail—3.6
Huckaby—1.3
Jim Thompson—1.9
Jordan—1.9
Little Horse—3.6
Llama—4.4
Lower Chimney Rock—4.3
Marg's Draw—0.9
Mitten Ridge—3.8
Munds Wagon—1.3
Mystic—3.1
Overlook Point—1.5
Ridge Trail—2.6
Schuerman Mtn.—4.5
Sedona Cent.—4.4
Soldier Pass Arches—3.0
Soldier Pass Tr.—3.0
Submarine Rock—2.1
Sugarloaf Loop—2.85
Summit Route—4.3
Sunrise—1.5
Table Top—2.6
Teacup—3.0
Templeton—4.7
Thunder Mtn.—4.3
Wilson Cyn.—1.1
Wilson Mtn. South—1.1

5-10 Miles
A. B. Young—8.8
Arizona Cypress—5.2
Bear Mtn.—8.9
Bear Sign—9.6
Bell Rock—5.2
Bell Rock Pathway—6.2
Big Park Loop—6.2
Boynton Cyn.—7.8
Boynton Cyn. Vista—7.8
Casner Cyn.—6.6
Cockscomb Trail—8.2
Courthouse Butte—6.2
Crescent Moon—7.0
David Miller—8.6
Dawa—6.7
Deadman Pass—7.8
Devil's Bridge—6.5
Doe Mtn.—8.9
Dry Creek—9.6
Fay Cyn.—8.2
Herkenham—6.2
Hot Loop—9.4
H. S. Cyn.—8.6
Jacks Cyn.—9.4
Long Cyn. #122—6.7
Lost Canyon—7.7
Mescal Mtn.—6.7
Munds Mtn.—6.6
Old Post—6.2
Purtymun—8.5
Rabbit Ears—9.4
Red Rock Loop—5.9
Red Rock State Park—8.8
Schnebly Hill—5.5
Secret Canyon—8.6
Slide Rock—6.9
Sterling Pass—6.2
Two Fences—5.2
Van Deren Cabin—7.7

10-20 Miles
Apache Maid—17.0
Baldwin—11.3
Beaverhead—11.2
Bell Trail—17.0
Casner Mtn. South—19.0
Cockscomb Butte—10.7
Cookstove—12.7
Harding Spring—11.4
Honanki—16.2
Kel Fox—12.6
Long Cyn. #63—18.0
Loy Cyn.—15.5
Palatki—13.5
Pumphouse Wash—13.5
Robbers Roost—18.8
Rupp Trail—10.7
Sacred Mtn.—18.1
Telephone—10.9
Thomas Point—10.5
Turkey Creek—11.9
Twin Pillars—11.9
V-Bar-V—17.4
Weir Trail—17.0
West Fork—10.5
White Mesa—17.0

More Than 20 Miles
Dead Horse—21.5
Dogie—20.3
Jail Trail—20.1
Lime Kiln—22.4
Mooney—20.9
Parsons—34.3
Raptor Hill—21.5
Rattlesnake Cyn.—23.0
West Clear Creek—29.5

Vultee Arch—9.6
Wilson Mtn. North—5.3
Woods Cyn.—8.7

Master Trail Map of

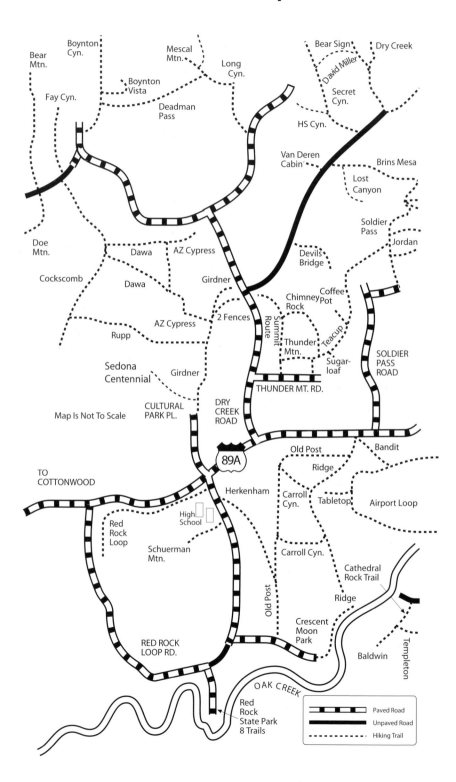

Trails Closest to Sedona

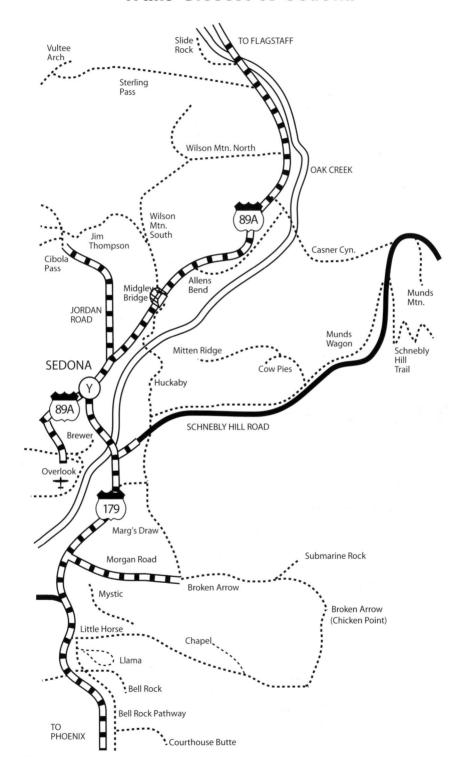

Oak Creek Canyon Recreation Sites

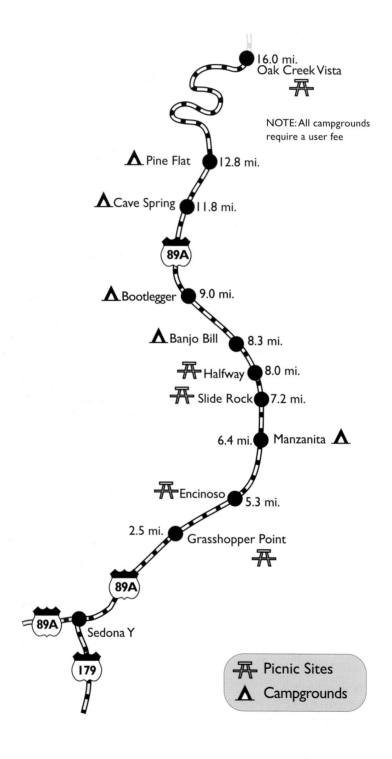

16.0 mi.
Oak Creek Vista

NOTE: All campgrounds require a user fee

Pine Flat 12.8 mi.

Cave Spring 11.8 mi.

89A

Bootlegger 9.0 mi.

Banjo Bill 8.3 mi.

Halfway 8.0 mi.

Slide Rock 7.2 mi.

6.4 mi. Manzanita

Encinoso 5.3 mi.

2.5 mi. Grasshopper Point

89A

89A Sedona Y

179

Picnic Sites
Campgrounds

Changes for this Edition

Our first edition of this book appeared in 1992 using a format that we have followed ever since: a complete description of each hike on facing pages, with the text on the left-hand page and the top of the right-hand page and a map on the bottom of the right-hand page. This was embellished with a color section in the middle of the book to give readers an idea of what some of the places described in the book look like.

In this, our 8th edition, we have taken a giant step forward. If it is true that a picture is worth a thousand words, then we have added more than 100,000 words to the book at the same time that we reduced the amount of text. How can this be? By the inclusion of a photograph of each trail above the trail map. We think this will give users a much better idea of what they will find on a trail. In order to make room for the photos we had to increase the size of the book, from 8½ x 5½ to 9 x 6. Then we had to reduce the amount of text so that it all fit on the left-hand page and left room for a photo caption.

The change required us to revisit the trails so that Sherry could photograph them for the book. Most of this work was done in the winter of 2003-2004, so you will see Dick wearing a jacket in many of the shots. Dick was the model, not because of his looks but because he was available. Sherry suffered the lot of all photographers: when you are behind the camera, you are never in the picture. We think the results of all this hard work are worthwhile because the photos have made the book more useful and more enjoyable and they will help hikers in making their selections. We removed the center color section because we felt that it was no longer necessary, and color is very expensive. By removing the color section we are able to keep the price of the book low.

We deleted the Page Springs Creekside Walk (not worth the long drive), Oak Creek-Verde Confluence (the area is filling up with homes), and the wonderful Rachel's Knoll (closed), the Goosenecks (too hard to find) and Hidden Cabin (too hard to find). We added the Llama Trail, the Sedona Centennial Trail and the Weir Trail, all of which are system trails. The Llama Trail is under construction but should be finished by the time you have this book in your hands. By popular demand we have returned two hikes formerly in the book: Lost Canyon and Pumphouse Wash.

The Forest Service has worked on some of the trailheads but has not done much new trail construction since our last issue. We consult with these helpful people in order to keep up with the Sedona trail situation. They have plans for more trails and trailheads, so we will keep readers informed of changes.

Sedona continues to be a very active hiking destination, with thousands of visitors enjoying its wealth of trail experiences. This book will open the treasure chest of Sedona hiking for you. We hope you like it!

A. B. Young Trail #100

General Information
Location Map B5
Munds Park and Wilson Mt. USGS Maps
Coconino Forest Service Map

Driving Distance One Way: 8.8 miles *14.0 km* (Time 20 minutes)
Access Road: All cars, Paved all the way
Hiking Distance One Way: 1.6 miles *2.6 km* (Time 80 minutes)
How Strenuous: Hard
Features: Views

NUTSHELL: This is a steep trail up the west wall of Upper Oak Creek Canyon near Bootlegger Campground in upper Oak Creek Canyon.

DIRECTIONS:
From the Sedona Y (the intersection of Highways 179 and 89A) Go:
North on Highway 89A for 8.8 miles *14.0 km* (MP 383) to the Bootlegger Campground **(1)**. Forget about parking inside the campground. Go past it slightly and park on the shoulder on the right-hand side of Highway 89A.

TRAILHEAD: Walk through Bootlegger Campground, where you will see a set of steps going down to the creek. You must wade or try to hop across the creek on boulders. There is a trailhead on the other shore, marked with a sign.

DESCRIPTION: Once you get across the creek you will see an old road running parallel to the creek. This old road was formerly the main road through Oak Creek Canyon and it is not the hiking trail. Your trail goes uphill.

The trail started its life as a cattle path, but was improved during the 1930s with CCC labor. It is very steep.

An interesting thing about the hike is that you pass through three life zones. Down at the creek, there is the lush riparian life zone. As you begin to climb, you get into a high desert life zone. At the top, you are in a pine forest. Once you rise above the trees at creekside, you are on an exposed face with no shade—a very hot hike in the summer.

You get some fine views as you go. At the top, you will notice that the trail continues. For the purposes of this book, we have ended the trail at the top, but you can continue southwest about 1.25 miles *2.0 km* to the East Pocket fire lookout tower. If this tower is occupied, the ranger may be willing to have you come up and share the tremendous views. This part of the rim is called East Pocket.

Photo: The distinctive zigzag lines made by the A. B. Young Trail as it makes its way up the canyon wall are clearly visible here.

A. B. Young Trail #100

Elevation
6800
5200

| Miles: 1.6 | Hard |

Elevation change 1600 ft.

N

WILDERNESS REDROCK/SECRET MOUNTAIN

WEATHER
Spring: Good
Summer: OK many days
Fall: Good
Winter: Poor, snowy
REPORT

1.6 mi.

T

Oak Creek

Bootlegger
Campground

Sedona
8.8 mi.
89A
MP 383
P

Y

Driving Distance One Way, Miles: 8.8
Hiking Distance One Way, Miles: 1.6

Airport Loop Trail

General Information
Location Map E4
Sedona USGS Map
Coconino Forest Service Map

Driving Distance One Way: 1.5 miles *2.4 km* (Time 10 minutes)
Access Road: All cars, Paved all the way
Hiking Distance, Complete Loop: 3.6 miles *5.8 km* (Time 2 hours)
How Strenuous: Moderate
Features: 360-degree views

NUTSHELL: This trail takes you around the circumference of Airport Mesa, so that you see all of Sedona.

DIRECTIONS:
From the Sedona Y (the intersection of Highways 179 and 89A) Go:
Southwest on Highway 89A for 1.0 mile *1.6 km,* to Airport Road **(1)**. Turn left onto Airport Road and drive uphill to the 1.5 mile *2.4 km* point where you turn left into the parking lot.

TRAILHEAD: At the 3-panel trailhead sign.

DESCRIPTION: Walk uphill on the main **Overlook Point Trail**. When you reach the crest, turn to your right, and you will see the Airport Loop Trail running along the side of the mesa.

The trail hugs the 4600-foot contour on Airport Mesa. It circles the mesa and gives you open views, so this is a great scenic hike. At first you hike along the southeast face of the mesa, looking down on Oak Creek and the Bell Rock area. At about 1.5 miles *2.4 km* you reach the end of this face of the mesa on a toe.

You then curve around to the north and at 1.6 miles *2.6 km* reach the **Table Top Trail** junction. Here the airport fence is to your right and you are near the end of the runway.

At 2.3 miles *3.7 km* the trail dips and you will see Bandit's grave on the right side of the trail where there is a metal cross and a mound of stones. We surmise that Bandit was a well-beloved dog. A short distance farther you will reach the intersection with the **Bandit Trail**, coming in to your left. Pass this and keep going around the mesa. The trail rises.

At 3.6 miles *5.8 km* you return to the airport road directly across from the parking lot where you began. The end seems unfinished, as the trail abruptly stops where it bangs into a guardrail. There are no trail signs here. Hop over the guardrail and walk across the road to the parking lot.

Photo: The Airport Loop Trail is wide open in most places, with very little shrubbery to block the views. This makes it a fine choice for viewing the Sedona area as you circle the mesa.

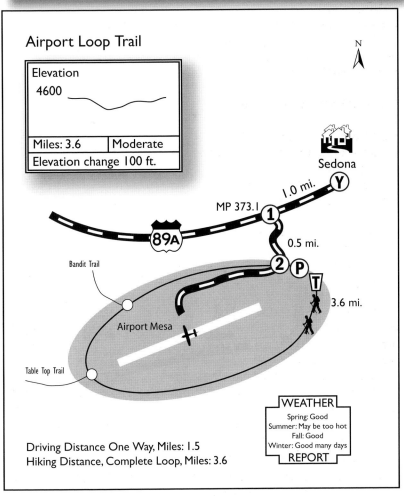

Airport Loop Trail

N

Elevation
4600

| Miles: 3.6 | Moderate |
| Elevation change 100 ft. | |

Sedona

1.0 mi.

Y

MP 373.1

89A

1

0.5 mi.

2 P T

3.6 mi.

Bandit Trail

Airport Mesa

Table Top Trail

WEATHER
Spring: Good
Summer: May be too hot
Fall: Good
Winter: Good many days
REPORT

Driving Distance One Way, Miles: 1.5
Hiking Distance, Complete Loop, Miles: 3.6

Allen's Bend Trail #111

General Information
Location Map D5
Munds Park USGS Map
Coconino Forest Service Map

Driving Distance One Way: 2.3 miles *3.7 km* (Time 10 minutes)
Access Road: All cars, Paved all the way
Hiking Distance One Way: 0.5 miles *0.8 km* (Time 30 minutes)
How Strenuous: Easy
Features: Creekside walk, Small Indian ruin, easy to reach, natural "sidewalk"

NUTSHELL: An easy, yet delightful ramble with Oak Creek on one side and red cliffs on the other.

DIRECTIONS:
From the Sedona Y (the intersection of Highways 179 and 89A) Go:
   North on Highway 89A 2.3 miles *3.7 km* (MP 376.5) then turn right into the Grasshopper Point Recreation Area **(1)**. You must pay a fee at the entry hut. There is no offsite parking.

TRAILHEAD: At the two-panel trailhead map/sign by the picnic tables on the lower lot. There is a toilet at the parking area.

DESCRIPTION: The ticket booth is sometimes staffed; at other times you self-pay at a dispenser. If the lower lot is open, drive down a paved road to a parking lot that has capacity for a couple of dozen cars. It also has a toilet.
   From the lower lot the signed trailhead is easily visible. The trail does not go down toward Oak Creek. Instead, it hugs the west wall of the canyon. At first it moves along the base of redrock cliffs along a redrock ledge where stones have been mortared into place to pave the trail and to make steps. The creek is to your right (E) at all times, anywhere from 20 to 100 yards away. The trail is shaded all the way and the creek—if by nothing other than its sound—offers refreshment. This is a good trail when the weather is too hot for more exposed hikes.
   There are several unofficial side trails going to the creek, which you may try. About midway the trail moves away from the cliffs onto a broad open area where there was an orchard. Look to your left here for a small Indian ruin in a shallow cave.
   At 0.4 miles *0.6 km* you reach a fork. The official trail goes left, uphill, while the unofficial trail goes down to the creek. Take the left fork, where you will enter a leveled area that was formerly a campground. The trail ends here, where it joints the **Casner Canyon** trail.

Photo: Being able to walk alongside this interesting redrock cliff is one of the delights of this easy trail. You also walk close Oak Creek and can easily get to the water.

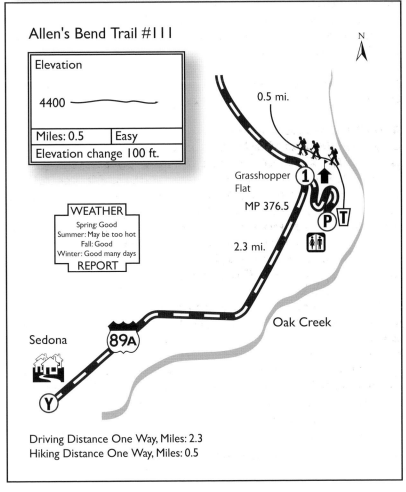

Allen's Bend Trail #111

Elevation	
4400 —	
Miles: 0.5	Easy
Elevation change 100 ft.	

N

0.5 mi.

Grasshopper Flat

MP 376.5

2.3 mi.

WEATHER
Spring: Good
Summer: May be too hot
Fall: Good
Winter: Good many days
REPORT

Oak Creek

Sedona

89A

Y

Driving Distance One Way, Miles: 2.3
Hiking Distance One Way, Miles: 0.5

Apache Maid Trail #15

General Information
Location Map G6
Casner Butte and Apache Maid USGS Maps
Coconino Forest Service Map

Driving Distance One Way: 17.0 miles *27.2 km* (Time 30 minutes)
Access Road: All cars, Last 0.1 mile *0.2 km* is a good gravel road
Hiking Distance One Way: 4.2 miles *6.72 km* (Time 2.5 hours)
How Strenuous: Hard
Features: Views of Wet Beaver Creek country, Rock Art

NUTSHELL: You hike the Bell Trail for 2.2 miles *3.5 km* and then branch off to climb this old cattle trail to the top of Casner Butte south of Sedona.

DIRECTIONS:
From the Sedona Y (the intersection of Highways 179 and 89A) Go:
   South on Highway 179 (toward Phoenix) for 14.7 miles *23.5 km* (MP 298.9), to the I-17 intersection **(1)**. Go straight here rather than getting on I-17. Follow paved road FR 618 until you see a sign for Beaver Creek Ranger Station and trailheads at 16.9 miles *27.1 km* **(2)**. Turn left. The new (opened in the spring of 2004) parking lot is at 17.0 miles *27.2 km*.

TRAILHEAD: Signed and marked at the parking lot.

DESCRIPTION: From the trailhead, you hike the Bell Trail. It goes up the canyon along Wet Beaver Creek, sometimes near it, sometimes away from it, but always following its path. Even when you are not near the creek, you can hear water running, a pleasant sound in desert country. The waterway is lined with tall sycamores and cottonwoods.
   The trail is an old jeep road, broad and easy to walk. As you go along the trail, note the canyon walls: they contain the same redrock as in Sedona in the lower layers but the top is covered with a thick cap of lava. If it weren't for that top layer of hard rock, this country would be just as eroded and colorful as Sedona. At 0.8 miles *1.2 km*, look for a large boulder on the left side of the trail for some nice rock art. It's on the side facing away from you.
   At the 2.2 mile *3.5 km* point you will hit a fork where the Apache Maid Trail #15 branches to the left and climbs Casner Butte. Please enter your name in the trail log. The trail makes a steep climb, rising about 1,400 feet in 2.0 miles *3.2 km* to our recommended stopping point. You will be rewarded by good views at the top, but the trail itself is not very interesting. The trail continues for miles, but we recommend stopping where you top out or perhaps just cruising along the rim for the views.

Photo: There is a logbook at the trail junction where the Apache Maid Trail starts. Here you leave the relatively flat Bell Trail and begin a steep climb.

Apache Maid Trail #15

Elevation

5400

4000

Miles: 4.2	Hard
Elevation change 1400 ft.	

WEATHER
Spring: Good
Summer: Will be too hot
Fall: Good
Winter: Good many days
REPORT

Sedona

Y

179 MP 298.9 **17**

14.7 mi. **1**

WET BEAVER CREEK WILDERNESS

To Montezuma Well

618

2.2 mi.

2

Bell Trail TH
White Mesa TH
Apache Maid TH
Weir Trail TH

2.0 mi.

0.1 mi. **P** **T**

2.2 mi.

Driving Distance One Way, Miles: 17.0
Hiking Distance One Way, Miles: 4.2

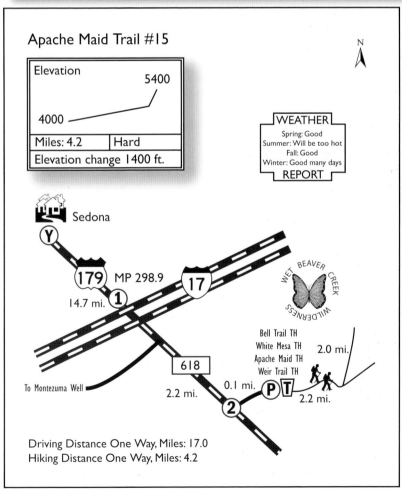

Arizona Cypress Trail

General Information
Location Map D3
Loy Butte and Wilson Mt. USGS Maps
Coconino Forest Service Map

Driving Distance One Way: 5.2 miles *8.3 km* (Time 15 minutes)
Access Road: All paved
Hiking Distance One Way: 2.7 miles *4.3 km* (Time 1.25 hours)
How Strenuous: Moderate
Features: Interesting ramble through the Dry Creek Canyon area.

NUTSHELL: Located near Sedona on good paved roads, this trail winds around an interesting area, passing through stands of Arizona Cypress trees. It connects to other trails.

DIRECTIONS:
From the Sedona Y (the intersection of Highways 179 and 89A) Go:
Southwest on Highway 89A (toward Cottonwood) for 3.2 miles *5.1 km* (MP 371) to Dry Creek Road **(1)**. Turn right on Dry Creek Road and drive to the 5.2 mile *8.3 km* point, where FR 152, the Vultee Arch Road, branches off to the right **(2)**. Don't take the Vultee Arch Road. Look to your left, below the road, and you will see a small trail sign on a post. Park at the side of the road as near to this sign as you can get **(P)**. There is no designated parking.

TRAILHEAD: Start at the **Girdner Trail** at the sign mentioned above.

DESCRIPTION: At 1.1 miles *1.8 km* you will pass the trailhead for the **Two Fences** trail, reaching the start of the Arizona Cypress trail at the 1.25 mile *2.0 km* point.
　　You turn right (NW), hugging the base of a large hill. Soon you cross over a small wash and after that will reach Dry Creek. From this point the trail follows the course of Dry Creek until the end, crossing Dry Creek four times. You walk through an Arizona Cypress forest here, the trees marked by their bark, which scales off in curly shreds.
　　At 1.75 miles *2.8 km* you reach a marker for the **Dawa Trail**, to your left. At 2.1 miles *3.4 km* you will find the marker for the **OK Trail**. Soon after this you will see that you are walking along an old jeep road.
　　The end of the trail, at a barbed wire fence with a stepover gate and trail sign, is at 2.7 miles *4.3 km*–a funny place to end because it is nowhere, just a point on the road. There is no parking area nor directional signs. If you walk the road for 0.5 miles *0.8 km* you will come out on the Dry Creek Road a few feet south of the stop sign at the Long Canyon Road junction.

Photo: Parts of this trail cross a creekbed, which is usually dry, and take you through an impressive Arizona Cypress forest.

Arizona Cypress Trail

Elevation
4600 ⌇⌇⌇

Miles: 2.7	Moderate
Elevation change 200 ft.	

N

WEATHER
Spring: Good
Summer: May be too hot
Fall: Good
Winter: Good many days
REPORT

OK Trail

Dawa Trail

Arizona Cypress
0.6 mi.

Cockscomb Trail

0.35
Arizona Cypress

Dawa Trail

0.5 mi.

Girdner Trail

P

Vultee Arch Road

152

Dry Creek Road

Cockscomb Trail

Arizona Cypress

0.15

1.1 mi.

T

2

Two Fences Trail

2.0 mi.

Girdner Trail

Sedona

Stop
Light

Y

89A

1

3.2 mi.

MP 371

Driving Distance One Way, Miles: 5.2
Hiking Distance One Way, Miles: 2.7

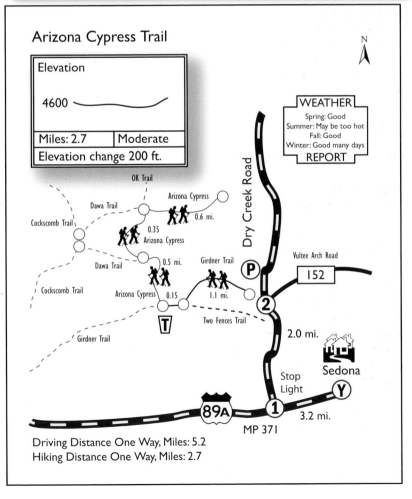

Baldwin Trail

General Information
Location Map F4
Sedona USGS Map
Coconino Forest Service Map

Driving Distance One Way: 11.3 miles *18.1 km* (Time 30 minutes)
Access Road: All cars, Last 1.0 miles *1.6 km* good dirt road
Hiking Distance One Way: 1.75 miles *2.8 km* (Time 1 hour)
How Strenuous: Moderate
Features: Rock formations, Views, Oak Creek

NUTSHELL: You hike along the face of Cathedral Rock to Oak Creek; then curve around a redrock butte to join the Verde Valley School Road.

DIRECTIONS:
From the Sedona Y (the intersection of Highways 179 and 89A) Go:
    South on Highway 179 (toward Phoenix) for 7.2 miles *11.5 km* (MP 306.1), to the Verde Valley School Road, where there is a stoplight **(1)**. Turn right (W) onto Verde Valley School Road. Follow it to the 11.3 mile *18.1 km* point where there is a sign marking the **Turkey Creek Trail (2)**. Just beyond the sign you will see FR 9216B, a dirt road to your left **(3)**. Take FR 9216B, turning left into the first parking area.

TRAILHEAD: Walk back to the main road, cross it, and turn to your right (SE). Walk the road for 250 paces until you see the trail marker to your left.

DESCRIPTION: You will see massive Cathedral Rock, one of the favorite, most-photographed of all Sedona landmarks, to the northeast as you start. To your left is a smaller, round-topped red butte. The trail goes through a pass between these two formations.
    The approach to the pass is fairly level until you get to the area between the buttes, where it moves up and down a bit, but nothing very difficult. There is a profusion of social trails here, so follow the markers.
    At 1.25 miles *2.0 km*, you emerge through the pass, go through a fence and meet the end of the **Templeton Trail**. Turn left. You will hear the sound of nearby Oak Creek, but will never go to the water. At 1.4 miles *2.2 km* take the left fork up, marked with an arrow, rather than going down to the right, toward the water. The correct trail hugs the base of the redrock butte.
    At 1.75 miles *2.8 km* you meet the Verde Valley School Road. You can backtrack for a total hike of 3.5 miles *5.6 km*, or you can turn to the left and walk the road to your car for a loop of 2.5 miles *4.0 km*. If you walk the road, be careful because there are blind spots.

Photo: The Baldwin Trail is in the area of Cathedral Rock, one of the most photographed of all Sedona landmarks. You are treated to superb views of the rock such as the one Sherry took here, using junipers as a frame.

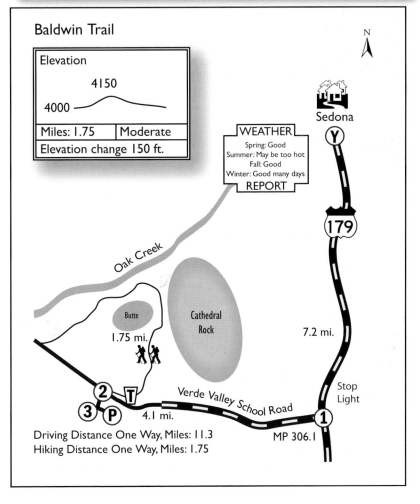

Baldwin Trail

Elevation

4150

4000 ———

| Miles: 1.75 | Moderate |
| Elevation change 150 ft. | |

N

WEATHER
Spring: Good
Summer: May be too hot
Fall: Good
Winter: Good many days
REPORT

Sedona

Y

179

Oak Creek

Butte

Cathedral
Rock

1.75 mi.

7.2 mi.

Verde Valley School Road

2
3 P
T

4.1 mi.

Stop
Light

1

MP 306.1

Driving Distance One Way, Miles: 11.3
Hiking Distance One Way, Miles: 1.75

Bandit Trail

General Information
Location Map E4
Sedona USGS Map
Coconino Forest Service Map

Driving Distance One Way: 2.6 miles *4.2 km* (Time 10 minutes)
Access Road: All cars, Paved all the way
Hiking Distance One Way: 0.9 miles *1.4 km* (Time 35 minutes)
How Strenuous: Moderate
Features: Views, Near town, Interesting pet grave

NUTSHELL: This short trail takes you up onto the hip of Airport Mesa and connects with the **Airport Loop Trail**, giving you access to a trail system.

DIRECTIONS:
From the Sedona Y (the intersection of Highways 179 and 89A) Go:
 Southwest on Highway 89A for 2.1 miles *3.4 km*, to a stoplight **(1)**. Turn left on Shelby Drive, go 0.5 miles *0.8 km* (just past Stanley Steamer) and turn right into the parking lot of the La Entrada, at 2155 Shelby Drive. At the back of the parking lot are three trailhead parking signs. Park at one of them.

TRAILHEAD: Just off the parking lot, where there is a sign and map.

DESCRIPTION: As you walk the trail you will almost immediately come to the junction with the **Old Post Trail**, going to your right. Soon after this you will reach the junction where the Bandit Trail starts, marked with a trail sign, where you turn to the left.
 The Bandit Trail then skirts the boundary of private land, bringing you up close to the fence around a storage yard, where you cross a drainage ditch. This is an ugly, industrial part of the trail. Then you begin to climb, making a steep ascent on to the shoulder of Airport Mesa, and moving away from the buildings. At 0.6 miles *1.0 km* you will intersect the **Airport Loop Trail**.
 This is the official end of the Bandit Trail, but it isn't much of a hike to this point. From the trail junction you have nice views of West Sedona, but otherwise the trail has only been a warm-up. We recommend that you continue for a while longer, making the brief climb to Bandit's grave, so that you can see how the trail got its name.
 Turn to the right, still climbing, on the joint Airport Loop trail. At 0.9 miles *1.4 km* to your left at the side of the trail you will find a metal cross with a nameplate reading "Bandit" and a small mound of stones. There is nothing more to explain the site, but it would seem that Bandit was a well-loved pet. This is where we recommend that hikers end the Bandit Trail.

Photo: This is Bandit's Grave, a touching monument to a beloved pet. Ironically, it is not on the Bandit Trail, although you will hike the Bandit Trail to reach it.

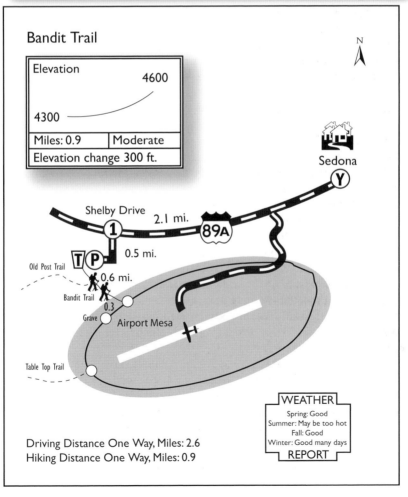

Bandit Trail

N

Elevation	
4300 ———	4600
Miles: 0.9	Moderate
Elevation change 300 ft.	

Sedona

Y

Shelby Drive   2.1 mi.

1   **89A**

0.5 mi.

Old Post Trail

T P

0.6 mi.

Bandit Trail

0.3

Grave   Airport Mesa

Table Top Trail

Driving Distance One Way, Miles: 2.6
Hiking Distance One Way, Miles: 0.9

WEATHER
Spring: Good
Summer: May be too hot
Fall: Good
Winter: Good many days
REPORT

Bear Mountain Trail #54

General Information
Location Map C2
Wilson Mountain USGS Map
Coconino Forest Service Map

Driving Distance One Way: 8.9 miles *14.3 km* (Time 20 minutes)
Access Road: All cars, Last 1.2 miles *2.0 km* bumpy dirt road
Hiking Distance One Way: 2.4 miles *3.8 km* (Time 2 hours)
How Strenuous: Hard, Very steep
Features: Views, Redrocks

NUTSHELL: We enjoy this hike because it is one of the best for getting into the redrock cliffs that characterize Sedona. The views are terrific. **A personal favorite**.

DIRECTIONS:
From the Sedona Y (the intersection of Highways 179 and 89A) Go:
    SW on Highway 89A (toward Cottonwood) for 3.2 miles *5.1 km* (MP 371) then turn right on Dry Creek Road **(1)** taking it to the 6.1 mile *9.8 km* point, where Dry Creek Road joins the Long Canyon Road **(2)**. Turn left on FR 152C and go to the 7.7 mile *12.3 km point*, where it joins the Boynton Canyon Road **(3)**. Turn left on the Boynton Pass Road, FR 152C, a bumpy dirt road. Stop at the 8.9 mile *14.3 km* point, just before a cattle guard. Parking is on the right.

TRAILHEAD: The Bear Mt. Trail shares its parking space with the **Doe Mt. Trail**, and you will see signs for both trails there. Crawl through the "window frame" in the fence to begin the Bear Mt. Trail #54.

DESCRIPTION: We think of this hike as having two levels, the red level and the white level. You first hike across flat land, crossing three gullies, to the base of the mountain. Then you make a stiffish climb to the top of the red level. We love this part because you are right in amongst the redrocks for close views of superb redrock formations.

    You walk around the base of the redrock cliffs and then make another steep climb up to the white level. The trail up to the white level is quite interesting. As you begin it, you think, "I can't get there from here." But you can. Once on top of the white level you are above the redrock. There is nothing much to see at hand, but there are breathtaking views of the redrock below you from the rim. The trail winds through low-growing manzanita shrubs to end on a knob from which you will have jaw-dropping views in all directions.

Photo: One of the delights of this fine trail is being able to touch some of the interesting rock formations.

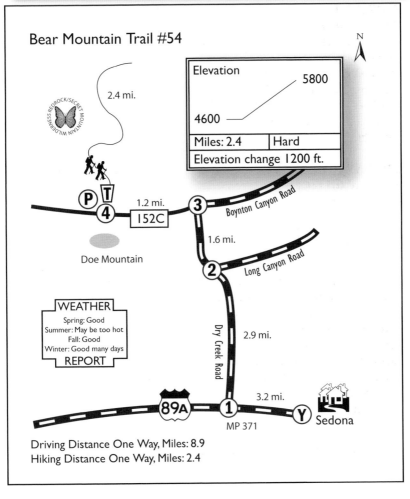

Bear Mountain Trail #54

N

2.4 mi.

REDROCK/SECRET MOUNTAIN WILDERNESS

Elevation	
5800	
4600	
Miles: 2.4	Hard
Elevation change 1200 ft.	

P T
4
152C   1.2 mi.   3   Boynton Canyon Road

Doe Mountain

1.6 mi.

2   Long Canyon Road

WEATHER
Spring: Good
Summer: May be too hot
Fall: Good
Winter: Good many days
REPORT

Dry Creek Road   2.9 mi.

3.2 mi.

89A   1   Y   Sedona
MP 371

Driving Distance One Way, Miles: 8.9
Hiking Distance One Way, Miles: 2.4

Bear Sign Trail #59

General Information
Location Map C4
Loy Butte and Wilson Mountain USGS Maps
Coconino Forest Service Map

Driving Distance One Way: 9.6 miles *15.4 km* (Time 45 minutes)
Access Road: Last 4.4 miles *7.0 km* bumpy unpaved road
Hiking Distance One Way: 3.2 miles *5.2 km* (Time 90 minutes)
How Strenuous: Moderate
Features: Secluded canyon, Beautiful redrocks

NUTSHELL: Located north of Sedona, this is a wilderness hike that follows a streambed to the base of the Mogollon Rim.

DIRECTIONS:
From the Sedona Y (the intersection of Highways 179 and 89A) Go:
    Southwest on Highway 89A (toward Cottonwood) for 3.2 miles *5.1 km* (MP 371) to Dry Creek Road **(1)** where you turn right and drive to the 5.2 mile *8.3 km* point **(2)**. Turn right on FR 152, the Vultee Arch Road, and follow it to the 9.6 mile *15.4 km* point, a parking loop, with the **Vultee Arch** Trailhead at the tip. Go past it. Parking for the Bear Sign and **Dry Creek** trails is a few yards beyond the Vultee parking area.

TRAILHEAD: At the parking area. There is a rusty sign: Dry Creek #52.

DESCRIPTION: You will walk across a little arroyo and around the toe of a hill for about 0.1 miles *0.16 km*, where you will reach Dry Creek. At the entry point, the canyon cut by Dry Creek is rather shallow and wide. Turn right (N) and follow the trail up the creek.
    At 0.6 miles *1.0 km*, you reach a point where the creek forks at a reef. The left-hand channel is the Bear Sign Trail, and the right fork is the **Dry Creek Trail**. There is a trail sign here. Now the canyon deepens with giant redrock buttes on both sides of the creek. As you walk, the trail climbs gradually and you cross the creekbed several times. The trail ends where it intersects a channel running east and west.
    Both the Bear Sign Trail and its neighboring Dry Creek Trail take you far away from habitation, and are nice if you want to get away into pristine country. Both trails head toward the Mogollon Rim and bump right against the base of it. The beauty of such trails is that they take you into wild and primitive country.
    At the 3.1 mile *5.0 km* point, look for the new **Dave Miller Trail**, which connects Bear Sign to the **Secret Canyon Trail**.

Photo: You will find shade in a pine forest on this wilderness trail.

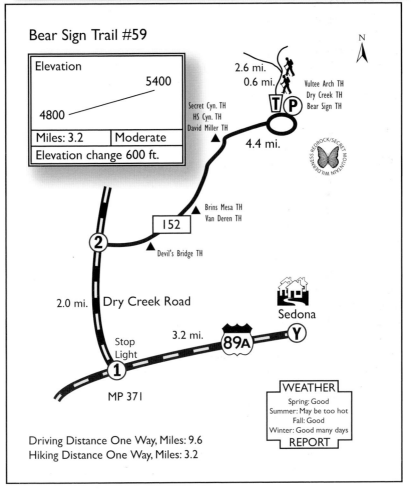

Bear Sign Trail #59

Elevation

5400

4800

Miles: 3.2	Moderate
Elevation change 600 ft.	

N

2.6 mi.
0.6 mi.

Vultee Arch TH
Dry Creek TH
Bear Sign TH

Secret Cyn. TH
HS Cyn. TH
David Miller TH

T P

4.4 mi.

REDROCK/SECRET MOUNTAIN WILDERNESS

Brins Mesa TH
Van Deren TH

152

2

Devil's Bridge TH

2.0 mi. Dry Creek Road

Sedona

3.2 mi.

89A

Y

Stop
Light

1

MP 371

Driving Distance One Way, Miles: 9.6
Hiking Distance One Way, Miles: 3.2

WEATHER

Spring: Good
Summer: May be too hot
Fall: Good
Winter: Good many days

REPORT

Beaverhead Route

General Information
Location Map G5
Casner Butte and Lake Montezuma USGS Maps
Coconino Forest Service Map

Driving Distance One Way: 11.2 miles *18.0 km* (Time 20 minutes)
Access Road: All paved
Hiking Distance One Way: 2.0 miles *3.2 km* (Time 45 minutes)
How Strenuous: Hard
Features: Historic road, Views

NUTSHELL: This hike climbs 1,000 feet to the top of the Mogollon Rim on an ancient Hopi trail that became a wagon road in the 1870s.

DIRECTIONS:
From the Sedona Y (the intersection of Highways 179 and 89A) Go:
South on Highway 179 (toward Phoenix) 11.2 miles *18.0 km* (MP 302.2) and then turn left on a gravel driveway **(1)**. Follow the drive to the gate in the barbed wire fence, drive through it for another 0.1 mile *0.16 km* and park.

TRAILHEAD: Unmarked. You walk the old road.

DESCRIPTION: Walk up the dirt road a distance of 0.1 miles *0.16 km*. There you will see a road to your right, going uphill, that has been blocked by a dirt ridge. Walk over the hump and you will pick up the old road.
    You walk a trail used by the Hopis for over 1,200 years. The route went from the Hopi mesas via Sunset Crossing (Winslow), Chavez Pass, Stoneman Lake, and Rattlesnake Canyon to the top of the Mogollon Rim just above your head. It ended at Camp Verde (with a branch to Jerome). The hardest challenge was to find a way down from the top of the Rim to the Verde Valley. This hike follows the path they chose.
    Spanish explorers used the trail in the late 1500s, then army scouts in the 1860s. It was improved as a military wagon road linking Fort Whipple and Santa Fe in the 1870s. Private operators became interested in the road and ran a stage line over it from 1876 to 1882. In 1884 a branch to Flagstaff was added. Until the Schnebly Hill Road was built in 1902, the Beaverhead Road was the only wagon road from Sedona to Flagstaff.
    As you reach the rim the road becomes incredibly rocky. At 1.0 miles *1.6 km* you come to The Slot, which looks like a trench lined with rocks. It runs for at least another mile. Many a wagon wheel must have broken here.
    The footing is so bad that we stop at 2.0 miles *3.2 km* where the trail comes against the edge of cliffs where there are tremendous views.

Photo: Imagine riding a stagecoach down this steep old road. The views behind you as you walk up the historic route are wonderful.

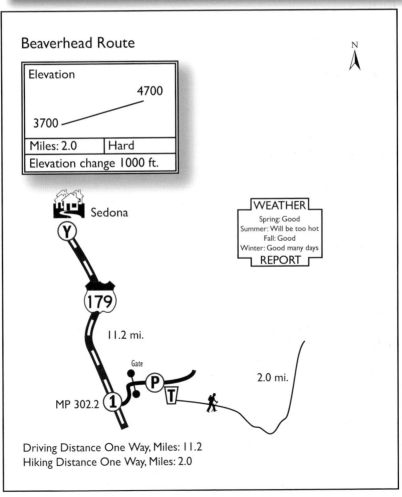

Beaverhead Route

N

Elevation

4700

3700

Miles: 2.0	Hard
Elevation change 1000 ft.	

Sedona

Y

179

WEATHER
Spring: Good
Summer: Will be too hot
Fall: Good
Winter: Good many days
REPORT

11.2 mi.

Gate

P

T

2.0 mi.

MP 302.2   1

Driving Distance One Way, Miles: 11.2
Hiking Distance One Way, Miles: 2.0

Bell Rock Trail

General Information
Location Map F4
Sedona USGS Map
Coconino Forest Service Map

Vortex

Driving Distance One Way: 5.2 miles *8.4 km* (Time 15 minutes)
Access Road: All cars, All paved
Hiking Distance, Complete Loop: 0.5/0.7 mile *0.8/1.1 km* (Time 30/45 minutes)
How Strenuous: Moderate
Features: Vortex Spot, Views

NUTSHELL: This landmark south of Sedona is one of the famed Vortex Spots. There is now a defined trail, new in 2003. There are really two trails here, the basic trail and the upper trail.

DIRECTIONS:
From the Sedona Y (the intersection of Highways 179 and 89A) Go:
   South on Highway 179 (toward Phoenix) a distance of 5.2 miles *8.4 km* (MP 308.4) **(1)**. (Drive to the Yavapai County line, then turn left).

TRAILHEAD: Go through the entryway. In a few steps you will intersect a trail. Turn right and walk about 100 paces to a two-wing signboard. Then go left about 30 paces to a cairn with a trail marker. This is the trailhead.

DESCRIPTION: From the trailhead climb right up the redrock behind the marker. You will see big cairns (rock baskets) marking the way. The redrock around Sedona was laid down in layers and has weathered in ledges that are almost like stairsteps. This is especially true on Bell Rock, with its conical slopes. The cairns lead hikers to a broad ledge that is perfect for sightseeing, and then loops back to the starting point. On the ledge you will see a sign for the Upper Bell Rock Trail. This makes a rather scary climb up a slickrock face to another broad ledge, where you turn left and walk toward the cairn that you will see on a lower level. Getting up and down the Upper Trail requires some scrambling and adds about 0.20 miles *0.32 km* to the hike. You will see hiker-made cairns delineating climbs up to even higher levels. If you take one of these, you are on your own. Please stay on the rock and do not damage the vegetation.
   Bell Rock is a vortex site. We know of no particular place that is regarded as *the* vortex spot on Bell Rock. Other vortex sites covered in this book are shown in the Index.

Photo: This popular trail takes you right up the side of Bell Rock so that you can enjoy a personal encounter with this favorite place.

Bell Rock Trail

N

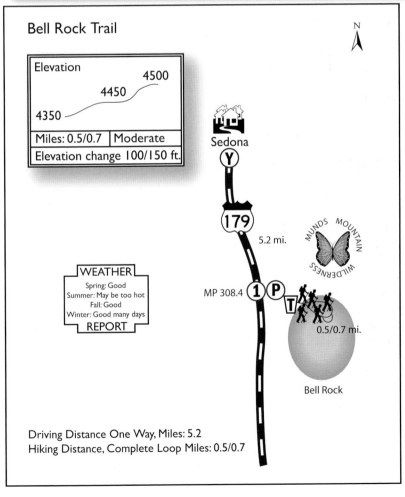

Elevation	
4350 — 4450 4500	
Miles: 0.5/0.7	Moderate
Elevation change 100/150 ft.	

Sedona

Y

179

5.2 mi.

MUNDS MOUNTAIN WILDERNESS

MP 308.4 1 P
T

0.5/0.7 mi.

Bell Rock

Driving Distance One Way, Miles: 5.2
Hiking Distance, Complete Loop Miles: 0.5/0.7

Bell Rock Pathway Trail #96

General Information
Location Map F4
Sedona USGS Map
Coconino Forest Service Map

Driving Distance One Way: 6.2 miles *9.9 km* (Time 20 minutes)
Access Road: All cars, All paved
Hiking Distance One Way: 3.7 miles *5.9 km* (Time 2.0 hours)
How Strenuous: Moderate
Features: Views

NUTSHELL: This trail was designed to connect the Village of Oak Creek with the trail system around Sedona. It starts just north of the Village of Oak Creek and winds its way north parallel to Highway 179, passing **Courthouse Butte** and **Bell Rock** along the way, to end at the **Little Horse** trailhead.

DIRECTIONS:
From the Sedona Y (the intersection of Highways 179 and 89A) Go:
   South on Highway 179 (toward Phoenix) for a distance of 6.2 miles *9.9 km* (MP 307.4) to a place south of Bell Rock, just short of the Village of Oak Creek, where you will see a road to your left **(1)**. This road is the entrance to the parking lot for the Bell Rock Pathway. Turn into it and park.

TRAILHEAD: At the parking lot. It is signed.

DESCRIPTION: The Bell Rock Pathway is as wide as a road and makes for easy hiking. It runs north to Bell Rock parallel to Highway 179. At a point 0.6 miles *1.0 km* from the beginning, you will be almost to the base of Bell Rock. Here you will find a distinct but much narrower trail running to your right, toward Courthouse Butte. Take the fork to the left (W) here, circling the base of Bell Rock. You will pass very close to Bell Rock, along its shoulder, and will enjoy viewing the famous landmark.
   A short distance beyond Bell Rock you enter the most scenic part of the trail, where you swing away from the highway onto some attractive redrock ledges. The views open up here and you will enjoy looking at Bell Rock, Courthouse Butte, and to the west, Little Park Heights.
   Soon the trail moves over close to the road again, and continues north, toward Twin Buttes. The famous Chapel of the Holy Cross is located on the south face of Twin Buttes, and you can see it as you approach.
   The trail ends at the trailhead for the Little Horse trail, where there is a large parking area and a toilet.

Photo: This wide easy trail takes you close to Bell Rock and Courthouse Butte, two of Sedona's favorite rock formations.

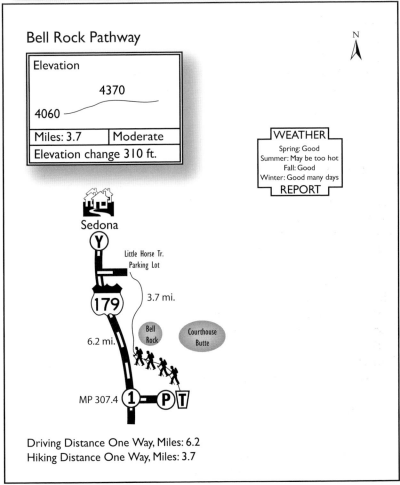

Bell Rock Pathway

N

Elevation

4370

4060

Miles: 3.7	Moderate
Elevation change 310 ft.	

WEATHER
Spring: Good
Summer: May be too hot
Fall: Good
Winter: Good many days
REPORT

Sedona

Y

Little Horse Tr.
Parking Lot

179

3.7 mi.

6.2 mi.

Bell
Rock

Courthouse
Butte

MP 307.4 (1)—(P)(T)

Driving Distance One Way, Miles: 6.2
Hiking Distance One Way, Miles: 3.7

Bell Trail #13

General Information
Location Map G6
Apache Maid and Casner Butte USGS Maps
Coconino Forest Service Map

Driving Distance One Way: 17.0 miles *27.2 km* (Time 30 minutes)
Access Road: All cars, Last 0.1 mile *0.2 km* is a good gravel road
Hiking Distance One Way: 6.8 miles *10.9 km* (Time 4 hours)
How Strenuous: Hard
Features: Permanent Stream, Steep-walled canyon, Redrocks

NUTSHELL: You hike along a historic cattle trail following the course of Wet Beaver Creek through a scenic canyon southeast of Sedona.

DIRECTIONS:
From the Sedona Y (the intersection of Highways 179 and 89A) Go:
   South on Highway 179 (toward Phoenix) for 14.7 miles *23.5 km* (MP 298.9), to the I-17 intersection **(1)**. Go straight rather than getting on I-17. Follow paved FR 618 until you see a sign for Beaver Creek Ranger Station and trailheads at 16.9 miles *27.1 km* **(2)**. Turn left and drive to the new parking area (opened in the spring of 2004) at 17.0 miles *27.2 km*.

TRAILHEAD: At the parking area.

DESCRIPTION: Cattle rancher Charles Bell built this trail in 1932 to take cattle to the top of the Mogollon Rim in the spring and return them in fall.
   At about 0.8 miles *1.2 km*, look for a large boulder on the left side of the trail. Facing away from you are a number of interesting petroglyphs.
   At 1.7 miles *2.7 km* you will find the **White Mesa Trail #86** to your left. You enter the wilderness here. At the 2.2 mile *3.5 km* point you will hit a fork where the **Apache Maid Trail #15** branches to the left and climbs Casner Butte.
   Just beyond this fork you will find the junction with the **Weir Trail #85** which goes to the right, down to the water. Go straight. You now enter the finest part of the trail, where you walk in the redrocks.
   At 3.5 miles *5.6 km* you reach Bell Crossing where the trail narrows and crosses Wet Beaver creek. Go upstream about 100 yards to check out a large pool known as The Crack. This is a good place to end a day hike.
   From the crossing, the trail goes 3.3 miles *5.3 km* farther and 1,200 feet higher up to the top of The Rim. The full hike is scenic, but is much longer and harder. We recommend stopping at the crossing for most day hikers.

Photo: Dick is looking at petroglyphs on a boulder at the side of this wide easy-to-walk trail.

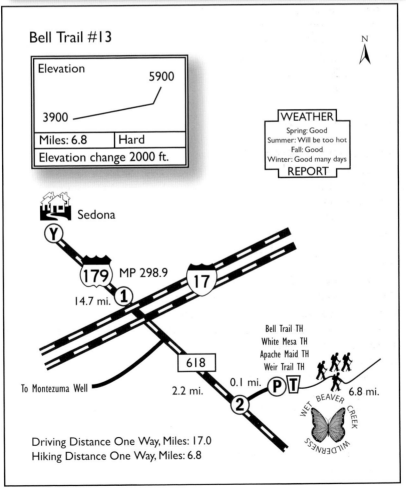

Bell Trail #13

Elevation

5900

3900

Miles: 6.8	Hard
Elevation change 2000 ft.	

N

Sedona

Y

179 MP 298.9 17

14.7 mi. ①

618

To Montezuma Well

2.2 mi. 0.1 mi. P T

②

Bell Trail TH
White Mesa TH
Apache Maid TH
Weir Trail TH

6.8 mi.

WET BEAVER CREEK WILDERNESS

Driving Distance One Way, Miles: 17.0
Hiking Distance One Way, Miles: 6.8

Big Park Loop Trail

General Information
Location Map F5
Sedona USGS Map
Coconino Forest Service Map

Driving Distance One Way: 6.2 miles *9.9 km* (Time 20 minutes)
Access Road: All cars, All paved
Hiking Distance, Complete Loop: 2.6 miles *4.2 km* (Time 1.2 hours)
How Strenuous: Moderate
Features: Nice side trail from the Bell Rock Pathway.

NUTSHELL: This trail takes you along the Bell Rock Pathway area, starting at the Village of Oak Creek, but when it reaches Courthouse Rock, it skirts it to the east, and then loops back to the parking area.

DIRECTIONS:
From the Sedona Y (the intersection of Highways 179 and 89A) Go:
    South on Highway 179 (toward Phoenix) for 6.2 miles *9.9 km* (MP 307.4) **(1)** and then turn left into the trailhead parking lot (signed).

TRAILHEAD: At the parking lot.

DESCRIPTION: You start off hiking the main **Bell Rock Pathway Trail** and at 0.1 miles *0.16 km* reach the junction with the Big Park Loop Trail. Turn to the right, following the sign, but be careful, because it looks as if two paths go to the right. Take the one that curls up toward Courthouse Rock, even though it looks like the less-traveled trail. The area is criss-crossed with informal trails, so be sure to pay attention to the trail signs and cairns.

    At 0.6 miles *1.0 km* you reach the junction with the **Courthouse Butte Loop Trail**, at the base of Courthouse Rock. Turn right. You will now walk along the base of this beautiful butte, and will have fine views of its highly sculpted faces. About midway along the rock, you will see a wide unmarked trail to your right going out across a flat open area. Ignore this and stay on the real trail. You will walk past the butte and into a streambed where the water has worn down to the red slickrock. On the other side of this streambed you will find the place where you are to turn right. It is signed and marked with a cairn.

    From this turn the nature of the trail changes and you walk through heavy brush and low-growing trees across two ridges. At 2.4 miles *3.8 km* you come out of the trees onto an open flat and meet a trail sign. From here you return to the starting sign for the Big Park Loop Trail. From this sign it is 0.1 miles *0.16 km* back to the trailhead, making a total walk of 2.6 miles *4.2 km.*

Photo: This trail takes you to Courthouse Butte, then turns to make a loop back to the trailhead.

Big Park Loop Trail

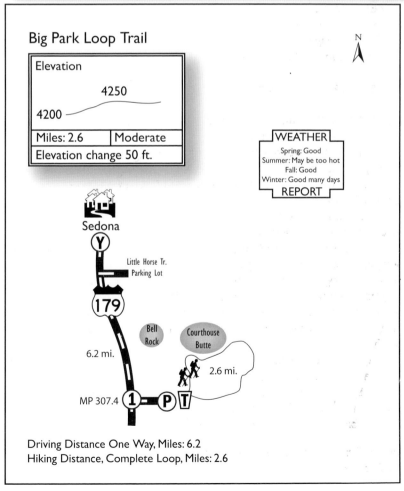

Elevation

4250

4200

Miles: 2.6	Moderate
Elevation change 50 ft.	

N

WEATHER
Spring: Good
Summer: May be too hot
Fall: Good
Winter: Good many days
REPORT

Sedona
Y

Little Horse Tr.
Parking Lot

179

Bell
Rock

Courthouse
Butte

6.2 mi.

2.6 mi.

MP 307.4 1 — P T

Driving Distance One Way, Miles: 6.2
Hiking Distance, Complete Loop, Miles: 2.6

Boynton Canyon Trail #47

General Information
Location Map C3
Wilson Mountain USGS Map
Coconino Forest Service Map

Driving Distance One Way: 7.8 miles *12.5 km* (Time 20 minutes)
Access Road: All cars, All paved
Hiking Distance One Way: 3.75 miles *6.0 km* (Time 90 minutes)
How Strenuous: Moderate
Features: Indian Ruins, Vortex

NUTSHELL: This wonderful canyon is easily reached by paved roads. **A personal favorite.**

DIRECTIONS:
From the Sedona Y (the intersection of Highways 179 and 89A) Go:
Southwest on Highway 89A (toward Cottonwood) a distance of 3.2 miles *5.1 km* (MP 371), then make a right turn onto Dry Creek Road **(1)**. Follow it to the 6.1 mile *9.8 km* point, where it joins Long Canyon Road **(2)**. Take a left here, staying on FR 152C. At the 7.7 mile *12.3 km* point, you reach another junction **(3)**. Go right. At 7.8 miles *12.5 km*, Turn right into the trail parking lot.

TRAILHEAD: Three-panel map, sign and toilet at the parking area.

DESCRIPTION: Follow the signs from the parking lot. The early part of this trail overlooks the Enchantment Resort. The trail winds along the east face of the canyon, hugging the towering ruin-dotted red cliffs so as to skirt the resort property.
At just under 1.25 miles *2.0 km* you will come downhill and see the Enchantment fence to your left. From the Enchantment fence, the trail turns away from the cliffs and follows along the canyon floor. It is much wider and easier to walk from this point.
Soon after this you will cross a shallow wash, beyond which the vegetation changes, because the elevation rises and the sheltering canyon walls make this part of the trail cooler.
At about 3.5 miles *5.6 km*, the trail pinches down as the canyon narrows. This is a good stopping place. However, you can bushwhack another 0.25 mile *0.4 km* to the head of Boynton, in a box against the side of Secret Mountain. The streambed forks here. Take the right fork and you will soon see a primitive path, almost a tunnel, through the lush growth at stream level. You will emerge into the box, ringed with towering cliffs.

Photo: The first part of this trail takes you past colorful cliffs on your right and the Enchantment Resort on your left. Several of the buildings of the resort are visible here.

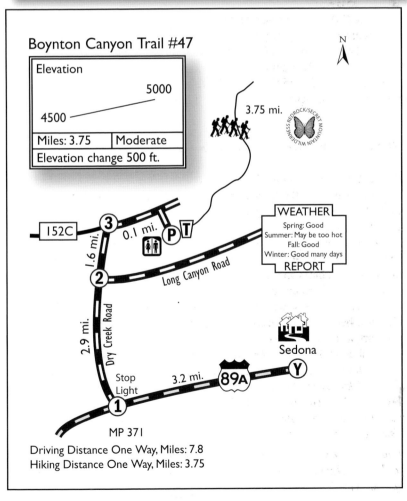

Boynton Canyon Trail #47

N

Elevation

5000

4500

| Miles: 3.75 | Moderate |
| Elevation change 500 ft. | |

3.75 mi.

REDROCK/SECRET MOUNTAIN WILDERNESS

152C

3

0.1 mi.

P T

1.6 mi.

WEATHER

Spring: Good
Summer: May be too hot
Fall: Good
Winter: Good many days

REPORT

2

Long Canyon Road

2.9 mi.

Dry Creek Road

Sedona

Stop Light

3.2 mi.

89A

Y

1

MP 371

Driving Distance One Way, Miles: 7.8
Hiking Distance One Way, Miles: 3.75

Boynton Canyon Vista Trail

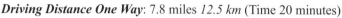

General Information
Location Map C3
Wilson Mountain USGS Map
Coconino Forest Service Map

Driving Distance One Way: 7.8 miles *12.5 km* (Time 20 minutes)
Access Road: All cars, All paved
Hiking Distance One Way: 0.75 miles *1.2 km* (Time 40 minutes)
How Strenuous: Easy
Features: Vortex site, Views of Boynton Canyon

NUTSHELL: This easily reached hike near Sedona takes you to a redrock saddle decorated with landmark rock formations.

DIRECTIONS:

From the Sedona Y (the intersection of Highways 179 and 89A) Go:
　　Southwest on Highway 89A (toward Cottonwood) a distance of 3.2 miles *5.1 km* (MP 371), to Dry Creek Road **(1)**, where you take a right turn onto Dry Creek Road. Follow it to the 6.1 mile *9.8 km* point, where it joins Long Canyon Road **(2)**. Take a left here, staying on FR 152C. At the 7.7 mile *12.3 km* point, you reach another junction **(3)**. Go right. At 7.8 miles *12.5 km* turn right into the trailhead parking area.

TRAILHEAD: Three-panel map, sign and toilet at the parking area.

DESCRIPTION: The **Boynton Canyon Trail** and the Boynton Canyon Vista trail share a common trailhead.
　　From the trailhead you will hike to a redrock formation, look up and to your right and you will see your destination, which is a large redrock formation with two spires sticking up. Between the spires is a saddle or gap. You will hike around to the back side of this formation, and up to the saddle.
　　As you start the hike, both trails blend. You walk uphill a short distance, then veer off to the right on the Vista Trail, which climbs steadily as it goes to the top of the toe of the rock formation. It then winds around to the back side.
　　Your objective is always in plain sight. Once you reach the top, you can see over into Boynton Canyon, which is mostly filled with the Enchantment Resort. There are views to the other side too, which are very nice. This is an easy little hike.

Photo: You walk to the saddle between the two spires on the left and the spire on the right. The saddle is considered to be a Vortex site. Whether you believe in such things or not, it is a wonderful viewpoint.

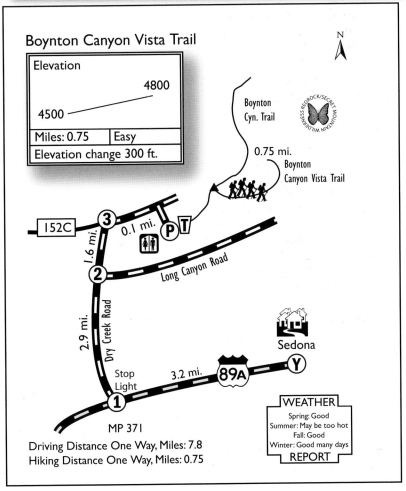

Boynton Canyon Vista Trail

N

Elevation	
4500 ————— 4800	
Miles: 0.75	Easy
Elevation change 300 ft.	

Boynton Cyn. Trail

REDROCK/SECRET MOUNTAIN WILDERNESS

0.75 mi.
Boynton Canyon Vista Trail

152C ③ 0.1 mi. P T

1.6 mi.

② Long Canyon Road

2.9 mi.

Dry Creek Road

Stop Light

3.2 mi. 89A Y

Sedona

①

MP 371

Driving Distance One Way, Miles: 7.8
Hiking Distance One Way, Miles: 0.75

WEATHER
Spring: Good
Summer: May be too hot
Fall: Good
Winter: Good many days
REPORT

Brewer Trail

General Information
Location Map E4
Sedona USGS Map
Coconino Forest Service Map

Driving Distance One Way: 1.5 miles *2.4 km* (Time 10 minutes)
Access Road: All cars, Paved all the way
Hiking Distance One Way: 1.0 miles *1.6 km* (Time 45 minutes)
How Strenuous: Moderate
Features: Views from Airport Mesa

NUTSHELL: This trail takes you from Airport Mesa to Brewer Road.

DIRECTIONS:
From the Sedona Y (the intersection of Highways 179 and 89A) Go:
   Southwest on Highway 89A for 1.0 miles *1.6 km*, to Airport Road **(1)**. Turn left onto Airport Road and drive uphill to the 1.5 mile *2.4 km* point and turn left into the parking lot.

TRAILHEAD: Through the gap in the cable fence.

DESCRIPTION: From the parking lot walk through the gap in the cable fence and turn left, walking the trail that you will see running along next to the cables. Ignore all trails to your right that go uphill. You will walk around the knolls and come to a place where the trail seems to end. Keep looking. You will see your trail continuing along the face of the red knoll to your left. Trust it.
   Walk out on the face of the rock. The trail runs fairly level until it gets past the base of the butte and then begins to descend. You go from 4,600 feet down to 4,200 feet from this point.
   At 0.8 miles *1.3 km* you will come into a clearing where there is an old stone water tank. The trail gets tricky here. Be sure to turn to your left before you walk past the tank. Turn to your left and you will see the true trail going through the shrubbery.
   From the tank you go downhill even farther, reaching Brewer Road at 1.0 miles *1.6 km*. The point where the trail joins the road is 0.6 miles *1.0 km* from the junction of Brewer Road with Highway 89A. If coming in from the Highway 89A/Brewer Road junction, you drive Brewer Road, looking for the Wesleyan Church, which will be to your left. Just beyond the church there is a gravel parking apron on the left. The trail is just across Brewer Road, marked by a one-panel trailhead sign. Look sharp, for the sign blends into the bushes and is not easy to see.

Photo: The Brewer Trail descends from Airport Mesa. The early part of the trail—the most interesting—takes you along this redrock ledge.

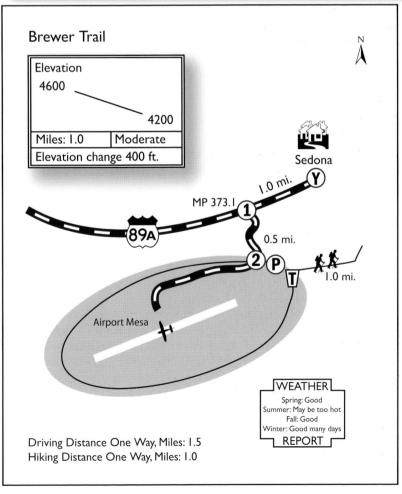

Brewer Trail

N

Elevation

4600

4200

Miles: 1.0	Moderate
Elevation change 400 ft.	

Sedona

1.0 mi.

MP 373.1

1

89A

0.5 mi.

2 **P**

T

1.0 mi.

Airport Mesa

WEATHER
Spring: Good
Summer: May be too hot
Fall: Good
Winter: Good many days
REPORT

Driving Distance One Way, Miles: 1.5
Hiking Distance One Way, Miles: 1.0

Brins Mesa Trail #119

General Information
Location Map D4
Wilson Mountain USGS Map
Coconino Forest Service Map

Driving Distance One Way: 1.9 miles *3.0 km* (Time 10 minutes)
Access Road*:* All cars, Last 0.6 miles *1.0 km* dirt road
Hiking Distance One Way*:* 4.3 miles *6.9 km* (Time 2.5 hours)
How Strenuous*:* Moderate
Features*:* Easy to reach, Good views

NUTSHELL: Starting at a point beyond the end of Jordan Road, you hike to the top of Brins Mesa, enjoy its fine views, then cross the mesa top and descend the other side, where the trail meets the Vultee Arch Road.

DIRECTIONS:
From the Sedona Y (the intersection of Highways 179 and 89A) Go:
   North on Highway 89A (toward Flagstaff) for 0.3 miles *0.5 km* to Jordan Road **(1)**. Take Jordan Road to its end, at 1.1 miles *1.8 km* **(2)**. Turn left at the stop sign, on West Park Ridge, which ends at 1.3 miles *2.1 km*. Keep going on the unpaved road. You reach the parking lot at 1.9 miles *3.0 km*.

TRAILHEAD: At the parking area, where there is a three-panel sign.

DESCRIPTION: The trail is a jeep road at first, taking you to the foot of Brins Mesa in 1.0 mile *1.6 km*. Now the trail gets strenuous as you climb the mesa, a 500-foot rise. As you go up, look behind you to enjoy views. You'll reach the top at 1.5 miles *2.4 km*. Ignore the trail to the right and go straight ahead.
   On top keep following the main trail (which looks like a jeep road) as it continues across the mesa to the west. You can tell that there is a canyon to your left. This is the Soldier Pass area. At 2.2 miles *3.5 km* there is a signpost without a sign, marking the turn for a connector going 0.25 miles *0.4 km* to join the **Soldier Pass Trail.** Go straight.
   At 2.8 miles *4.5 km* the Brins Mesa trail drops strongly, winding through a lovely Arizona Cypress forest to join the Vultee Arch Road, at the second Brins Mesa trailhead. This sets up a two-car hike, parking a car at each end. To get to the second trailhead from the Y, drive SW on Highway 89A for 3.2 miles *5.1 km* (MP 371) then turn right on Dry Creek Road and proceed to the 5.2 mile *8.4 km* point, where you turn right on FR 152, the Vultee Arch Road, and follow it to the 7.7 mile *12.4 km* point. Pull off to the right into the big parking area, where you will see a Brins mesa trailhead sign.

Photo: After you reach the top of Brins Mesa, wonderful sights unfold.

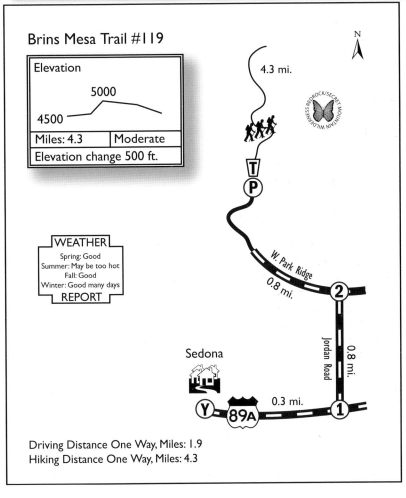

Brins Mesa Trail #119

Elevation

5000

4500

Miles: 4.3	Moderate
Elevation change 500 ft.	

4.3 mi.

REDROCK/SECRET MOUNTAIN WILDERNESS

N

T
P

W. Park Ridge
0.8 mi.

Jordan Road

0.8 mi.

WEATHER

Spring: Good
Summer: May be too hot
Fall: Good
Winter: Good many days

REPORT

Sedona

Y **89A** 0.3 mi. **1**

2

Driving Distance One Way, Miles: 1.9
Hiking Distance One Way, Miles: 4.3

Broken Arrow Trail #125

General Information
Location Map E5
Sedona USGS Map
Coconino Forest Service Map

Driving Distance One Way: 2.1 miles *3.4 km* (Time 10 minutes)
Access Road: All cars, Last 0.1 mile *0.16 km* good dirt road
Hiking Distance One Way: 1.5 miles *2.4 km* (Time 60 minutes)
How Strenuous: Moderate
Features: Redrocks, Views, Sinkhole

NUTSHELL: This trail is located in Sedona's "backyard" at the south end of Marg's Draw. It winds around redrock cliffs and canyons, ending at Chicken Point, with a stop at Devil's Dining Room along the way. **A Personal Favorite**

DIRECTIONS:
From the Sedona Y (the intersection of Highways 179 and 89A) Go:
   South on Highway 179 (toward Phoenix) for 1.4 miles *2.3 km* (MP 312.1) to Morgan Road in the Broken Arrow Subdivision **(1)**. Turn left (E) on Morgan Road and follow it to its end, at 2.0 miles *3.2 km*; then go another 0.1 miles *0.16 km* to the parking area.

TRAILHEAD: At the parking lot.

DESCRIPTION: From the parking lot, you walk southwest across the road and follow the markers and cairns west and south. The trail soon moves over near the base of the nice redrock cliffs of Battlement Mesa and climbs up onto a ledge, winding around the base of the mesa.
   At 0.5 miles *0.8 km* you will come downhill to a sinkhole protected by a fence. This is the Devil's Dining Room, a local landmark. At 0.75 miles *1.2 km* you will reach a trail junction. From this point the trail to the left goes down to **Submarine Rock**, while the trail to the right goes to Chicken Point. Take the right fork. You will make a mild climb, enjoying several nice viewpoints.
   From this trail junction the Broken Arrow trail winds around the base of Twin Buttes heading south. The trail moves near some gorgeous red spires and sculptured cliff faces and we think you will especially enjoy this last leg of the hike. At 1.45 miles *2.3 km* you come to a gap in the butte, where you have a great view. From here it is a short drop down to Chicken Point, where you can go out onto a red slickrock and enjoy even more views.

Photo: The Broken Arrow Trail offers variety, such as a passage across this redrock ledge, rounded and smoothed by water and wind.

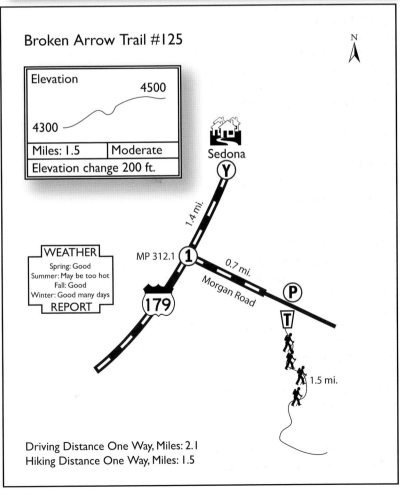

Broken Arrow Trail #125

N

Elevation	
4300 —	4500
Miles: 1.5	Moderate
Elevation change 200 ft.	

Sedona
Y

1.4 mi.

MP 312.1 **1**

0.7 mi.

Morgan Road

WEATHER
Spring: Good
Summer: May be too hot
Fall: Good
Winter: Good many days
REPORT

179

P

T

1.5 mi.

Driving Distance One Way, Miles: 2.1
Hiking Distance One Way, Miles: 1.5

Carroll Canyon Trail

General Information
Location Map E4
Sedona USGS Map
Coconino Forest Service Map

Driving Distance One Way: 2.6 miles *4.2 km* (Time 10 minutes)
Access Road: All vehicles, All paved
Hiking Distance, Complete Loop: 4.3 miles *6.9 km* (Time 2 hours)
How Strenuous: Moderate
Features: Connects to other trails around Airport Mesa

NUTSHELL: This trail shows hikers the best part of Carroll Canyon near Airport Mesa.

DIRECTIONS:
From the Sedona Y (the intersection of Highways 179 and 89A) Go:
SW on Hwy 89A for 2.1 miles *3.4 km,* to a stoplight **(1)**. Turn left on Shelby Drive and take it for 0.5 miles *0.8 km* (just past Stanley Steamer Dr.), then turn right into the parking lot of La Entrada, at 2155 Shelby Drive. At the back of the parking lot you will see trailhead parking signs.

TRAILHEAD: Orphan. Access via the **Old Post Trail**.

DESCRIPTION: Take the footpath going into the trees from the parking area. Almost immediately you will see a sign for the Old Post Trail. Turn right and follow this trail, which is a connector to the desired trail. At 0.5 miles *0.8 km* you will come to the trail junction, where you turn left on the Carroll Canyon Trail, which heads off into the trees. At 0.7 miles *1.1 km* you will come to a sign showing that the Carroll Canyon Trail splits. We suggest that you take the left fork.

At 1.3 miles *2.1 km* you reach a T-junction where you meet the **Ridge Trail** at the base of Airport Mesa. Go right here, on the joint Ridge-Carroll Canyon trails. At 1.6 miles *2.6 km* turn right, away from the Ridge Trail. The Carroll Canyon Trail goes down, crossing the canyon at a shallow place. Soon after you make the crossing, Carroll Canyon, which has been nothing more than a wash up to now, deepens, with attractive cliffs.

You will walk along the rim of the cliffs on the north bank for a while, and then veer away from the canyon to the west. As you come over a ridge, you will meet the **Old Post Trail** at 2.6 miles *4.2 km*. Turn right.

From here the Old Post and Carroll Canyon trails are combined, following the old mail road. This old mail road ends at the 2.8 miles *4.5 km* point. You then follow the Old Post Trail as a footpath back to the parking lot.

Photo: Here Dick is on the rim of Carroll Canyon, the most scenic part of this trail, which is part of a network of trails near Airport Mesa.

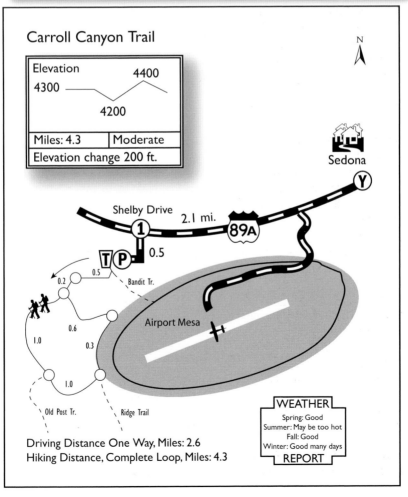

Carroll Canyon Trail

N

Elevation 4300 — 4400 4200	
Miles: 4.3	Moderate
Elevation change 200 ft.	

Sedona

Shelby Drive

Y

2.1 mi.

1

89A

T P 0.5

0.5

0.2

Bandit Tr.

Airport Mesa

0.6

1.0

0.3

1.0

Old Post Tr.

Ridge Trail

Driving Distance One Way, Miles: 2.6
Hiking Distance, Complete Loop, Miles: 4.3

WEATHER
Spring: Good
Summer: May be too hot
Fall: Good
Winter: Good many days
REPORT

Carruth Trail

General Information
Location Map D4
Sedona USGS Map
Coconino Forest Service Map

Driving Distance One Way: 2.1 miles *3.4 km* (Time 10 minutes)
Access Road: All cars, All paved
Hiking Distance, Complete Loop: 0.9 miles *1.4 km* (Time 20 minutes)
How Strenuous: Easy
Features: Easy to reach, Views, Plant identification signs

NUTSHELL: This urban trail is gentle and short, but interesting.

DIRECTIONS:
From the Sedona Y (the intersection of Highways 179 and 89A) Go:
Southwest on Highway 89A (toward Cottonwood) for 1.5 miles *2.4 km* (MP 371.3), then turn right on Posse Ground Road **(1)**. Follow it to the 1.8 mile point *2.9 km* where there is a V-intersection in front of the Posse Grounds Community Park **(2)**. Go right. At 2.1 miles *3.4 km* you will meet Carruth Drive **(3)**. Turn right and drive a few yards and then park on the left-hand shoulder. You will see the trail marker a few feet down the street.

TRAILHEAD: It is signed.

DESCRIPTION:
This is a short hike in an urban setting. In fact, you are in a pocket of land surrounded by subdivisions and are close to a park; so there are houses and people in sight and hearing at all times. Nevertheless, the trail provides a very pleasant walk. Little signs identify many of the trailside plants.

The trail heads in a northerly direction, toward Coffee Pot Rock. Immediately there is a fork: go left. The trail then hugs a high ridge so you have good views all along the trail.

At the 0.25 mile *0.4 km* point, you will find the Marie Brown Handrail and a set of stairs, a thoughtful touch, meeting the special needs of some hikers. At the top of the steps turn right. You will pass by a picnic ramada. At the 0.33 mile *0.5 km* point you reach a sign indicating that the trail becomes a loop. Go to the right and soon you will come upon a nice stone bench, a great place to sit and enjoy the nice views. Shortly beyond the bench a connecting trail goes off to the right, downhill, to join the **Sunrise Trail**. Follow the trail carefully on top as there are many false social trails. Finish the loop, coming back to the place where it began and then retrace your path to the stair and handrail and thus back to your car.

Photo: The Carruth Trail is an urban trail but is quite enjoyable, with some lovely views out over scenic countryside.

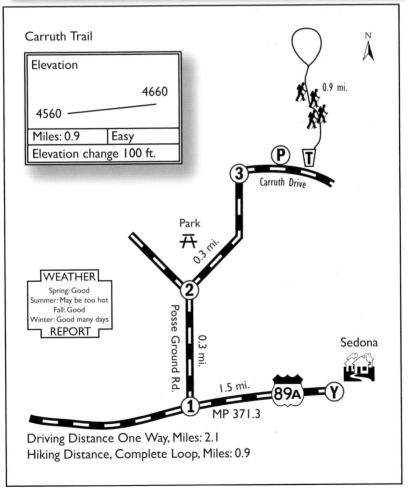

Carruth Trail

Elevation

4660

4560

Miles: 0.9 | Easy
Elevation change 100 ft.

0.9 mi.

N

P T

Carruth Drive

Park

0.3 mi.

WEATHER
Spring: Good
Summer: May be too hot
Fall: Good
Winter: Good many days
REPORT

Posse Ground Rd.

0.3 mi.

Sedona

1.5 mi.

89A Y

MP 371.3

Driving Distance One Way, Miles: 2.1
Hiking Distance, Complete Loop, Miles: 0.9

Casner Canyon Trail #11

General Information
Location Map D5
Munds Park USGS Map
Coconino Forest Service Map

Driving Distance One Way: 6.6 miles *10.6 km* (Time 30 minutes)
Access Road: All cars, Last 5.3 mi. *8.5 km* rough unpaved road
Hiking Distance One Way: 3.0 miles *4.8 km* (Time 2 hours)
How Strenuous: Hard
Features: Views, Historic cattle trail

NUTSHELL: This steep scenic livestock trail takes you from the top of Schnebly Hill Road down to Oak Creek. For experienced hikers only.

DIRECTIONS:
From the Sedona Y (the intersection of Highways 179 and 89A) Go:
    South on Highway 179 (toward Phoenix) for 0.3 miles *0.5 km* (MP 313.1) to the Schnebly Hill Road, just across the bridge past Tlaquepaque **(1)**. Turn left on the Schnebly Hill Road, which is paved for the first 1.0 mile *1.6 km* and then turns into a dirt road that is sometimes very rough. Drive to the top, 6.6 miles *10.6 km* and park at the big parking lot at the Schnebly Hill Vista.

TRAILHEAD: At the parking lot, but there are no signs.

DESCRIPTION: From the parking lot walk north to the corner of the barbed wire fence. Go through the gate into a chute between two fences with a pen at the entry and walk to the end where you pass through another pen. When you clear the fences you will see cairns. Follow them closely. You need them.
    The little-used trail is faint here. You walk northward over rocky country to the head of Casner Canyon and enter the canyon. The trail is now easy to follow. The canyon walls are sheer, with tree cover. Soon you reach a point where the walls to your left end and you see superb redrock formations. You break out of the tree cover here and for the rest of the trail there is no shade. You are exposed to the sun. This trail would be murder on a hot sunny day!
    The part of the trail shown in the photo is next, below the treeline, making a straight line down the canyon. The views are great but watch your footing. Near the end you come down to the bottom of the canyon and then must cross Oak Creek, which means wading and boulder hopping. On the other side you will see the trail going up to Highway 89A on an old road.
    Our favorite way to do this hike is to use two cars. Park one on the shoulder of Highway 89A at MP 376.8, a place that is 2.6 mi. *4.2 km* north of the Y and take the other to Schnebly Hill Vista, then make the hike as written.

Photo: Sherry took this photo from the Schnebly Hill Road. It shows the Casner Canyon Trail making a straight diagonal line down the canyon.

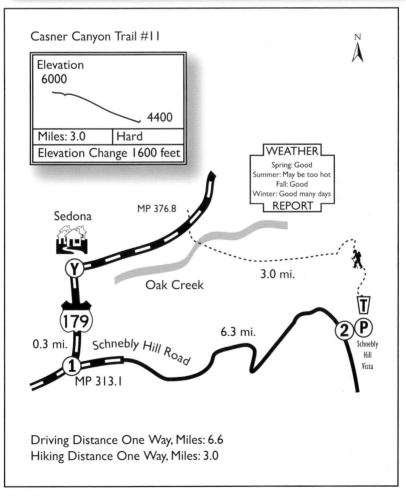

Casner Canyon Trail #11

N

Elevation
6000

4400

Miles: 3.0	Hard
Elevation Change 1600 feet	

WEATHER
Spring: Good
Summer: May be too hot
Fall: Good
Winter: Good many days
REPORT

Sedona

MP 376.8

Y

Oak Creek

3.0 mi.

179

T

0.3 mi.

Schnebly Hill Road

6.3 mi.

2 P

1

Schnebly
Hill
Vista

MP 313.1

Driving Distance One Way, Miles: 6.6
Hiking Distance One Way, Miles: 3.0

Casner Mountain Trail #8

General Information
Location Map C1
Loy Butte and Clarkdale USGS Maps
Coconino Forest Service Map

Driving Distance One Way: 19.0 miles *30.4 km* (Time 30 minutes)
Access Road: All cars, Last 9.6 miles *15.4 km* good dirt road
Hiking Distance One Way: 2.0 miles *3.2 km* (Time 1.5 hours)
How Strenuous: Hard
Features: Views

NUTSHELL: This hike takes you to the top of a mountain overlooking Sycamore Canyon and the Sedona back country.

DIRECTIONS:
From the Sedona Y (the intersection of Highways 179 and 89A) Go:
   On Highway 89A (toward Cottonwood) for 9.4 miles *15.0 km* (MP 364.2) to Point **(1)**. Turn right onto FR 525. Drive it to the 12.2 mile *19.5 km* Point **(2)**. Turn left on FR 525C. At 12.7 miles *20.3 km* Point **(3)** turn right. At 15.2 miles *24.3 km* Point **(4)** the Bill Gray Road (FR 761) goes left. Stay on FR 525C to the 19.0 mile *30.4 km* Point **(5)**, where you will see the small rusty trail sign (right). There is a small parking space.

TRAILHEAD: The trailhead is marked with a sign. The trail follows the power line up the south face of Casner Mountain, and you can see clearly from the start of the hike where the trail goes.

DESCRIPTION: Casner Mountain is bare of shade trees and the trail takes you up its south face; so you are in full sunlight with no shade. Take a hat and plenty of water and don't try this hike on a hot day. The trail follows along a jeep road created for the construction of the power line. You will climb about 0.4 miles *0.65 km* to join the power line, then hike across a shelf.
   From the end of the shelf, the trail goes straight up the mountain to about the halfway point, where the pitch becomes quite steep, and from there the trail serpentines. At the 1.6 mile *2.6 km* point you come to a sharp switchback at the west edge of the mountain where you break over a shoulder so that you suddenly see into Sycamore Canyon. It is a vast and soul-stirring view.
   From this point you will make the final push and stop at the top, at the highest point. Though Casner Mountain looks like a free-standing mountain when you start the hike, it is attached to the Mogollon Rim by Buck Ridge. The power line runs across this ridge and you can continue hiking the power line road for 4.0 miles *6.4 km* to the rim.

Photo: Sherry took this shot from the bank of Black Tank, with Casner Mountain towering in the distance. The trail climbs the south face.

Casner Mountain Trail #8

N

Elevation

6836

4750

Miles: 2.0	Hard
Elevation Change 2086 feet	

2.0 mi.

525C ⑤ Ⓟ Ⓣ

3.8 mi.

Bill Gray Road 761 ④

525C

2.5 mi.

WEATHER
Spring: Good
Summer: May be too hot
Fall: Good
Winter: Poor: snow, mud
REPORT

③ 0.5 ② 525

2.8 mi.

Sedona

525

① 9.4 mi. 89A Ⓨ
MP 364.2

Driving Distance One Way, Miles: 19.0
Hiking Distance One Way, Miles: 2.0

Cathedral Rock Trail #170

General Information
Location Map F4
Sedona USGS Map
Coconino Forest Service Map

Vortex

Driving Distance One Way: 4.1 miles *6.6 km* (Time 15 minutes)
Access Road: All cars, All paved
Hiking Distance One Way: 0.7 miles *1.1 km* (Time 45 minutes)
How Strenuous: Hard
Features: Views, Redrocks

NUTSHELL: This trail provides an exciting but hard climb to a saddle on Cathedral Rock, from which there are superb views.

DIRECTIONS:
From the Sedona Y (the intersection of Highways 179 and 89A) Go
     South on Highway 179 for 3.4 miles *5.5 km* (MP 310.2) and then turn right on the Back O' Beyond Road **(1)**. Follow it to the 4.1 mile *6.6 km* point, where you will see a marked and fenced parking area to your left.

TRAILHEAD: At the parking lot. There is a three-panel sign.

DESCRIPTION: The sign at the entry warns that this hike is for experienced hikers only and requires some strenuous climbing. We have seen some very unathletic people make the hike, however. Some of them huffed and puffed, but they made it. Timid or out-of-shape hikers may be satisfied to stop wherever they reach their personal limits. From the parking lot you will cross a little streambed and then make a 150-foot climb to the Vista, a bare redrock shelf with great views. A short distance up the trail from the Vista you will intersect the **Templeton Trail**. Go to the right. Then in a few paces turn left at the cairn where your trail leaves the Templeton Trail. Now the hike becomes very steep and there are places where you have to scramble up rock faces. There are toeholds cut into key places and we find the ascent to be thrilling rather than daunting.
     The route climbs to the saddle between two major clusters of spires near the top of Cathedral Rock. There are several places as you climb where you reach level open spaces and can pause to enjoy the great views. Once the saddle is in sight, you will be spurred to finish the climb so that you can see what is on the other side. The saddle is magnificent. There is room to move around, with wonderful views to the east and west and mighty cliffs framing the north and south sides. There are some perfectly placed rocks, made to order for sitting, viewing and meditating. This is regarded as a vortex site.

Photo: This hiking experience can be summed up in three words: vertical but wonderful.

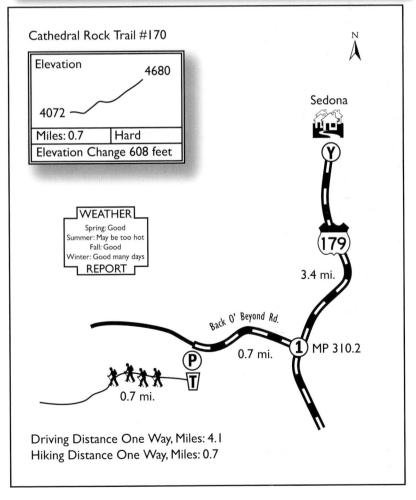

Cathedral Rock Trail #170

N

Elevation	
4072 —	4680
Miles: 0.7	Hard
Elevation Change 608 feet	

Sedona

Y

179

3.4 mi.

WEATHER
Spring: Good
Summer: May be too hot
Fall: Good
Winter: Good many days
REPORT

Back O' Beyond Rd.

1 MP 310.2

0.7 mi.

P
T

0.7 mi.

Driving Distance One Way, Miles: 4.1
Hiking Distance One Way, Miles: 0.7

Chapel Trail

General Information
Location Map E5
Sedona USGS Map
Coconino Forest Service Map

Driving Distance One Way: 3.6 miles *5.8 km* (Time 10 minutes)
Access Road: All cars, All paved
Hiking Distance One Way: 2.4 miles *3.84 km* (Time 1.2 hours)
How Strenuous: Moderate
Features: Views, Access to world-famed Chapel of the Holy Cross

NUTSHELL: This trail branches off from the Little Horse Trail at the base of Twin Buttes and takes you along a scenic route to the parking lot at the foot of the Chapel of the Holy Cross.

DIRECTIONS:
From the Sedona Y (the intersection of Highways 179 and 89A) Go:
    South on Highway 179 (toward Phoenix) for 3.6 miles *5.8 km* (MP 309.8) **(1)** and then turn left into the **Little Horse Trail** parking lot.

TRAILHEAD: At the parking lot, with signs.

DESCRIPTION: There are full facilities at the parking place. The Chapel Trail is shown on the trailhead map. To reach it you hike the Little Horse Trail, which is signed and marked with cairns, to the trail junction. The hike to the junction is nothing special. You do not have any sweeping views, as you are down in the trees. You will find the trail junction at the 1.5 mile *2.4 km* point, which is at the base of Twin Buttes. It is marked with a small wooden sign.
    The trail goes up on redrock ledges in places, where you are up high enough to see over the screen of trees, and for the first time on this hike you can enjoy views. Near at hand, you can look up to your right onto the gorgeous cliff faces of Twin Buttes. We really enjoy this part of the hike—by far the best part.
    However, the enjoyment of the trail is moderated by the fact that it passes by the backyards of several homes that have been built in the area in the last few years. You are not trespassing if you stay on the trail but you still may feel as if you are intruding on the privacy of the homeowners.
    The trail ends at the lower parking lot, from where it is a simple matter to walk up to the Chapel and enjoy its unique beauty and tranquility.

Photo: After following the Little Horse Trail to the Chapel Trail junction, you walk along the base of Twin Buttes to the Chapel of the Holy Cross, famed Sedona landmark.

Chapel Trail

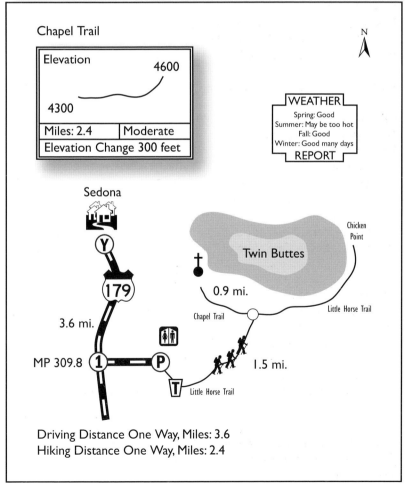

Elevation

4600

4300

Miles: 2.4	Moderate
Elevation Change 300 feet	

N

WEATHER
Spring: Good
Summer: May be too hot
Fall: Good
Winter: Good many days
REPORT

Sedona

Y

179

Chicken Point

Twin Buttes

0.9 mi.

3.6 mi.

Chapel Trail

Little Horse Trail

MP 309.8 1 P

Little Horse Trail

1.5 mi.

Driving Distance One Way, Miles: 3.6
Hiking Distance One Way, Miles: 2.4

Chimney Rock Pass Trail

General Information
Location Map D4
Sedona and Wilson Mountain USGS Maps
Coconino Forest Service Map

Driving Distance One Way: 4.3 miles *6.9 km* (Time 15 minutes)
Access Road: All cars, All paved
Hiking Distance, Complete Loop: 2.25 miles *3.6 km*
How Strenuous: Moderate
Features: Rock formations, Views

NUTSHELL: Chimney Rock is a prominent landmark in Sedona. This trail takes you to the top of the ridge from which the spire rises for fine views.

DIRECTIONS:
From the Sedona Y (the intersection of Highways 179 and 89A) Go:
Southwest on Highway 89A (toward Cottonwood) for 3.2 miles *5.1 km* (MP 371) to Dry Creek Road **(1)**. Turn right on Dry Creek Road and proceed to the 3.7 mile *5.9 km* point **(2)**. Turn right Thunder Mountain Road at the entrance to the Thunder Mountain subdivision. Drive to the 4.3 miles *6.9 km* point **(3)**, and then turn left into the trail parking lot.

TRAILHEAD: At the parking area. There is a 3-panel sign with a map of the trails in the area.

DESCRIPTION: From the parking area, walk north, toward the redrock buttes. At 0.1 miles *0.2 km* you reach a trail junction with a sign, where the **Thunder Mountain Trail** goes to the right. Go straight here.

You will climb to the top of a little pass at 0.35 miles *0.56 km*. The **Summit Route Trail** goes to the left just beyond here. The **Lower Chimney Rock Trail** goes downhill. Turn to the right.

From now on you will ascend to the ridge topped by Chimney Rock. The trail is well designed so that the climb is easy. The approach is very scenic; you will enjoy it. The trail does not go to the chimney, but to a ridge top, a fine place, giving you good views from both sides.

When you are ready to finish the hike, go down the other side. You will reach a trail junction in about 0.25 miles *0.4 km*, where you turn right. In another 0.15 miles *0.24 k*m you will reach a trail junction where a trail goes down to your left to a big green water tank. Pass this and go straight ahead.

You will complete your loop when you reach the junction with the trail from the parking lot, marked with a signpost, where you turn left and go back to your car.

Photo: Here is the view of Chimney Rock that you will have while beginning the climb up to its base. It looks like a single spire from a distance, but is actually a cluster of three joined columns.

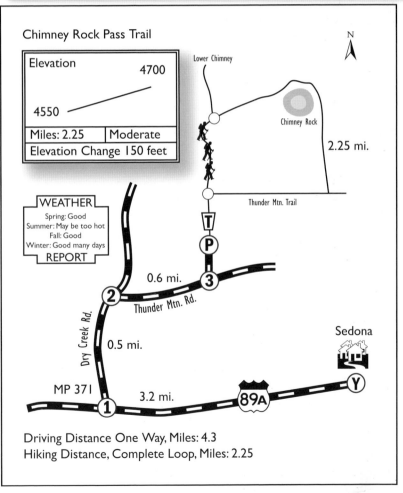

Chimney Rock Pass Trail

N

Elevation

4700

4550

Miles: 2.25 | Moderate

Elevation Change 150 feet

Lower Chimney

Chimney Rock

2.25 mi.

Thunder Mtn. Trail

WEATHER
Spring: Good
Summer: May be too hot
Fall: Good
Winter: Good many days
REPORT

0.6 mi.

Thunder Mtn. Rd.

Dry Creek Rd.

0.5 mi.

Sedona

MP 371

3.2 mi.

89A

Y

Driving Distance One Way, Miles: 4.3
Hiking Distance, Complete Loop, Miles: 2.25

Cibola Pass Trail

General Information
Location Map D4
Munds Park, Wilson Mountain USGS Maps
Coconino Forest Service Map

Driving Distance One Way: 1.9 miles *3.0 km* (Time 10 minutes)
Access Road: All cars. Last 0.4 miles *0.6 km* dirt road
Hiking Distance, Complete Loop: 2.25 miles *3.6 km* (Time 40 minutes)
How Strenuous: Moderate
Features: Easy to reach, all-weather road, pleasant hike near town, good views

NUTSHELL: Starting from the old shooting range at the end of Jordan Road, this trail branches west, climbs over a pass on Cibola Ridge and goes over to connect to the Jordan Trail.

DIRECTIONS:
From the Sedona Y (the intersection of Highways 179 and 89A) Go:
    North on Highway on 89A (toward Flagstaff) for 0.3 miles *0.5 km* to Jordan Road, in the middle of uptown Sedona **(1)**. Turn left (N) and take Jordan Road to its end, at 1.1 miles *1.8 km* **(2)**. Turn left at the stop sign, onto Park Ridge Drive, a paved road, which goes through a subdivision and ends at 1.3 miles *2.1 km*. Keep going on the unpaved road. At the 1.9 mile *3.0 km* point, you will come to the parking area and trailhead.

TRAILHEAD: You drove past the trailhead on the way to the parking area. Backtrack to it on foot.

DESCRIPTION: The trail at first dips down into the bottom of a little wash, and then climbs, passing through an attractive forest of Arizona cypress. You will rise high enough to have views out over the Brins Mesa area, which is quite scenic, rimmed by beautiful red and white cliffs.
    At the 0.5 mile *0.8 km* point, you come to the top of Cibola Ridge, where there is a barbed wire fence. Turn right at the fence and follow it for about 30 paces to a gate. You pass through the gate and then descend the other side of the ridge, through another cypress forest to reach a junction with the **Jordan Trail** at 1.0 miles *1.6 km*. This is the end of the Cibola Pass Trail. You can turn right and hike another 0.4 miles *0.64 km* to Devil's Kitchen. Or you can turn left and follow the Jordan Trail back to the parking lot, a hike of about 1.25 miles *2.0 km*. We prefer turning to the left and returning home on the Jordan Trail. It gives the hiker very nice views of the impressive red cliffs on the edge of Cibola Ridge.

Photo: Pictured here is the rock formation known as the Cibola Mittens. The Cibola Pass Trail is located in this area.

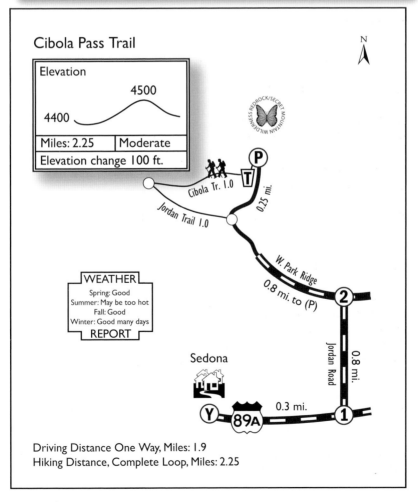

Cibola Pass Trail

N

Elevation

4500

4400

| Miles: 2.25 | Moderate |
| Elevation change 100 ft. | |

REDROCK/SECRET MOUNTAIN WILDERNESS

Cibola Tr. 1.0

Jordan Trail 1.0

0.25 mi.

W. Park Ridge

0.8 mi. to (P)

WEATHER
Spring: Good
Summer: May be too hot
Fall: Good
Winter: Good many days
REPORT

Sedona

Jordan Road

0.8 mi.

0.3 mi.

89A

Driving Distance One Way, Miles: 1.9
Hiking Distance, Complete Loop, Miles: 2.25

Cockscomb Butte Route

General Information
Location Map D3
Wilson Mountain USGS Map
Coconino Forest Service Map

Driving Distance One Way: 10.7 miles *17.1 km* (Time 20 minutes)
Access Road: All cars, Last 3.0 miles bumpy dirt roads
Hiking Distance One Way: 0.75 miles *1.2 km* (Time 1.0 hour)
How Strenuous: Moderate
Features: Views

NUTSHELL: The Cockscomb is one of the southernmost redrock buttes in the Sedona area. After a short, level approach, you make a 400 foot climb to enjoy exploring the top and take in the wonderful views.

DIRECTIONS:
From the Sedona Y (the intersection of Highways 179 and 89A) Go:
    Southwest on Highway 89A for 3.2 miles *5.1 km* (MP 371) and then turn right on Dry Creek Road **(1)**. Follow it to the 6.1 mile *9.8 km* point, where it joins Long Canyon Road **(2)**. Turn left. At the 7.7 mile *12.3 km* point **(3)**, turn left on FR 152C, a dirt road. At the 9.7 mile *15.5 km* point **(4)**, turn left on FR 9583 and follow it to the 10.7 mile *17.1 km* point, a locked gate. Park on the shoulder so that you do not block access to the gate.

TRAILHEAD: Walk up to the gate, turn right, and follow the barbed wire fence. You will see a well-worn path around the ranch fence.

DESCRIPTION: The ranch was the Tree Farm, but will be subdivided. At about the 0.35 mile *0.6 km* point the trail moves away from the fence, bearing southeast, and heads toward the Cockscomb. You are almost at the foot of the Cockscomb at this point, and will meet the system **Cockscomb Trail** here. From the place where you can no longer see the fence, look for a path going to the right (S) and heading uphill. It is usually marked with cairns. It is at 0.4 miles *0.7 km*. This is a hiker-made trail, and receives enough use so that the path is well-worn and easily discernible.
    The trail has been level up to here. You will now climb 400 feet to the top. Look carefully. We never have any trouble following this trail, but you want to keep checking the cairns, because there is only one route to the top. The trail winds up the face and "around the corner" where you will find some natural stairsteps and hiker-built steps to the top. The top is small, easy to explore, and has many clear areas for excellent views out over the countryside.

Photo: The trail winds up the north face of Cockscomb Butte, which is on the left side of the photo.

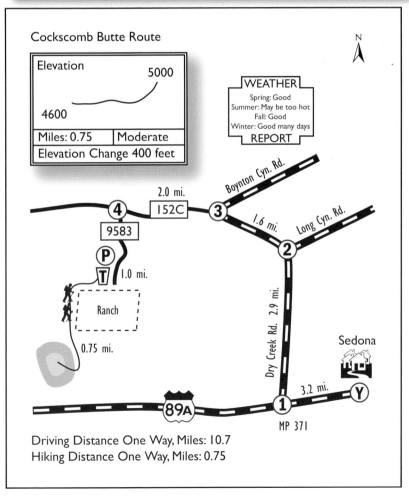

Cockscomb Butte Route

N

Elevation

5000

4600

| Miles: 0.75 | Moderate |
| Elevation Change 400 feet | |

WEATHER
Spring: Good
Summer: May be too hot
Fall: Good
Winter: Good many days
REPORT

Boynton Cyn. Rd.

2.0 mi.

152C

④ ③

9583

1.6 mi.

Long Cyn. Rd.

②

P
T
1.0 mi.

Ranch

Dry Creek Rd. 2.9 mi.

Sedona

0.75 mi.

3.2 mi.

89A

① Y

MP 371

Driving Distance One Way, Miles: 10.7
Hiking Distance One Way, Miles: 0.75

Cockscomb Trail

General Information
Location Map D3
Wilson Mt. USGS Map
Coconino Forest Service Map

Driving Distance One Way: 8.2 miles *13.2 km* (Time 25 minutes)
Access Road: All cars, Last 0.5 mile *0.8 km* fair dirt road
Hiking Distance One Way: 3.0 miles *4.8 km* (Time 1.5 hours)
How Strenuous: Moderate
Features: Views of Doe Mountain and the Cockscomb

NUTSHELL: This trail is easy to reach and goes into interesting backcountry around Doe Mountain and the Cockscomb. If you want to hike to the top of the Cockscomb, take the **Cockscomb Butte Route** described in this book.

DIRECTIONS:
From the Sedona Y (the intersection of Highways 179 and 89A) Go:
   Southwest on Highway 89A (toward Cottonwood) for 3.2 miles *5.1 km* (MP 371) and then turn right on Dry Creek Road **(1)**. Follow it to the 6.1 mile *9.8 km* point, the Long Canyon Road junction **(2)**. Turn left. At the 7.7 mile *12.3 km* point, you intersect the Boynton Canyon Road **(3)**. Turn left onto the unpaved road. At the 8.2 mile *13.2 km* point you will see the driveway for the **Fay Canyon Trail**, to your right. Drive past this turnoff for a few feet and turn to the left on the first road beyond it **(4)**, FR 9586. It takes you directly to the parking area.

TRAILHEAD: The parking area. There are trail signs to guide you from there.

DESCRIPTION: You will walk closed jeep roads for 0.5 miles *0.8 km* to a horse gate. Walk through the gate. The trail runs under a power line and gives nice views into scenic country around Thunder Mountain and the Dry Creek areas. At 1.5 miles *2.4 km* the **Dawa Trail** comes in from your left and joins you for a few yards, then branches off to the left. The Cockscomb Trail now turns southwest and runs along the base of Doe Mountain. In this area the trail is an old jeep road, so it is wide and easy to walk.

   At 3.0 miles *4.8 km* the trail ends at a fence corner, where there is a sign for the **Rupp Trail**. Forest Service officials told us that they are not certain about the Cockscomb Trail from this point, because decisions hinge on the development of the old Tree Farm property that runs south from Doe Mountain. The fence corner where the trail stops is a boundary of that land.

Photo: The Cockscomb is a familiar Sedona landmark. This trail takes you near it, but not to its top.

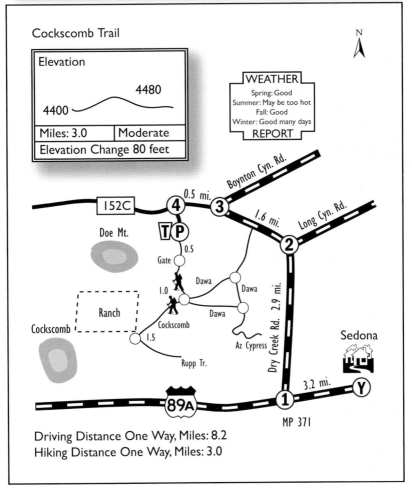

Cockscomb Trail

Elevation

4480

4400

| Miles: 3.0 | Moderate |
| Elevation Change 80 feet | |

N

WEATHER
Spring: Good
Summer: May be too hot
Fall: Good
Winter: Good many days
REPORT

152C

Boynton Cyn. Rd.

0.5 mi.

4 — 3

1.6 mi.

Long Cyn. Rd.

Doe Mt.

T P

0.5

Gate

Dawa

Dawa

2

1.0

Dawa

Ranch

Cockscomb

Dawa

Dry Creek Rd. 2.9 mi.

Cockscomb

1.5

Az Cypress

Sedona

Rupp Tr.

89A

1

3.2 mi.

Y

MP 371

Driving Distance One Way, Miles: 8.2
Hiking Distance One Way, Miles: 3.0

Coffee Pot

General Information
Location Map D4
Sedona and Wilson Mt. USGS Maps
Coconino Forest Service Map

Driving Distance One Way: 2.85 miles *4.6 km* (Time 10 minutes)
Access Road: All cars, All paved
Hiking Distance One Way: 1.0 miles *1.6 km* (Time 45 minutes)
How Strenuous: Easy
Features: Rock formations, Views

NUTSHELL: Coffee Pot Rock is a familiar Sedona landmark. This trail allows you easy access to its base.

DIRECTIONS:
From the Sedona Y (the intersection of Highways 179 and 89A) Go:
Southwest on Highway 89A (toward Cottonwood) for 1.9 miles *3.0 km* (MP 372.7 then turn right on Coffee Pot Drive (at stoplight) **(1)**. Follow it to the 2.5 mile *4.0 km* point where you turn left on Sanborn **(2)** and proceed west to the 2.65 mile *4.2 km* point **(3)**, where you turn right on Little Elf Drive. At the end of Little Elf, the 2.85 mile *4.6 km* point, turn right on Buena Vista and drive a few yards, turning left into the first road you see, which goes into the parking lot.

TRAILHEAD: At the parking area, but the sign does not show this trail.

DESCRIPTION: From the parking area walk north. The trail splits and you may be confused. Go right at the first fork and keep moving north toward the distant cliffs. You will reach a power line at 0.5 miles *0.8 km* where there is a T-intersection with the **Thunder Mountain Trail**. Turn right on Thunder Mountain Trail.
Next you will come to a signpost for the **Sugarloaf Loop Trail**. Go past it, and shortly beyond, at 0.6 miles *1.0 km* you will see the unmarked junction for the Coffee Pot Trail. A circle of stones surrounds a bush here. Turn left. Even though the trail is unofficial, it is well traveled and easy to follow, using an old jeep road. Whenever you come to a side path (there are several), just remember where Coffee Pot Rock is and keep moving toward it.
The trail goes to the base of the cliffs and then moves along a ledge toward Coffee Pot. The cliffs here are gorgeous. As the trail nears Coffee Pot it becomes rougher and you have to watch carefully to follow it. Eventually the ledge you walk on pinches out. Here you can look up and see the spout of Coffee Pot towering above your head. There are great views.

Photo: The coffeepot is easy to see from this perspective, with its domed lid and prominent spout. You will hike out onto a ledge underneath the spout.

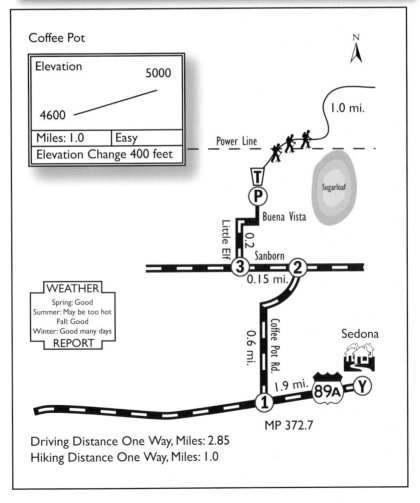

Coffee Pot

N

Elevation

5000

4600

Miles: 1.0 | Easy
Elevation Change 400 feet

1.0 mi.

Power Line

Sugarloaf

T P

Buena Vista

Little Elf

0.2

Sanborn

3 — 2

0.15 mi.

WEATHER
Spring: Good
Summer: May be too hot
Fall: Good
Winter: Good many days
REPORT

Coffee Pot Rd.

0.6 mi.

Sedona

1.9 mi. 89A Y

1

MP 372.7

Driving Distance One Way, Miles: 2.85
Hiking Distance One Way, Miles: 1.0

Cookstove Trail #143

General Information
Location Map B5
Mountainaire USGS Map
Coconino Forest Service Map

Driving Distance One Way: 12.7 miles *20.4 km* (Time 20 minutes)
Access Road: All cars, All paved
Hiking Distance One Way: 0.75 miles *1.2 km* (Time 45 minutes)
How Strenuous: Hard
Features: Views

NUTSHELL: This trail starts at the Pine Flat Campground north of Sedona and climbs the east wall of upper Oak Creek Canyon.

DIRECTIONS:
From the Sedona Y (the intersection of Highways 179 and 89A) Go:
  North on Highway 89A (toward Flagstaff) for a distance of 12.7 miles *20.4 km* (MP 386.9) to the Pine Flat Campground **(1)**. On your left at the upper end of the campground on the shoulder of the highway, you will see a standpipe with flowing water. Park anywhere near the standpipe. There are wide aprons on both shoulders in this area.

TRAILHEAD: On the east side of the road just across Highway 89A from the standpipe. It is marked by a rusty sign.

DESCRIPTION: The Cookstove Trail is one of four trails in upper Oak Creek Canyon that climb the east wall of the canyon. Others are **Harding Spring, Purtymun, Thomas Point.** They are all strenuous hikes.
  The trail starts by the road and immediately begins to climb. At first the trail parallels Cookstove Draw. At 0.1 miles *0.16 km* you get a great view down into the draw, where there is a small waterfall at times. Then the trail veers away from Cookstove Draw. The forest through which this trail passes is typical for upper Oak Creek Canyon, with pine at the beginning, changing into mixed pines and firs as you climb. The climbing is steady, as if the builders of the trail wanted to get to the top in a straight line.
  When you top out, you are in a spot where you get good views of the west wall of Oak Creek Canyon, though the views are not as good as the views you get at the top of the nearby Harding Spring trail.
  The elevation at the top is 6,600 feet, almost as high as Flagstaff, and the climate is similar. This hike can often be pleasant in summer when hiking in Sedona would be too hot.

Photo: The Cookstove Trail climbs the east wall of Oak Creek Canyon. Near the top, as pictured here, you enter a zone of cool pines.

Cookstove Trail #143

Elevation	
Miles: 0.75	Hard
Elevation change 1000 ft.	

Elevation: 6600 / 5600

N

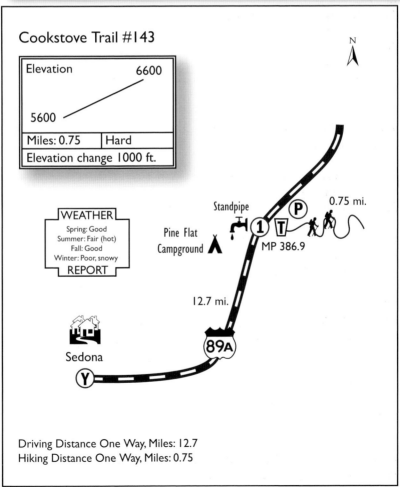

WEATHER
Spring: Good
Summer: Fair (hot)
Fall: Good
Winter: Poor, snowy
REPORT

Standpipe

Pine Flat
Campground

0.75 mi.

1 T P

MP 386.9

12.7 mi.

89A

Sedona

Y

Driving Distance One Way, Miles: 12.7
Hiking Distance One Way, Miles: 0.75

Courthouse Butte Loop Trail

General Information
Location Map F5
Sedona and Munds Mt. USGS Maps
Coconino Forest Service Map

Driving Distance One Way: 6.2 miles *9.9 km* (Time 20 minutes)
Access Road: All cars, All paved
Hiking Distance, Complete Loop: 4.3 miles *6.9 km* (Time 2.0 hours)
How Strenuous: Moderate
Features: Views

NUTSHELL: This fine trail takes you up close and personal to Courthouse Butte and Bell Rock, two of Sedona's prime landmarks.

DIRECTIONS:
From the Sedona Y (the intersection of Highways 179 and 89A) Go:
    South on Highway 179 (toward Phoenix) for 6.2 miles *9.9 km* (MP 307.4) to a place south of Bell Rock, just short of the Village of Oak Creek **(1)**, where you will see a trail sign. Turn left into the parking area.

TRAILHEAD: Use the Bell Rock Pathway as the trailhead.

DESCRIPTION: There is a nice shelter with map at the parking area showing the details of the network of trails here. Walk the Bell Rock Pathway north for 0.5 miles *0.8 km* to a signed trail junction. The Courthouse Butte Loop starts here. Turn right. The trail makes a circle around Courthouse Butte, hugging the base of this beautiful formation.
    At 1.5 miles *2.4 km* you will come to a streambed of native redrock. You are now in the Munds Mountain Wilderness Area. As you walk out onto the streambed, turn left (N) and walk about 75 paces along the far side. Here you will find the trail again, coming off of the rock and running along a shelf of soil a few yards away from the stream bottom.
    This area is our favorite part of the hike, because it is quiet, scenic and natural, quite different from the bustle around Bell Rock. You will make a climb on the next leg of the hike, but it is not very steep, finally emerging on a ridge top where there is a round redrock knob just to your right.
    From this point, you walk west along the north side of the butte, rejoining the Bell Rock Pathway near Highway 179 and there are always a lot of people around. You simply turn south and walk back to the parking place.

Photo: You will make a complete circuit around famous Courthouse Butte on this fine trail.

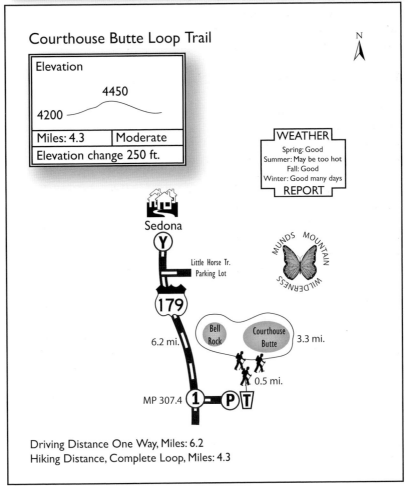

Courthouse Butte Loop Trail

N

Elevation

4450

4200

| Miles: 4.3 | Moderate |

Elevation change 250 ft.

WEATHER
Spring: Good
Summer: May be too hot
Fall: Good
Winter: Good many days
REPORT

Sedona

Y

Little Horse Tr.
Parking Lot

179

MUNDS MOUNTAIN
WILDERNESS

6.2 mi.

Bell
Rock

Courthouse
Butte

3.3 mi.

0.5 mi.

MP 307.4   1   P T

Driving Distance One Way, Miles: 6.2
Hiking Distance, Complete Loop, Miles: 4.3

Cow Pies

General Information
Location Map E5
Munds Mt. and Munds Park USGS Maps
Coconino Forest Service Map

Driving Distance One Way: 3.8 miles *6.1 km* (Time 20 minutes)
Access Road: High clearance cars, Last 2.5 miles *4.0 km* rough dirt road
Hiking Distance One Way: 1.5 miles *2.4 km* (Time 40 minutes)
How Strenuous: Easy
Features: Views, Fascinating rock formations and sculptures, Vortex

NUTSHELL: The Cow Pies are redrock formations just west of the Schnebly Hill Road, only 3.8 miles *6.1 km* east of uptown Sedona. If you like redrocks, you will love the Cow Pies. **A personal favorite**.

DIRECTIONS:
From the Sedona Y (the intersection of Highways 179 and 89A) Go:
    South on Highway 179 (toward Phoenix) for a distance of 0.3 miles *0.5 km* (MP 313.1) to the Schnebly Hill Road **(1)**. It is just across the bridge past Tlaquepaque. Turn left onto the Schnebly Hill Road. It is paved for the first 1.0 mile *1.6 km* and then turns into a dirt road that is sometimes bad. At 3.8 miles *6.1 km* **(2)** turn right into the marked parking area.

TRAILHEAD: There is a trail sign at the parking area.

DESCRIPTION: Walk across the road to start the trail. The Cow Pies are rounded buttes, a unique Sedona experience, easy to reach and hike on.
    At 0.2 miles *0.3 km* you will come onto a redrock shelf littered with small black stones, bits of broken lava.
    At 0.43 miles *0.7 km* you come out on a ledge. The trail you have been following goes in a straight line (see **Mitten Ridge**). Quit the trail and turn to the left. Walk west, to your left, on the level area to the end of the ledge, where at 0.52 miles *0.8 km* you will find a land bridge linking it to the largest pie.
    You will top out on the largest pie at about 0.6 miles *1.0 km*. From this point there is no trail. You just walk around and explore. In fact, it is so easy to walk around on these formations that you won't realize how substantial they are until you get to their edges and look down
    The farthest extension of these rocks takes you out about 1.5 miles *2.4 km* from the parking place. This is one of the few places where it is fun not to have an official trail and to be free to roam around at will exploring whatever takes your fancy.

Photo: We love this hike and enjoy being right on the famous Sedona redrock. After a rain numerous small pools are formed, reflecting the cliffs beyond.

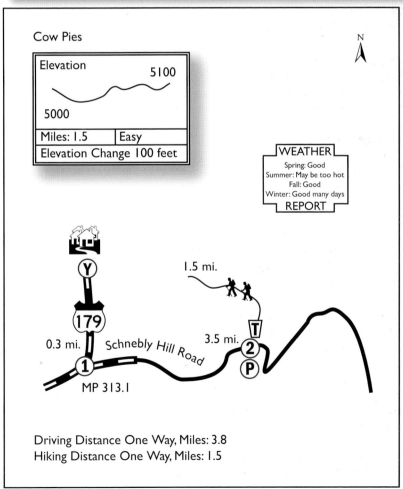

Cow Pies

N

Elevation

5100

5000

Miles: 1.5	Easy
Elevation Change 100 feet	

WEATHER

Spring: Good
Summer: May be too hot
Fall: Good
Winter: Good many days

REPORT

1.5 mi.

Y

179

0.3 mi.

Schnebly Hill Road

3.5 mi.

T

2

P

1

MP 313.1

Driving Distance One Way, Miles: 3.8
Hiking Distance One Way, Miles: 1.5

Crescent Moon Creek Walk

General Information
Location Map F4
Sedona USGS Map
Coconino Forest Service Map

Driving Distance One Way: 7.0 miles *11.2 km* (Time 20 minutes)
Access Road*:* All cars, All paved
Hiking Distance One Way: 1.0 miles *1.6 km* (Time 30 minutes)
How Strenuous*:* Easy
Features*:* Easy to reach, Views of Cathedral Rock, Creekside stroll

NUTSHELL: You drive to Crescent Moon Ranch, and then walk along the banks of Oak Creek in the shadow of Cathedral Rock.

DIRECTIONS:
From the Sedona Y (the intersection of Highways 179 and 89A) Go:
　　Southwest on Highway 89A (toward Cottonwood) a distance of 4.2 miles *6.8 km* (MP 368.9) to the Upper Red Rock Loop Road (stop light) **(1)**. Turn left and follow the Loop to the 6.0 mile *10.0 km* point **(2)**, and turn left, following the paved road to Crescent Moon Ranch Park which you reach at 7.0 miles *11.2 km* **(P)**. You must pay a fee at the entrance. Park inside.

TRAILHEAD: No marked trail; follow the pink sidewalk.

DESCRIPTION: Travelers used to ford Oak Creek here, where a redrock shelf gave firm footing. Countless photos of Cathedral Rock taken from the crossing made Sedona's beauties known to the world.
　　Try to park near the entrance booth. Follow the pink sidewalk down toward the creek, at the west end of the park. Then turn and walk along the pink sidewalk easterly. There are several places where benches have been placed so that you can take your time, sit and meditate or just enjoy the experience of being in this lovely place. The sidewalk ends about 0.25 miles *0.4 km* and a dirt footpath continues.
　　You enter the site of the old Chavez Ranch next, with old buildings. Of particular interest is a water wheel. From this point, the trail moves nearer the creek. We particularly enjoy an area where the trail moves across a broad redrock shelf. Keep following the trail. There are many side paths, but it doesn't matter, they all go to the same place, confined by the creek on one side and an irrigation ditch on the other.
　　The trail ends at a big curve, where the creek splits and a power line crosses it. This is a very pleasant, easy walk that people of all ages can enjoy.

Photo: The Crescent Moon Ranch park provides one of the best places from which to photograph world famous Cathedral Rock.

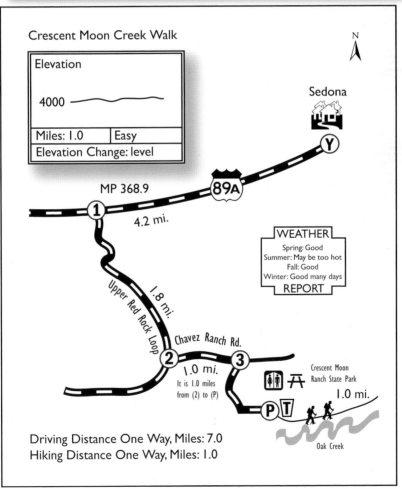

Crescent Moon Creek Walk

N

Elevation

4000

Miles: 1.0	Easy
Elevation Change: level	

Sedona

MP 368.9

89A

(1)

4.2 mi.

Upper Red Rock Loop

1.8 mi.

WEATHER
Spring: Good
Summer: May be too hot
Fall: Good
Winter: Good many days
REPORT

Chavez Ranch Rd.

(2)   (3)

1.0 mi.
It is 1.0 miles
from (2) to (P)

Crescent Moon
Ranch State Park

1.0 mi.

(P) (T)

Oak Creek

Driving Distance One Way, Miles: 7.0
Hiking Distance One Way, Miles: 1.0

David Miller Trail

General Information
Location Map C4
Wilson Mt. USGS Map
Coconino Forest Service Map

Driving Distance One Way: 8.6 miles *13.8 km* (Time 30 minutes)
Access Road: Most cars, Last 3.4 miles *5.4 km* rough dirt road
Hiking Distance, Complete Loop: 7.3 miles *11.7 km* (Time 4 hours)
How Strenuous: Hard
Features: Views, Remote canyons, Variety of terrain

NUTSHELL: This scenic trail links the **Secret Canyon Trail** to the **Bear Sign Trail,** for a loop hike in some of Sedona's wildest backcountry.

DIRECTIONS:
From the Sedona Y (the intersection of Highways 179 and 89A) Go:
Southwest on Highway 89A (toward Cottonwood) for 3.2 miles *5.1 km* (MP 371) to Dry Creek Road **(1)**. Turn right on Dry Creek and go to the 5.2 mile *8.3 km* point **(2)**. Turn right on FR 152, the Vultee Arch Road, and follow it to the 8.6 mile *13.8 km* point, where there is a sign for the Secret Canyon Trail turnoff **(3)**. Turn left into the parking area. (Very rough road).

TRAILHEAD: There is a signboard and map at the trailhead.

DESCRIPTION: You hike the Secret Canyon Trail to the 2.1 mile *3.4 km* point. The signed David Miller Trail joins here, to your right (N). The trail takes you uphill along a canyon through a dense forest of oak and cypress. At the 2.6 miles *4.2 km* point you break out above the forest for superb vistas. Before you is a notch at the top of a ridge between two buttes—your target, requiring a very steep climb.

You reach the top of the pass at the 2.9 mile *4.6 km* point. Then you begin a descent into Bear Sign Canyon. You will pass from desert into alpine landscape, hiking through cool pines and firs to the sign at the Bear Sign/ David Miller junction at 3.25 miles *5.2 km*. Turn right here, for a 3.1 mile *5.0 km* walk to the Bear Sign/Dry Creek Trailhead. From there you walk south on FR 152 for 1.0 mile *1.6 km* to the Secret Canyon Trailhead.

This is a long, tiring hike, so we like to use two cars. Drive both cars to the Bear Sign Trailhead. Park one car there. Then everybody piles into the second car, which is driven to the Secret Canyon Trailhead and parked.

David Miller was a young Forest Service employee who went out hiking by himself in 1997 and disappeared. In spite of the massive manhunt that was launched to find him, he was never found, and his location is a mystery.

Photo: Dick is resting near the high point of this great trail, and looking back at the Secret Canyon wilderness, a highly scenic wonderland.

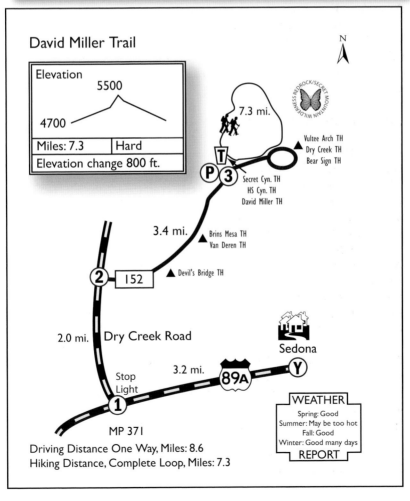

David Miller Trail

N

Elevation		
	5500	
4700		
Miles: 7.3	Hard	
Elevation change 800 ft.		

WILDERNESS REDROCK/SECRET MOUNTAIN

7.3 mi.

T
P 3

Vultee Arch TH
Dry Creek TH
Bear Sign TH

Secret Cyn. TH
HS Cyn. TH
David Miller TH

3.4 mi.

Brins Mesa TH
Van Deren TH

2 152

Devil's Bridge TH

2.0 mi. Dry Creek Road

Sedona

3.2 mi.

Stop
Light

89A Y

1

MP 371

Driving Distance One Way, Miles: 8.6
Hiking Distance, Complete Loop, Miles: 7.3

Dawa Trail

General Information
Location Map D3
Wilson Mt. USGS Map
Coconino Forest Service Map

Driving Distance One Way: 6.7 miles *10.7 km* (Time 15 minutes)
Access Road: All cars, All paved
Hiking Distance, Complete Loop: 2.5 miles *4.0 km* (Time 2.5 hours)
How Strenuous: Moderate
Features: Connections to other trails

NUTSHELL: The Dawa Trail makes a nice loop in the Doe Mountain area, connecting to three other trails.

DIRECTIONS:
From the Sedona Y (the intersection of Highways 179 and 89A) Go:
Southwest on Highway 89A (toward Cottonwood) for 3.2 miles *5.1 km* (MP 371) to the Dry Creek Road **(1)**. Turn right onto Dry Creek Road and drive it to the 6.1 mile *9.8 km* point, a stop sign **(2)**. Turn left and drive to the 6.7 mile *10.7 km* point, where you see a wide apron in front of a gap in a barbed wire fence to your left **(3)**. Park.

TRAILHEAD: On the other side of the fence, where there is a 2-panel trailhead sign.

DESCRIPTION: Follow the trail from the sign. At 0.1 miles *0.16 km* you come to a V-fork. Go straight here. The **OK Trail** goes to the left. The Dawa Trail is an old road. There are many old roads, so keep a lookout. Because this trail is popular with bikers, the best way to follow the trail is by following bike tracks
At 1.1 miles *1.8 km*, near Doe Mountain, you come to a T-shaped trail junction, where the Dawa joins the **Cockscomb Trail**. Turn left, as the Dawa and the Cockscomb run together for a short distance. In about ten yards, turn left, as the Dawa leaves the other trail. From now on you will walk near a power line.
At 2.1 miles *3.4 km* you reach Dry Creek and go across. On the other side, a few yards from the bank, is a T-trail junction with the **Arizona Cypress Trail**. Turn left here. At 2.4 miles *3.8 km* you will cross Dry Creek again, at a point where it has two channels. On the far side of the second channel is a T-junction with the OK Trail. Turn left and hike the OK Trail back to the parking place.
"Dawa" is a Hopi word, meaning "moon".

Photo: The trail is sandy here, with good views of some beautiful buttes.

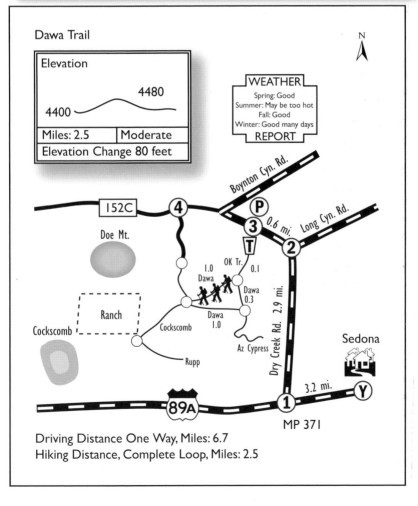

Dawa Trail

Elevation

4480

4400

Miles: 2.5 | Moderate

Elevation Change 80 feet

N

WEATHER
Spring: Good
Summer: May be too hot
Fall: Good
Winter: Good many days
REPORT

Boynton Cyn. Rd.

152C 4

P

3 0.6 mi. Long Cyn. Rd.

T

2

Doe Mt.

OK Tr. 0.1

1.0
Dawa

Dawa
0.3

Dry Creek Rd. 2.9 mi.

Sedona

Ranch

Dawa
1.0

Cockscomb

Cockscomb

Az Cypress

Rupp

89A

3.2 mi. Y

1

MP 371

Driving Distance One Way, Miles: 6.7
Hiking Distance, Complete Loop, Miles: 2.5

Dead Horse Ranch State Park Trails

General Information
Location Map F1
Clarkdale USGS Map
Coconino Forest Service Map

Driving Distance One Way: 21.5 miles *34.4 km* (Time 45 minutes)
Access Road: All cars, All paved
Hiking Distances: Tavasci Marsh 1.0 miles *1.6 km*, one-way, Verde River
Greenway 1.0 mile 1.6 *km* one-way
How Strenuous: Moderate (both trails)
Features: Easy to reach, Verde River access, Birdwatching, Toilets and
other amenities

NUTSHELL: This state park, located near Cottonwood, has nice facilities, including trails. Upon entrance to the park, visitors are given a map showing a number of hiking trails. Most of these are simply intra-park trails designed to move visitors from one part of the park to another. Two of the trails, the Tavasci Marsh and the Verde River Greenway trails, are worthy of an entry in this article. Two other trails originating in the park, the **Lime Kiln Trail** and the **Raptor Hill Trail**, are given full chapters.

DIRECTIONS:
From the Sedona Y (the intersection of Highways 179 and 89A) Go:
   Southwest on Highway 89A for 18.6 miles *29.8 km*, to the stoplight at the junction of Highways 279 and 89A in Cottonwood. Go straight on Historic Highway 89A (Main Street). At 20.6 miles *33.0 km*, just past the cemetery, turn right on 10th Street, which is signed for the park **(1)**. The entrance to the park is at 21.5 miles *34.4 km*, where you must pay an entrance fee **(2)**.

TRAILHEADS:
   (1) Verde River Greenway Trail—Pass the Sanitation Station and turn on the second turn to the right **(3)**, into the Mesquite Day Use Area, and drive to first striped parking area to the left. The trail starts at the head of the handicapped parking space that is not by the toilet.
   (2) Tavasci Marsh Trail—Turn left at the second road to the left **(4)**, where you will see a Tavasci Marsh sign. Drive to the parking lot at the end.

DESCRIPTIONS:
   (1) Verde River Greenway Trail. 1.0 miles *1.6 km*. Level. Moderate. At the start there is no trailhead sign, only a lath-type marker with a hiker symbol. The trail takes you downhill to a streambed which you cross three times on plank bridges. Then you climb stairsteps and emerge onto a parking lot west of the Lagoon. From here the trail is close to the river but never goes to the river's edge, staying on the cliffs above. At the Lagoon take the right fork and then the left. The trail is away from the riverbank but there are

many places where you can walk to the right and see the river. Then the trail moves away from the river and becomes a sandy path through stands of tall cottonwoods and sycamores, an excellent birding area. Deep sand here makes walking hard. At 1.0 miles *1.6 km* is a trail fork. We recommend you go back the way you came at this point.

(2) Tavasci Marsh Trail. 1.0 miles *1.6 km*. Fairly level. Moderate. Takes you to an observation deck on a marsh, the Verde's best bird watching spot. At the start, you can take the River Route, downhill left, or the Road Route, uphill through the gate. The paths merge. This is a good hike for kids.

Photo: There is a photo from Dead Horse Ranch State Park on page 252.

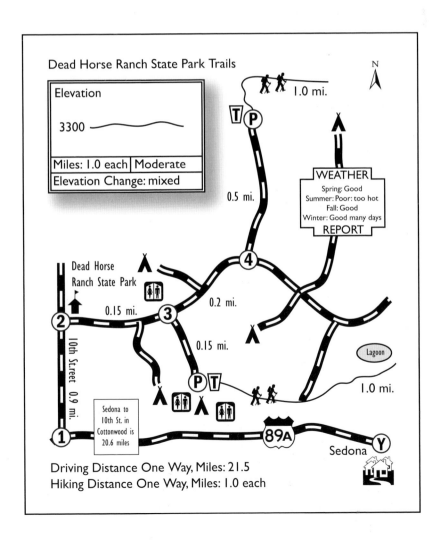

Deadman Pass Trail

General Information
Location Map C3
Wilson Mountain USGS Map
Coconino Forest Service Map

Driving Distance One Way: 7.8 miles *12.5 km* (Time 20 minutes)
Access Road: All cars, All paved
Hiking Distance One Way: 1.4 miles *2.2 km* (Time 45 minutes)
How Strenuous: Moderate
Features: Easy to reach, Redrock views, uncrowded

NUTSHELL: You hike along an old jeep trail through dense thickets of manzanita, admiring the buttes of Boynton on one side and Mescal Mountain on the other, then joining the Long Canyon Trail.

DIRECTIONS:
From the Sedona Y (the intersection of Highways 179 and 89A) Go:
Southwest on Highway 89A (toward Cottonwood) for 3.2 miles *5.1 km* (MP 371), and then make a right turn onto Dry Creek Road (1). Follow it to the 6.1 mile *9.8 km* point, where it joins Long Canyon Road (2). Turn left. At the 7.7 mile *12.3 km* point, you reach another junction (3). Go right. At 7.8 miles *12.5 km*, turn right into the trailhead parking lot.

TRAILHEAD: At the parking area. There is a toilet.

DESCRIPTION: We don't know how Deadman Pass got its name. The pass is a natural corridor leading between the buttes that form the east side of Boynton Canyon and the west side of Mescal Mountain. At its end, the Deadman Pass trail joins the **Long Canyon Trail**.
At its beginning, the trail runs along under a power line. The trail carves a path through thick forests of manzanita and other desert shrubs, which are incredibly dense here. On your left, you will enjoy enchanting views of the cliffs of the Boynton Cliffs. We particularly admire the sheer red walls on this face of this butte, though it features pillars and alcoves as well.
To your right is Mescal Mountain. Its cliffs are not nearly so impressive, but it is still very scenic. The trail undulates, following the natural curvature of the terrain—no cuts or fills here—gradually climbing to a high point at the end of Mescal Mountain. From here you will enjoy views to the north. From the high point, the trail curls around the tip of Mescal Mountain and descends, crossing under the powerline, then joins the Long Canyon Trail on the flat. There is a sign at the trail junction.

Photo: This moderate trail takes you through a passage between the cliffs of Boynton Canyon on the left and Mescal Mountain on the right. Very scenic.

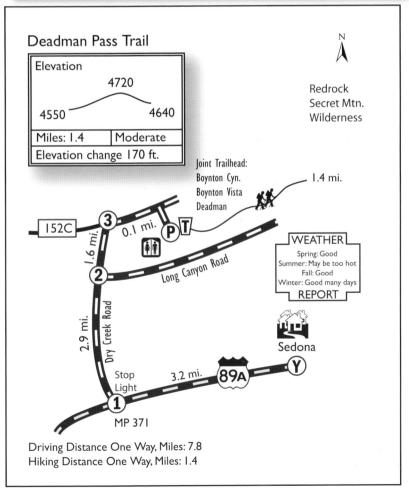

Deadman Pass Trail

Elevation

4720

4550   4640

Miles: 1.4	Moderate
Elevation change 170 ft.	

N

Redrock
Secret Mtn.
Wilderness

Joint Trailhead:
Boynton Cyn.
Boynton Vista
Deadman

1.4 mi.

152C   ③   0.1 mi.   P T

1.6 mi.

Long Canyon Road

②

WEATHER
Spring: Good
Summer: May be too hot
Fall: Good
Winter: Good many days
REPORT

2.9 mi.

Dry Creek Road

Sedona

Stop
Light   3.2 mi.   89A   Y

①

MP 371

Driving Distance One Way, Miles: 7.8
Hiking Distance One Way, Miles: 1.4

Devil's Bridge Trail #120

General Information
Location Map D4
Loy Butte and Wilson Mt. USGS Maps
Coconino Forest Service Map

Driving Distance One Way: 6.5 miles *10.4 km* (Time 30 minutes)
Access Road: All cars, Last 1.3 miles *2.1 km* bumpy dirt road
Hiking Distance One Way: 1.0 miles *1.6 km* (Time 30 minutes)
How Strenuous: Moderate
Features: Views, Arch

NUTSHELL: A short hike into a beautiful canyon where you climb sandstone stairs to a fascinating arch.

DIRECTIONS:
From the Sedona Y (the intersection of Highways 179 and 89A) Go:
　　Southwest on Highway 89A (toward Cottonwood) for 3.2 miles *5.1 km* (MP 371) then turn right on Dry Creek Road **(1)** and follow it to the 5.2 mile *8.3 km* point, where you take FR 152 to the right **(2)**. FR 152 is a dirt road that can be rough, but is usually OK, even for ordinary cars. At 6.5 miles *10.4 km* turn right on the signed dirt road to the parking lot **(3)**.

TRAILHEAD: At the big three-panel trailhead marker and map.

DESCRIPTION: You walk up an old road into a gorgeous canyon.
　　The trail rises gently as you hike to and then climb the redrock cliffs on the south wall. The path itself is interesting as it climbs up the cliff, using some natural steps made by erosion and adding to these by cementing in sandstone slabs to form stairs.
　　At 0.7 miles *1.1 km* you come to an undercut cliff where the trail forks. To go to the bottom of the arch, take the trail to the left. To go to the top of the arch take the trail to the right, uphill. Most hikers will want to do both. It is only about 0.2 miles *3.2 km* to the bottom of the arch on the lower trail and no climbing is required. Return to the junction and hike to the top. Here you will find the steep sandstone staircase.
　　At the top enjoy the great views into colorful backcountry, both the canyon in which you are located and the Dry Creek Basin beyond it. Turn left and follow the trail to the top of the arch. It is dangerous to walk on the arch, so admire it from a distance.
　　The trail is officially rated as 1.0 mile *1.6 km* long, but if you go to the bottom of the arch and the top and do some exploring along the top, you can easily add 0.5 miles *0.8 km* or more to this hike.

Photo: A side trail takes you under this interesting arch, as shown here. The main trail allows you to walk on top of it.

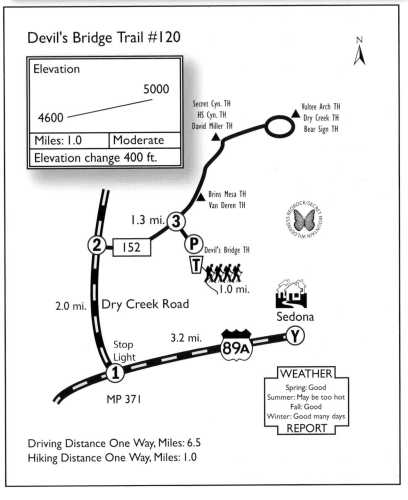

Devil's Bridge Trail #120

Elevation

5000
4600

| Miles: 1.0 | Moderate |

Elevation change 400 ft.

N

Secret Cyn. TH
HS Cyn. TH
David Miller TH

Vultee Arch TH
Dry Creek TH
Bear Sign TH

Brins Mesa TH
Van Deren TH

REDROCK/SECRET MOUNTAIN WILDERNESS

1.3 mi. **3**

2 152

P Devil's Bridge TH

T

1.0 mi.

2.0 mi. Dry Creek Road

Sedona

Stop
Light

3.2 mi. **89A** **Y**

1

MP 371

WEATHER
Spring: Good
Summer: May be too hot
Fall: Good
Winter: Good many days
REPORT

Driving Distance One Way, Miles: 6.5
Hiking Distance One Way, Miles: 1.0

Doe Mountain Trail #60

General Information
Location Map D3
Wilson Mt. USGS Map
Coconino Forest Service Map

Driving Distance One Way: 8.9 miles *14.3 km* (Time 20 minutes)
Access Road: All cars, Last 1.2 miles *1.9 km* bumpy dirt road
Hiking Distance One Way: 1.8 miles *2.9 km* (Time 1 hour)
How Strenuous: Moderate
Features: Views

NUTSHELL: This small mesa situated west of uptown Sedona, is fairly easy to climb. Its weathered cliffs are a delight to explore and it provides great views. **A personal favorite**

DIRECTIONS:
From the Sedona Y (the intersection of Highways 179 and 89A) Go:
 Southwest on Highway 89A (toward Cottonwood) for 3.2 miles *5.1 km* (MP 371) then turn right on Dry Creek Road **(1)**. Drive it to the 6.1 mile *9.8 km* point, a stop sign **(2)**. Turn left here and go to the 7.7 mile *12.3 km point*, a junction where a road goes right to Boynton Canyon **(3)**. Turn left on the Boynton Pass Road. The paving ends, replaced by a bumpy dirt road. Park at the trail parking lot at the 8.9 mile *14.3 km* point, on the right **(4)**.

TRAILHEAD: Across the road.

DESCRIPTION: Doe Mountain is a small mesa standing by itself. It is one of the most southerly redrock formations in the west-of-Sedona area. Only the **Cockscomb** is farther south. The trail zigzags to the top of the mesa, climbing steadily.
 The top of Doe Mountain is not bare rock. Soil has formed through weathering and in some places is deep enough to support low-growing junipers and shrubs. The best part of this hike once you are on the top is to walk around the rim, the edge of which is mostly bare redrock with no trees to obstruct your views; so Doe Mountain is a terrific viewpoint and it is situated so that there are interesting things to see. The views of the town of Sedona are particularly good from here.
 In addition to the views of far off objects, you will see some wonderful things on Doe Mountain itself, where erosion has worked the cliff faces into some really fantastic rock sculptures.

Photo: The views from Doe Mountain can be spectacular. This shot looks to the west toward Bear Mountain on a late afternoon in January.

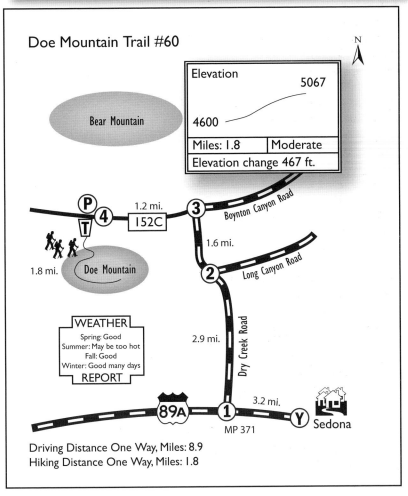

Doe Mountain Trail #60

N

Elevation

5067

4600

Miles: 1.8	Moderate
Elevation change 467 ft.	

Bear Mountain

P
T **④** —— 1.2 mi. —— **③** Boynton Canyon Road
152C

1.6 mi.

1.8 mi. Doe Mountain

② Long Canyon Road

WEATHER
Spring: Good
Summer: May be too hot
Fall: Good
Winter: Good many days
REPORT

2.9 mi.

Dry Creek Road

89A **①** —— 3.2 mi. —— **Y** Sedona
MP 371

Driving Distance One Way, Miles: 8.9
Hiking Distance One Way, Miles: 1.8

Dogie Trail #116

General Information
Location Map C1
Loy Butte and Sycamore Basin USGS Maps
Coconino Forest Service Map

Driving Distance One Way: 20.3 miles *32.5 km* (Time 45 minutes)
Access Road: All cars, 10.8 miles *17.3 km* of dirt road, last 1.0 mile *1.6 km* rough
Hiking Distance One Way: 5.4 miles *8.6 km* (Time 3.5 hours)
How Strenuous: Hard
Features: Sycamore Canyon access, Views, Wild backcountry

NUTSHELL: Reaching the trailhead requires a long drive over dirt roads, but takes you through scenic areas missed by the hordes. The hike itself takes you into an unspoiled scenic area with lots of redrock.

DIRECTIONS:
From the Sedona Y (the intersection of Highways 179 and 89A) Go:
   On Highway 89A (toward Cottonwood) for 9.4 miles *15.0 km* (MP 364.2) to Point **(1)**. Turn right onto FR 525. Drive it to the 12.2 mile *19.5 km* Point **(2)**. Turn left on FR 525C. At the 12.7 miles *20.3 km* Point **(3)** turn right. At 15.2 miles *24.3 km* FR 525C meets FR 761, the Bill Gray Road **(4)**. Go right, still on FR 525C. Stay on FR 525C to the trailhead **(5)** at the 20.3 mile *32.5 km* point, which has a parking area big enough to hold several cars.

TRAILHEAD: There is a three-panel sign with maps and bulletins at the trailhead. The trail starts at the sign.

DESCRIPTION: For the first 0.5 mile *0.8 km* of the hike you will make a gentle climb through an area that is quite scenic, winding around as you climb. You will reach a high point where you will find a rusty trailhead sign, a gate and a sign-in box. Please enter your name in the trail log.
   The trail now goes into a huge unspoiled backcountry area with breathtaking views and beautiful redrock formations. It is like Sedona before the urbanization. The path was built as a cattle trail, but the Forest Service has reworked it as a hiking trail, and it is much better.
   As a cattle trail, the Dogie went to a couple of tanks but as a hiking trail it bypasses the tanks so as not to disturb the wildlife. Beyond the tanks there is a giant redrock butte. As you round the toe of this, at about 2.0 miles *3.2 km* the terrain changes, as you enter a vast basin that slopes down to the brink of Sycamore Canyon. Going all the way to Sycamore Creek and back is strenuous. You may want to quit at some intermediate point.

Photo: You are able to enjoy redrock formations not visible from Sedona on this wilderness hike.

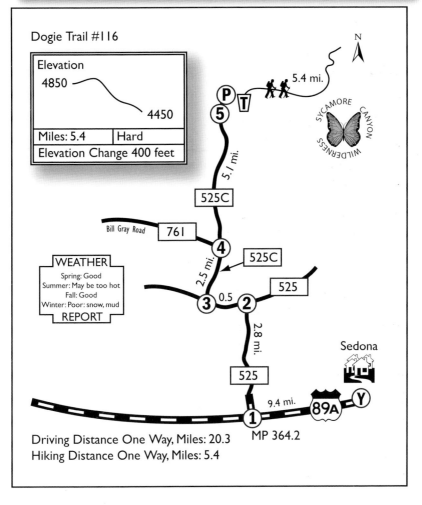

Dogie Trail #116

Elevation

4850

4450

Miles: 5.4	Hard
Elevation Change 400 feet	

N

P T   5.4 mi.

5

SYCAMORE CANYON WILDERNESS

5.1 mi.

525C

Bill Gray Road 761

4

2.5 mi.

525C

WEATHER

Spring: Good
Summer: May be too hot
Fall: Good
Winter: Poor: snow, mud

REPORT

3 0.5 2 525

2.8 mi.

Sedona

525

9.4 mi. 89A Y

1

MP 364.2

Driving Distance One Way, Miles: 20.3
Hiking Distance One Way, Miles: 5.4

Dry Creek Trail #52

General Information
Location Map C4
Loy Butte and Wilson Mt. USGS Maps
Coconino Forest Service Map

Driving Distance One Way: 9.6 miles *15.4 km* (Time 45 minutes)
Access Road: Most cars, Last 4.4 miles *7.0 km* bumpy unpaved road
Hiking Distance One Way: 2.0 miles *3.2 km* (Time 1 hour)
How Strenuous: Moderate
Features: Scenic canyon

NUTSHELL: This is a wilderness hike that follows the course of Dry Creek to its head at the base of the Mogollon Rim.

DIRECTIONS:
From the Sedona Y (the intersection of Highways 179 and 89A) Go:
　　Southwest on Highway 89A (toward Cottonwood) for 3.2 miles *5.1 km* (MP 371) to Dry Creek Road **(1)**. Turn right on Dry Creek Road and proceed to the 5.2 mile *8.3 km* point **(2)**. Turn right on FR 152, the Vultee Arch Road, and follow it to its end at the 9.6 mile *15.4 km* point. Here there is a parking loop, with the **Vultee Arch** Trailhead at the tip. Curve around and head back, and you will see the parking for the **Bear Sign** and Dry Creek trails to your right, just a few yards beyond the Vultee Arch parking spot.

TRAILHEAD: At the parking area

DESCRIPTION: From the parking place, walk across a little arroyo and around the toe of a hill for about 0.10 miles *0.16 km* where you will encounter Dry Creek. The canyon cut by Dry Creek is rather shallow and wide here. The trail goes up the creek in a northerly direction. The trail crosses the creekbed at least a dozen times.
　　As you walk, the trail gains elevation gradually. The trail is good and the walking is pretty easy. At 0.6 miles *1.0 km* you reach a point where the creek forks at a reef. The left hand channel is the **Bear Sign Trail** (marked by a sign) and the right fork is the Dry Creek Trail. From this point the canyon deepens and you are treated to the sight of giant redrock buttes on both sides.
　　The trail ends where it intersects a channel running east and west. We are informed that this channel can be hiked but it would be very steep and rugged, for advanced hikers only. To the east, it appears to go all the way to the top of the rim to East Pocket, where the East Pocket fire lookout tower is located.

Photo: Dry Creek isn't always dry, as Dick discovered on this winter hike. If the water isn't too high, it adds to the pleasure of this hike.

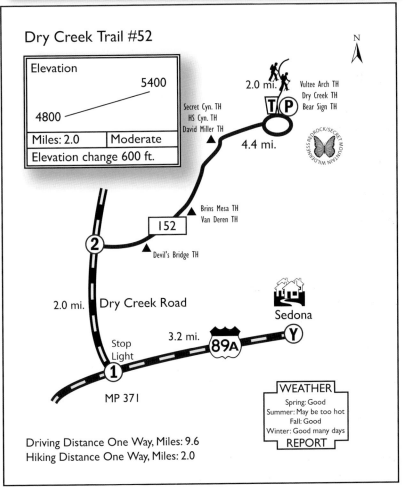

Dry Creek Trail #52

Elevation

5400

4800

Miles: 2.0	Moderate
Elevation change 600 ft.	

N

2.0 mi.

Vultee Arch TH
Dry Creek TH
Bear Sign TH

Secret Cyn. TH
HS Cyn. TH
David Miller TH

4.4 mi.

REDROCK/SECRET MOUNTAIN WILDERNESS

152

Brins Mesa TH
Van Deren TH

Devil's Bridge TH

2.0 mi.   Dry Creek Road

Sedona

Stop
Light

3.2 mi.   89A   Y

MP 371

WEATHER

Spring: Good
Summer: May be too hot
Fall: Good
Winter: Good many days

REPORT

Driving Distance One Way, Miles: 9.6
Hiking Distance One Way, Miles: 2.0

Fay Canyon Trail #53

General Information
Location Map C3
Wilson Mt. USGS Map
Coconino Forest Service Map

Driving Distance One Way: 8.2 miles *13.1 km* (Time 20 minutes)
Access Road: All cars, Last 0.5 miles *0.8 km* bumpy dirt road
Hiking Distance One Way: 1.2 miles *1.9 km* (Time 30 minutes)
How Strenuous: Moderate
Features: Views, Arch, Indian ruins

NUTSHELL: This hike is easy to reach and features a lovely canyon with a natural arch. **A personal favorite.**

DIRECTIONS:
From the Sedona Y (the intersection of Highways 179 and 89A) Go:
    Southwest on Highway 89A (toward Cottonwood) for 3.2 miles *5.1 km* (MP 371) then turn right on Dry Creek Road **(1)**. Follow it to the stop sign at 6.1 miles *9.8 km* **(2)**. Turn left and drive to the 7.7 mile *12.3 km* point, where you intersect the Boynton Canyon Road **(3)**. Turn left onto the unpaved Boynton Pass Road. At 8.2 miles *13.1 km* **(4)** turn right into the parking area.

TRAILHEAD: Three-panel sign/map at the parking area.

DESCRIPTION: The trail is gentle and wide. You will find a forest of oaks, many of them quite sizable. Though the canyon is short, about one mile long, it is broad and very scenic. There are impressive red cliffs on both sides with buff colored cliffs rimming the back of the canyon.
    At just over 0.5 miles *0.8 km*, a side trail branches off to the right (E) and makes a sharp climb up the east side of the canyon to Fay Arch. This trail is usually marked with cairns. The path to the arch is nothing like the main trail. It seems to have just been scratched out of the side of the canyon haphazardly. It is steep and there are places where the footing is tricky. Aunt Maude would have no trouble with the main trail along the canyon floor but the climb to the arch would be too much for her.
    There is a narrow slot between the arch and the wall from which it has broken away. You can stand underneath the gap and look up through it for an interesting view. The clamber up the side of the canyon would be worthwhile for the views even if there were no arch. Spectacular.
    After visiting the arch, return to the main trail and continue up the canyon. At its end it is blocked by a big rock slide.

Photo: The attractions of this canyon are plentiful, the trail is nice and easy and there is a side trip to an arch if you are willing to make a steep climb up a difficult trail.

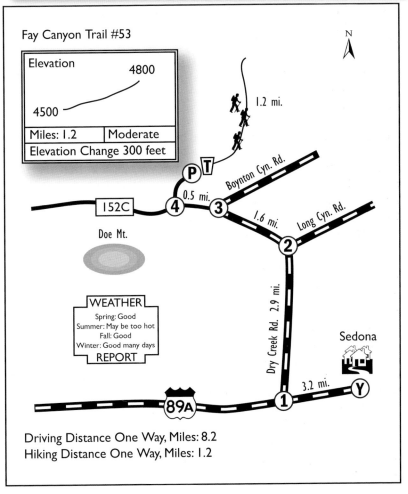

Fay Canyon Trail #53

Elevation
4800
4500

Miles: 1.2 | Moderate
Elevation Change 300 feet

1.2 mi.

N

P T
Boynton Cyn. Rd.
0.5 mi.
152C 4 3
1.6 mi.
Long Cyn. Rd.
2
Doe Mt.
Dry Creek Rd. 2.9 mi.
WEATHER
Spring: Good
Summer: May be too hot
Fall: Good
Winter: Good many days
REPORT
Sedona
89A 1 3.2 mi. Y

Driving Distance One Way, Miles: 8.2
Hiking Distance One Way, Miles: 1.2

Girdner Trail

General Information
Location Map E3
Sedona USGS Map
Coconino Forest Service Map

Driving Distance One Way: 4.4 miles *7.0 km* (Time 10 minutes)
Access Road: All vehicles, All paved
Hiking Distance One Way: 5.0 miles *8.0 km* (Time 2.5 hours)
How Strenuous: Hard
Features: Views, A means of enjoying Dry Creek's hidden canyon

NUTSHELL: The trail starts at the Sedona Cultural Park, winds through backcountry hills following Dry Creek, and ends at Dry Creek Road.

DIRECTIONS:
From the Sedona Y (the intersection of Highways 179 and 89A) Go:
Southwest on Highway 89 (toward Cottonwood) for 4.1 miles *6.6 km* (MP 369.9) **(1)**; then turn right onto Cultural Park Place. Go to the farthest parking lot, where you see a picnic table under a big roof supported by massive pillars. There is a 3-panel trailhead sign here **(2)**. Pull in and park.

TRAILHEAD: The trail starts at the sign.

DESCRIPTION: This trail is named for the Girdner family, early day ranchers. The trail heads off through a typical juniper forest. Soon you are out of sight of manmade things and are "out in the country."
You enter a hidden system of hills and valleys carved by tributaries of Dry Creek. The early portion of the trail is high enough to give nice views.
At about 1.0 miles *1.6 km* you begin to work down to Dry Creek, reaching it at the 1.25 mile *2.0 km* point. Dry Creek will be your companion for the next 2.0 miles *3.2 km*. The trail crosses the creek a dozen times.
Dry Creek's canyon is very pretty and we enjoy this hike along its banks. The Forest Service has done a nice job on the trail, making it follow the terrain in an intelligent manner. At 2.6 miles *4.2 km* you will pass through a gate with supports high enough to allow a mounted horse rider to ride through. At 3.0 miles *4.8 km* the **Rupp Trail** comes in from your left on an old jeep road. The Girdner Trail becomes a jeep road. You cross the creek again and then begin to swing away from it as the old road lifts out of the canyon, allowing you to see out again. The trail goes to a high viewpoint and then descends.
At 3.7 miles *5.9 km* the **Arizona Cypress** Trail branches to the left. At 3.8 miles *6.0 km* the **Two Fences** trail branches to the right. The trail ends at the Dry Creek Road just opposite the **Vultee Arch** road.

Photo: There's plenty to see on the longish Girdner Trail.

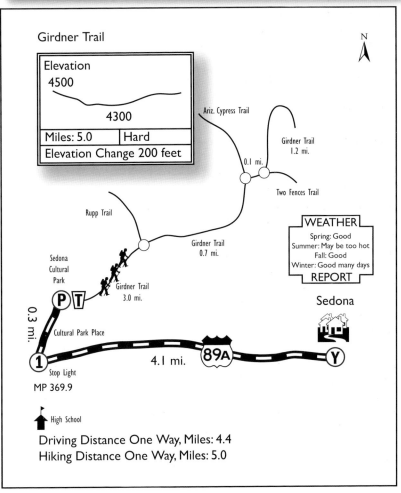

Girdner Trail

N

Elevation	
4500	
4300	
Miles: 5.0	Hard
Elevation Change 200 feet	

Ariz. Cypress Trail

Girdner Trail
1.2 mi.

0.1 mi.

Two Fences Trail

Rupp Trail

Girdner Trail
0.7 mi.

WEATHER

Spring: Good
Summer: May be too hot
Fall: Good
Winter: Good many days

REPORT

Sedona
Cultural
Park

P T

Girdner Trail
3.0 mi.

Sedona

0.3 mi.

Cultural Park Place

1

Stop Light

MP 369.9

89A

4.1 mi.

Y

High School

Driving Distance One Way, Miles: 4.4
Hiking Distance One Way, Miles: 5.0

Harding Spring Trail #51

General Information
Location Map B5
Mountainaire and Munds Park USGS Maps
Coconino Forest Service Map

Driving Distance One Way: 11.4 miles *18.2 km* (Time 20 minutes)
Access Road: All cars, All paved
Hiking Distance One Way: 0.8 miles *1.3 km* (Time 45 minutes)
How Strenuous: Hard
Features: Views

NUTSHELL: This is a marked and posted trail located just across Highway 89A from the Cave Spring Campground 11.4 miles *18.2 km* north of Sedona. It climbs the east wall of Oak Creek Canyon.

DIRECTIONS:
From the Sedona Y (the intersection of Highways 179 and 89A) Go:
     North on Highway 89A (toward Flagstaff) for a distance of 11.4 miles *18.2 km* (MP 385.6) to the entrance to the Cave Spring Campground, which is on your left (west) **(1)**. Pull in to the Cave Spring driveway and take an immediate right into a small parking area.

TRAILHEAD: On the east side of Highway 89A just across from the Cave Spring Campground entrance. It is marked by a rusty sign reading, "Harding Spring Trail #51."

DESCRIPTION: Like the other trails climbing the east wall of upper Oak Creek Canyon, the Harding Spring trail goes virtually straight up with little finesse. You start in a pine and spruce forest, reach a more open area as you climb above tree line, then get into a region of pine forest again at the top.
     The trail zigzags in such a way that it isn't a killer. Similar trails are the **Cookstove Trail,** the **Purtymun Trail** and the **Thomas Point Trail.**
     When you reach the top you will see a clear path over to the edge of the rim where you can enjoy tremendous views out over the canyon. This is a great place to sit and enjoy looking at this scenic wonderland.
     Harding Spring is named for O. P. Harding, a pioneer. He came to Flagstaff in 1884 and worked in construction. In 1889 he moved to Oak Creek and homesteaded, planting hundreds of fruit trees. He brought his fruit to Flagstaff, using this trail. In 1910 the Flagstaff newspaper reported that Harding, age 76, had walked from Oak Creek to Flagstaff. At his death in 1915 it was learned that he was a distinguished Union General in the Civil War, a fact he had kept hidden during his lifetime.

Photo: When you finish this hike, you have the feeling of being on top of the world. Dick is enjoying a rest while looking toward the high white spires of the west rim of Oak Creek Canyon.

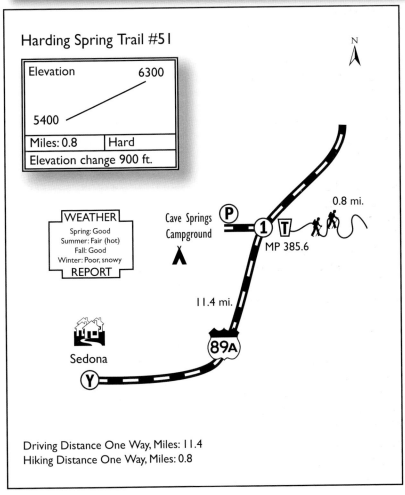

Harding Spring Trail #51

N

Elevation	6300
5400	
Miles: 0.8	Hard
Elevation change 900 ft.	

WEATHER
Spring: Good
Summer: Fair (hot)
Fall: Good
Winter: Poor, snowy
REPORT

Cave Springs
Campground

P

1 T
MP 385.6

0.8 mi.

11.4 mi.

89A

Sedona

Y

Driving Distance One Way, Miles: 11.4
Hiking Distance One Way, Miles: 0.8

Herkenham Trail

General Information
Location Map E4
Sedona USGS Map
Coconino Forest Service Map

Driving Distance One Way: 6.2 miles *9.9 km* (Time 20 minutes)
Access Road: All cars, All paved
Hiking Distance One Way: 2.0 miles *3.2 km* (Time 1 hour)
How Strenuous: Moderate
Features: Easy to reach, Views

NUTSHELL: This trail runs from the Chavez Ranch Road through a little pocket of Forest Service land up to the Sedona Red Rock High School.

DIRECTIONS:
From the Sedona Y (the intersection of Highways 179 and 89A) Go:
    Southwest on Highway 89A (toward Cottonwood) for 4.2 miles *6.8 km* (MP 368.9) then turn left on the Upper Red Rock Loop Road **(1)**. Follow it to the 6.0 mile *10.0 km* point **(2)**, where you turn left, heading toward Crescent Moon Ranch Park on a paved road. At the 6.2 mile *9.9 km* point turn left into a parking apron with a 2-panel trailhead sign **(3)**.

TRAILHEAD: At the trail sign.

DESCRIPTION: This is a Class 2 trail, with low to moderate use and limited signage. If you only have time to hike a few trails in Sedona, this one would not be on your list. If you have hiked the major trails and are the kind of hiker (as we are) who wants to do all the trails, then try it.
    Begin by walking along an old road that has been converted into the **Old Post Trail**. At the 0.7 mile *1.1 k*m point you reach a V-fork where the **Herkenham Trail** branches to the left. Take the left fork.
    Now the trail becomes strictly a footpath. You are heading toward Schuerman Mountain, which you can see from many points on the trail, following through country dotted with low-growing pinons and junipers.
    At 0.8 miles *1.3 km* the trail veers to the right. It doesn't look correct, as it is fainter than the trail that you leave. The real trail does not go into a ravine. If you go into a ravine, backtrack and look again. The trail works its way toward the Upper Red Rock Loop Road, and from the 1.5 mile *2.4 km* point is very near it. You can hear cars going by overhead to your left, but you can't see them until you are quite near the end of the trail. Eventually it comes to a point where it meets the road just across from the high school, at Scorpion Drive, at 2.0 miles *3.2 km*.

Photo: This trail is part of the network of trail around Airport Mesa. It is partly footpath and partly an old road.

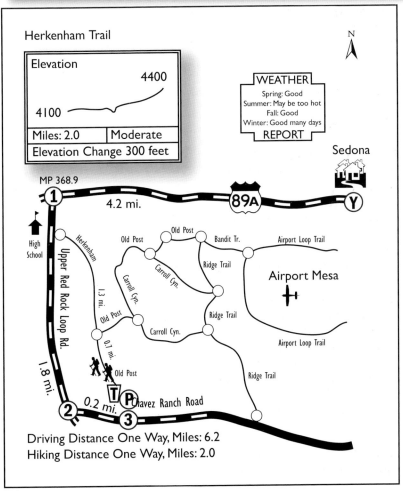

Herkenham Trail

Elevation
4400
4100

Miles: 2.0 | Moderate
Elevation Change 300 feet

WEATHER
Spring: Good
Summer: May be too hot
Fall: Good
Winter: Good many days
REPORT

N

Sedona

MP 368.9
1
4.2 mi.
89A
Y

High School

Upper Red Rock Loop Rd.

Herkenham

Old Post
Old Post
Bandit Tr.
Airport Loop Trail

Carroll Cyn.
Carroll Cyn.
Ridge Trail

Airport Mesa

1.3 mi.
Old Post
Carroll Cyn.
Ridge Trail

0.7 mi.
Old Post
Airport Loop Trail

1.8 mi.
Old Post
Ridge Trail

T P Chavez Ranch Road
2   0.2 mi.   3

Driving Distance One Way, Miles: 6.2
Hiking Distance One Way, Miles: 2.0

Honanki

General Information
Location Map C1
Loy Butte and Page Springs USGS Maps
Coconino Forest Service Map

Driving Distance One Way: 16.2 miles *25.9 km* (Time 45 minutes)
Access Road: All cars, Last 8.5 miles *13.6 km* bumpy dirt road
Hiking Distance One Way: 0.25 miles *0.4 km* (Time 10 minutes)
How Strenuous: Easy
Features: Best Indian ruins in the Sedona area

NUTSHELL: Located 16.2 miles *25.9 km* northwest of Sedona, this is a short hike to excellent Indian ruins.

DIRECTIONS:
From the Sedona Y (the intersection of Highways 179 and 89A) Go:
    Southwest on Highway 89A (toward Cottonwood) for 3.2 miles *5.1 km,* to a stoplight, then turn right on the Dry Creek Road **(1)**. Drive to a stop sign at 6.1 miles *9.8 km* **(2)**. Turn left and drive to a second stop sign at 7.7 miles *12.3 km* **(3)**. Go left on unpaved road FR 152C. You will come to third stop sign at 11.7 miles *18.7 km* **(4)**, where you turn right on FR 525. At 11.8 miles *18.9 km* is a V-fork where you go left on FR 525 **(5)**. You pass through the Hancock Ranch and reach the parking area (to your left) at the 16.2 mile point *25.9 km* **(6)**.

TRAILHEAD: At the entrance booth. There is a toilet.

DESCRIPTION: Our first experience in visiting Honanki (then called the Loy Butte Ruins) came in 1977. It was tough to find the site and even tougher to walk to it. Today it is easy to find and walking it is a pleasure. The Forest Service has done a lot of work on the place (including a name change). Now there is a pleasant wide trail. It splits soon after you begin. Don't worry about which fork to take, as they loop around to the ruins. Take one on the way to the ruins and the other on the return to the parking lot.
    The trail brings you to the ruins, which are in two alcoves. The larger and more imposing ruin is to your left. There are guard rails to prevent people from getting to the ruins and damaging them, but you get very close for a good look. The other alcove has smaller ruins but much more rock art, and you are allowed to get even closer to the ruins, though you can't enter any of the rooms.
    We appreciate the work that has been done to preserve this fine site yet make it accessible.

Photo: A visit to this special place gives you a close look at how the original inhabitants of the area lived hundreds of years ago.

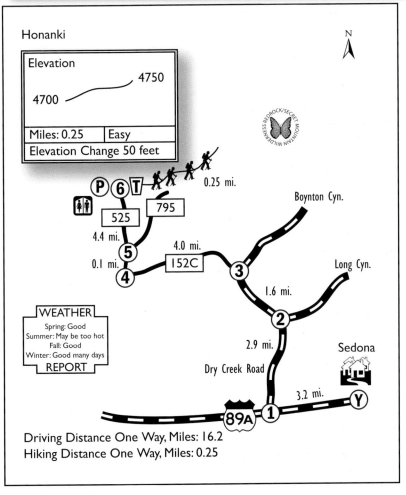

Honanki

N

Elevation

4750

4700

| Miles: 0.25 | Easy |
| Elevation Change 50 feet | |

WILDERNESS BEDROCK/SECRET MOUNTAIN

0.25 mi.

P 6 T

Boynton Cyn.

795

525

4.4 mi.

5

4.0 mi.

0.1 mi.

4

152C

3

Long Cyn.

1.6 mi.

2

WEATHER
Spring: Good
Summer: May be too hot
Fall: Good
Winter: Good many days
REPORT

2.9 mi.

Sedona

Dry Creek Road

89A

1

3.2 mi.

Y

Driving Distance One Way, Miles: 16.2
Hiking Distance One Way, Miles: 0.25

Hot Loop Trail #94

General Information
Location Map F5
Munds Mountain USGS Map
Coconino Forest Service Map

Driving Distance One Way: 9.4 miles *15.0 km* (Time 20 minutes)
Access Road: All cars, Last 0.1 miles *0.16 km* good dirt road
Hiking Distance One Way: 3.0 miles *4.8 km* (Time 2 hours)
How Strenuous: Hard
Features: Views

NUTSHELL: This trail climbs to the top of Wild Horse Mesa.

DIRECTIONS:
From the Sedona Y (the intersection of Highways 179 and 89A) Go:
    South on Highway 179 (toward Phoenix) for 7.2 miles *11.5 km* (MP 306.2) then turn left on Jack's Canyon Road **(1)** and follow it to the 9.3 miles *14.9 km* point, where there is a road to your right going to a corral **(2)**. Drive past the trailhead sign and park at the back of the parking area.

TRAILHEAD: At the end of the parking loop.

DESCRIPTION: There is a confusing assortment of unmarked trails. Go through the tall horse gate and walk alongside the loading chute, then follow the barbed wire fence to its end, where all trails merge in a gully. The trail now begins a steady climb.
    You reach the top of a saddle in 1.1 miles *1.8 km* where you have excellent views into the Village of Oak Creek area. Just over the other side of the ridge the landscape changes entirely—going from urban to wild in a few steps.
    The next portion is our favorite, where you pass through some nice redrocks, with thrilling views. The big canyon you can see is Woods Canyon. Your trail winds down and comes to a side canyon where you cross a slickrock face. Beyond this you intersect a trail at 1.75 miles *2.8 km*. To the right is the old part of the Hot Loop Trail, coming up from the **Woods Canyon Trail**. Turn left and climb to the top of Wild Horse Mesa. The trail to the top is difficult: it goes over loose lava stones, and makes a steep climb.
    When you finally struggle to the top of Wild Horse Mesa, the trail improves. At the 3.0 mile point *4.8 km* it is obvious that the rim of the mesa is to your left. Walk over to it and enjoy the view—a great vantage point from which to see Pine Valley, Jacks Canyon and Lee Mountain. For a day hike, this is a good stopping point, though the trail continues some 7.0 miles *11.2 km* to Jack's Point.

Photo: The trailhead area contains corrals, making this hike a favorite one for horse riders.

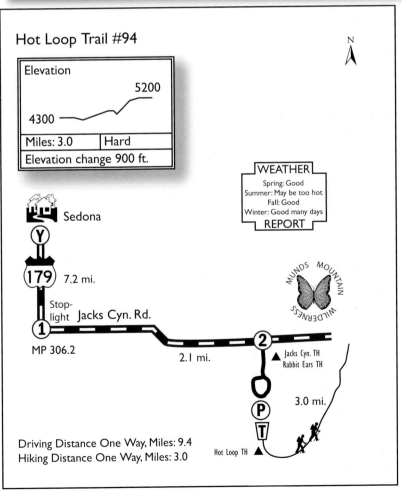

Hot Loop Trail #94

N

Elevation	
4300	5200
Miles: 3.0	Hard
Elevation change 900 ft.	

WEATHER
Spring: Good
Summer: May be too hot
Fall: Good
Winter: Good many days
REPORT

Sedona

Y

179 7.2 mi.

Stop-light Jacks Cyn. Rd.

1

MP 306.2

2.1 mi.

2

Jacks Cyn. TH
Rabbit Ears TH

3.0 mi.

P
T

MUNDS MOUNTAIN WILDERNESS

Driving Distance One Way, Miles: 9.4
Hiking Distance One Way, Miles: 3.0

Hot Loop TH

HS Canyon Trail #50

General Information
Location Map C4
Loy Butte and Wilson Mt. USGS Maps
Coconino Forest Service Map

Driving Distance One Way: 8.6 miles *13.8 km* (Time 30 minutes)
Access Road: Last 3.4 miles *5.4 km* rough dirt
Hiking Distance One Way: 2.0 miles *3.2 km* (Time 70 minutes)
How Strenuous: Moderate
Features: Views, Remote side canyon

NUTSHELL: This beautiful canyon, 8.6 miles *13.8 km* northwest of uptown Sedona, provides a delightful hike.

DIRECTIONS:
From the Sedona Y (the intersection of Highways 179 and 89A) Go:
Southwest on Highway 89A (toward Cottonwood) for 3.2 miles *5.1 km* (MP 371) then turn right on Dry Creek Road **(1)** and drive to the 5.2 mile *8.3 km* point **(2)**. Turn right on FR 152 and follow it to the 8.6 mile *13.8 km* point **(3)** where you turn left into the Secret Canyon trail turnoff.

TRAILHEAD: Hike the Secret Canyon Trail, which starts at the parking area, for 0.6 miles *1.0 km* to reach the HS Canyon trailhead.

DESCRIPTION: The **Secret Canyon Trail** goes over to Dry Creek and then proceeds along its drainage. If water is running in Dry Creek you may be unable to make this hike as the trail frequently crosses the creekbed.
At 0.6 miles *1.0 km* you will reach the H S Canyon trail junction. Turn left onto the HS Trail, which goes up the narrow H S Canyon. It goes mostly to the west toward the north face of Maroon Mountain, and you can see a huge fin of Maroon Mountain in the distance. H S Canyon is a pretty little canyon and not very well known. We have never encountered any other hikers on this trail, but usually find them on the better known Secret Canyon Trail.
An easy walk, the trail is mostly shaded by a pleasant forest. It climbs but the climb is so gradual that it is not exhausting. There are great views. The canyon walls here are lower than those flanking some of the other hikes in this book. As a result they seem to be on a more human scale, and consequently the canyon has a nice friendly feeling.
The trail takes you to the base of Maroon Mountain where it ends in a box canyon surrounded by thousand foot high white cliffs—truly an impressive place. The end of the trail gives a false appearance of climbing out of the canyon but that is an illusion, for it plays out against the mountain.

Photo: This trail takes you into a pleasant canyon mostly screened by trees. Every now and then a break in the vegetation allows wonderful views.

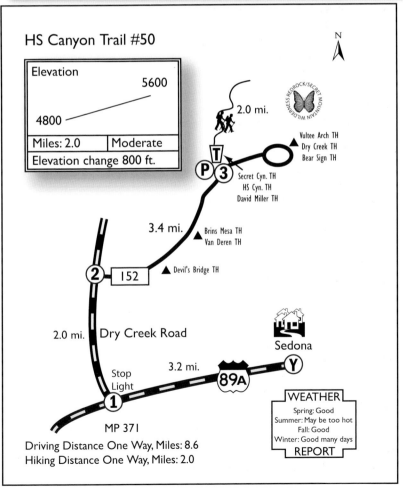

HS Canyon Trail #50

N

Elevation

5600

4800

Miles: 2.0	Moderate
Elevation change 800 ft.	

2.0 mi.

REDROCK/SECRET MOUNTAIN WILDERNESS

Vultee Arch TH
Dry Creek TH
Bear Sign TH

T
P 3

Secret Cyn. TH
HS Cyn. TH
David Miller TH

3.4 mi.

▲ Brins Mesa TH
Van Deren TH

2 152

▲ Devil's Bridge TH

2.0 mi.   Dry Creek Road

Sedona

3.2 mi.

Stop
Light

1

89A

Y

MP 371

Driving Distance One Way, Miles: 8.6
Hiking Distance One Way, Miles: 2.0

WEATHER
Spring: Good
Summer: May be too hot
Fall: Good
Winter: Good many days
REPORT

H. T. Trail

General Information
Location Map F4
Munds Mountain and Sedona USGS Maps
Coconino Forest Service Map

Driving Distance One Way: 3.6 miles *5.8 km* (Time 10 minutes)
Access Road: All cars, All paved
Hiking Distance One Way: 1.25 miles *2.0 km* (Time 45 minutes)
How Strenuous: Easy
Features: Easy to reach, Interesting passage under Highway 179.

NUTSHELL: This short trail leaves the Bell Rock Pathway, crosses under Hwy. 179, heads toward Cathedral Rock, and ends at the **Templeton Trail**.

DIRECTIONS:
From the Sedona Y (the intersection of Highways 179 and 89A) Go:
    South on Highway 179 (toward Phoenix) for a distance of 3.6 miles *5.8 km* (MP 309.8) **(1)**. Turn left into the trailhead parking lot, which is well posted on the highway. This is a major trailhead, with all facilities.

TRAILHEAD: At the parking lot (at least, you begin the hike there).

DESCRIPTION: When you start hiking you will come to a trail sign which shows that the **Little Horse Trail** and **Bell Rock** are to your right and the **Mystic Trail** is to your left. Turn right. At 0.3 miles *0.5 km* you will reach a V-fork where the Little Horse Trail turns off to your left. Go right.
    At 0.5 miles *0.8 km* you walk over a wooden bridge. On the other side to your right is the H. T. trail. The H. T. Trail itself is only 0.75 miles *1.2 km* long, but you have to walk 0.5 miles *0.8 km* to reach it. There is a small trail sign where the trail begins. Turn right onto the H. T. Trail.
    The trail goes down into a wash and passes through a short tunnel under Highway 179. We are told that H. T. stands for Highway Tunnel. On the other side of the tunnel you soon move up out of the drainage and onto a low ridge, moving south parallel to Highway 179.
    You have nice views of Cathedral Rock and the Transept from here. Soon you'll walk on an old jeep road, moving away from the highway. Look carefully at 0.9 miles *1.4 km*, where the trail turns to the right, off of the road, at a point where the road starts downhill. The place is marked with cairns.
    At 1.0 miles *1.6 km* you cross a streambed and begin to walk again on a jeep road, heading toward Cathedral Rock. The trail goes up over another ridge, and where it comes down on the other side, it ends, at 1.25 miles *2.0 km*, where it meets the Templeton Trail.

Photo: H. T. stands for Highway Tunnel, and here it is, with Dick standing at the far end. The tunnel passes under Highway 179.

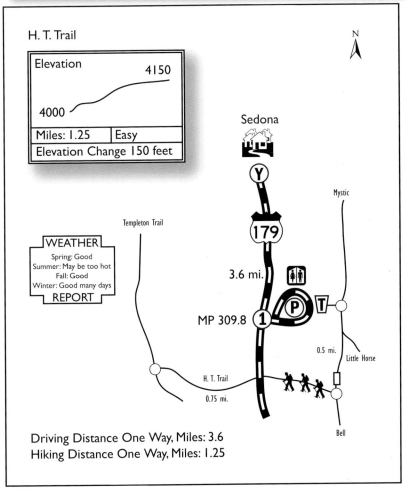

H. T. Trail

Elevation
4150
4000

Miles: 1.25 | Easy
Elevation Change 150 feet

N

Sedona

Mystic

Templeton Trail

WEATHER
Spring: Good
Summer: May be too hot
Fall: Good
Winter: Good many days
REPORT

179

3.6 mi.

MP 309.8 1 P T

0.5 mi.
Little Horse

H. T. Trail
0.75 mi.

Bell

Driving Distance One Way, Miles: 3.6
Hiking Distance One Way, Miles: 1.25

Huckaby Trail

General Information
Location Map D5
Sedona, Wilson Mtn., Munds Mtn. USGS Maps
Coconino Forest Service Map

Driving Distance One Way: 1.3 miles *2.1 km* (Time 5 minutes)
Access Road: All cars, All paved
Hiking Distance One Way: 3.0 miles *4.8 km* (Time 2.0 hours)
How Strenuous: Moderate or Hard (see below)
Features: Views, Hike into inner gorge of Oak Creek Canyon, Variety

NUTSHELL: This fine trail runs between Schnebly Hill and Midgley Bridge. The center part runs along the banks of Oak Creek.

DIRECTIONS:
From the Sedona Y (the intersection of Highways 179 and 89A) Go:
South on Highway 179 (toward Phoenix) for a distance of 0.3 miles *0.5 km* (MP 313.1) to the Schnebly Hill Road **(1)**. It is just across the bridge past Tlaquepaque. Turn left onto the Schnebly Hill Road. Drive to the 1.3 mile *2.1 km* point, where you will see a sign for the trailhead parking to your left **(2)**. Pull in and park. This is a major trailhead with signs, maps, and a toilet.

TRAILHEAD: At the parking area.

DESCRIPTION: The trail is fairly level to the fork with the **Margs Draw Trail**, but soon goes downhill on a steep old jeep road. You cross Bear Wallow Canyon on a redrock shelf at 0.5 miles *0.8 km* and go up the other side. You will climb steeply to the 1.0 mile *1.6 km* point. The trail leaves the jeep road and becomes a footpath, twisting up and around rolling hills.

In time you have fine views of Sedona, and at 1.1 miles *1.7 km* begin walking on bluffs overlooking the creek and the town. The high point is reached at 1.25 miles *2.0 km* and from here you can see an area burnt by a forest fire. The trail enters the burnt zone at 1.5 miles *2.4 km*. Shortly after this the trail winds downhill at a steep angle and reaches creek level.

The trail then goes north along the east bank of Oak Creek—a very nice part of the trail—to two footbridges over the creek. Caution: these bridges wash out in high water, and wading across the creek twice without them is slippery and even dangerous. If you can cross the creek, the trail climbs up under Midgley Bridge and you emerge at the bridge parking lot. This is a moderate hike if you use two cars, parking one at Midgley Bridge; but space at the bridge is very limited and often crowded, so you need two conditions: a berth at the parking lot and the footbridges in place.

Photo: The Huckaby Trail offers wonderful variety: an open trail through scrub to a fine overlook giving a view of uptown Sedona, a creekside ramble and a view of Midgley Bridge from the underside.

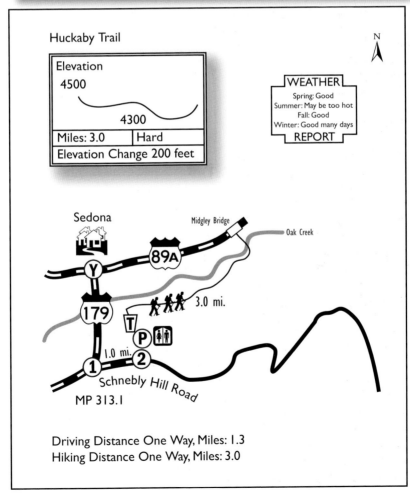

Huckaby Trail

Elevation

4500

4300

Miles: 3.0	Hard
Elevation Change 200 feet	

N

WEATHER
Spring: Good
Summer: May be too hot
Fall: Good
Winter: Good many days
REPORT

Sedona

Midgley Bridge

Oak Creek

89A

Y

179

3.0 mi.

T
P

1

2

1.0 mi.

Schnebly Hill Road

MP 313.1

Driving Distance One Way, Miles: 1.3
Hiking Distance One Way, Miles: 3.0

Jack's Canyon Trail #55

General Information
Location Map F5
Munds Mountain and Sedona USGS Maps
Coconino Forest Service Map

Driving Distance One Way: 9.4 miles *15.0 km* (Time 15 minutes)
Access Road: All cars, Last 0.1 mile *0.16 km* good dirt road
Hiking Distance One Way: 5.0 miles *8.0 km* (Time 2.5 hours)
How Strenuous: Hard
Features: Old cattle trail, Views

NUTSHELL: This 1890s cattle trail goes from an inhabited area into some remote back country, climbing to the top of the Mogollon Rim.

DIRECTIONS:
From the Sedona Y (the intersection of Highways 179 and 89A) Go:
  South on Highway 179 (toward Phoenix) for a distance of 7.2 miles *11.5 km* (MP 306.2) to Jack's Canyon Road (stoplight) **(1)**. Turn left (E) onto Jack's Canyon Road and follow it to the 9.3 miles *14.9 km* point, where you turn right on an unpaved road **(2)** into a corral area. Park at the 9.4 mile *15.0 km* point, where you will see a three-panel sign/map.

TRAILHEAD: On the other side of the tall pole gate, where there is a rusty sign reading, "Jack's Canyon #55."

DESCRIPTION: The first 1.0 miles *1.6 km* of the trail parallels the road, then skirts the Pine Valley subdivision. At the 1.5 miles *2.4 km* point you break into open country, mostly hiking on an old jeep road.
  The trail runs northeasterly to Jack's Canyon Tank at the 2.5 mile *4.0 km* point. From the tank the road ends and you follow a footpath down into the canyon floor, which you reach at 3.0 miles *4.8 km* where the trail turns northerly. The trail becomes more interesting and colorful, especially if there is water running in the canyon. The canyon is narrow and scenic and you walk on extensive patches of slickrock.
  You reach the end of this attractive canyon portion of the trail at about 5.0 miles *8.0 km*. We recommend that most hikers stop there.
  Beyond the 5.0 mile *8.0 km* point the trail makes a very steep climb of over 1,200 feet to the top of the Mogollon Rim where it meets the **Munds Mt. Trail**. The old-time cattlemen used to walk their cattle up and down this trail, to get to cool grazing at the top in summer and to warm up at the bottom in winter.

Photo: After clearing the subdivision area, this trail takes you out into the backcountry, part of it (shown here) on an old road.

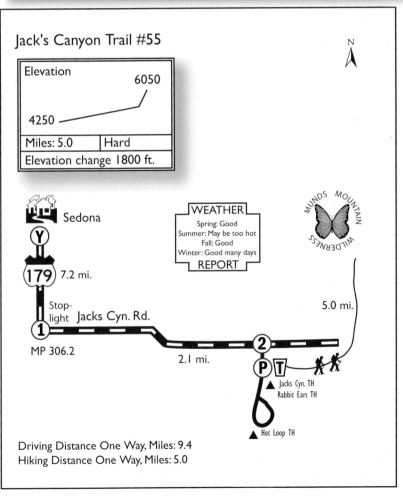

Jack's Canyon Trail #55

Elevation	6050
4250	
Miles: 5.0	Hard
Elevation change 1800 ft.	

N

Sedona

(Y)

(179) 7.2 mi.

Stop-
light Jacks Cyn. Rd.
(1)

MP 306.2

2.1 mi.

(2)

(P)(T)

▲ Jacks Cyn. TH
Rabbit Ears TH

▲ Hot Loop TH

5.0 mi.

MUNDS MOUNTAIN WILDERNESS

WEATHER
Spring: Good
Summer: May be too hot
Fall: Good
Winter: Good many days
REPORT

Driving Distance One Way, Miles: 9.4
Hiking Distance One Way, Miles: 5.0

Jail Trail

General Information
Location Map F1
Clarkdale USGS Map
Coconino Forest Service Map

Driving Distance One Way: 20.1 miles *32.2 km* (Time 45 minutes)
Access Road: All cars, All paved
Hiking Distance One Way: 0.5 miles 0.8 *km*, with an extension available
How Strenuous: Easy
Features: Easy to reach, Verde River access, Nature walk.

NUTSHELL: This trail starts at the old Cottonwood Jail, goes down to the Verde River on a wide old road, then follows the bank of the river to a bridge, where it officially ends.

DIRECTIONS:
From the Sedona Y (the intersection of Highways 179 and 89A) Go:
Southwest on Highway 89A for 18.6 miles *29.8 km*, to the stoplight in Cottonwood **(1)** at the junction of Highways 89A and 279. Go straight on Historic Highway 89A (Main Street) into the historic old town of Cottonwood. At 20.1 miles *32.2 km*, you will see a trail sign in front of a small building made of river rock **(2)**. Pull in and park in the lot by the building.

TRAILHEAD: Where you park. There is a trail sign at the gate. You may be able to get a trail guide brochure at the gate or in the visitor center.

DESCRIPTION: This is an easy walk. You go through the gate and follow an old road down to the river level. Along the way you will find some nicely executed metal signs shaped like a leaf. Each sign bears a number that is keyed in to the brochure. The signs allow you to identify the plants.

Once you reach the river level, you will walk along the south bank. There are heavy growths of cattails and other plants between you and the water in most places, but there are some breaks where you could go over and dip your toes in the aqua if you are so inclined. The trail here goes along river sand, not the best footing, but there are plans to apply some kind of fill.

The trail goes along the river to the bridge where 10th St. crosses the Verde on its way to **Dead Horse State Park**. The trail hooks to the right and rises up to Tenth Street at the bridge. Ignore this. You can stop at the bridge for a gentle but interesting hike. You also have the option of continuing to walk along the Riverwalk Trail, which follows the riverbank for about 0.75 miles *1.2 km* to Riverfront Park.

Photo: This friendly trailhead sign prepares you for this trail, which goes from the old Cottonwood Jail down to the Verde River and along its banks.

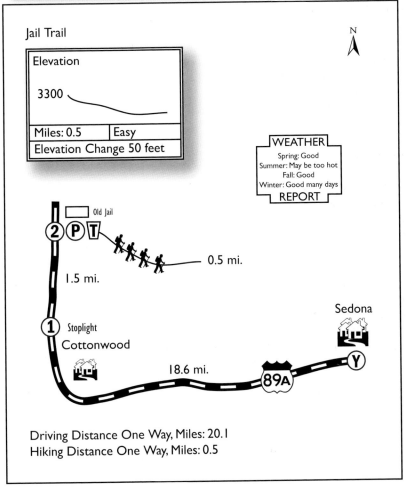

Jail Trail

N

Elevation	
3300	
Miles: 0.5	Easy
Elevation Change 50 feet	

WEATHER
Spring: Good
Summer: May be too hot
Fall: Good
Winter: Good many days
REPORT

Old Jail

2 P T

0.5 mi.

1.5 mi.

1 Stoplight
Cottonwood

18.6 mi.

89A

Sedona

Y

Driving Distance One Way, Miles: 20.1
Hiking Distance One Way, Miles: 0.5

Jim Thompson Trail #124

General Information
Location Map D5
Munds Park, Wilson Mountain USGS Maps
Coconino Forest Service Map

Driving Distance One Way: 1.9 miles *3.0 km* (Time 10 minutes)
Access Road: All cars. Last 0.4 miles *0.6 km* dirt road
Hiking Distance One Way: 3.0 miles *4.8 km* (Time 1.5 hours)
How Strenuous: Moderate
Features: Historic road, Good views

NUTSHELL: This historic road is easy to reach and provides superb views while you hike around the base of Steamboat Rock.

DIRECTIONS:
From the Sedona Y (the intersection of Highways 179 and 89A) Go:
  North on Highway on 89A (toward Flagstaff) for 0.3 miles *0.5 km* to Jordan Road, in the middle of uptown Sedona **(1)**. Turn left (N) and take Jordan Road to its end, at 1.1 miles *1.8 km* **(2)**. Turn left at the stop sign, onto Park Ridge Drive, a paved road, which goes through a subdivision and ends at 1.3 miles *2.1 km.* Keep going past the subdivision on the unpaved road. Drive it to the trailhead parking lot at 1.9 miles *3.0 km* **(3)**.

TRAILHEAD: You passed it as you drove to the parking area.

DESCRIPTION: Walk back down the road from the parking area and go left where you see the trail sign. At 0.24 miles *0.4 km*, you will intersect the Old Jim Thompson Road. Turn left here and go uphill. The downside leg of the road is blocked where it enters private property.
  You come to a gate at 0.5 miles *0.8 km*, and at this point have climbed high enough to begin to enjoy wonderful views.
  Soon you will stop climbing at the 4,800 foot level where the old road is wide and easy to walk. You will move right over to the base of Steamboat Rock and curve around it.
  At 1.2 miles *1.9 km* you will walk under a power line. At 2.2 miles *3.5 km* you will be just below Steamboat Tank, and can see deciduous trees sticking up from it. A short detour to it is worthwhile. The road ends where it comes down to **Wilson Canyon**.
  Jim Thompson was the first settler in Oak Creek, arriving at Indian Gardens in 1876. Later he made a homestead in Sedona. He built this road to link his two homes. First it ran along at creek level, but was washed away by floods, causing him to build this road, far above the creek, in 1887.

Photo: The Jim Thompson Trail takes you right up into the redrocks, where you enjoy highly sculpted rock formations up close and personal.

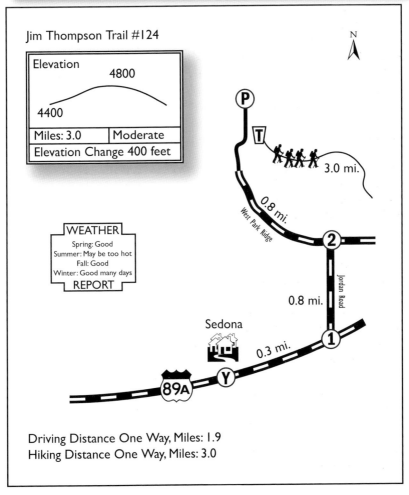

Jim Thompson Trail #124

Elevation
4800
4400

Miles: 3.0	Moderate
Elevation Change 400 feet	

N

P

T

3.0 mi.

0.8 mi.

West Park Ridge

2

Jordan Road

0.8 mi.

WEATHER
Spring: Good
Summer: May be too hot
Fall: Good
Winter: Good many days
REPORT

Sedona

1

0.3 mi.

89A Y

Driving Distance One Way, Miles: 1.9
Hiking Distance One Way, Miles: 3.0

Jordan Trail

General Information
Location Map D4
Munds Park, Wilson Mountain USGS Maps
Coconino Forest Service Map

Driving Distance One Way: 1.9 miles *3.0 km* (Time 10 minutes)
Access Road: All cars. Last 0.4 miles *0.6 km* dirt road
Hiking Distance One Way: 1.5 miles *3.1 km* (Time 50 minutes)
How Strenuous: Moderate
Features: Easy to reach, all-weather road, pleasant hike near town, good views

NUTSHELL: This trail curls around the southern tip of Cibola Ridge, ending at Devil's Kitchen on the **Soldier Pass Trail.**

DIRECTIONS:
From the Sedona Y (the intersection of Highways 179 and 89A) Go:
   North on Highway on 89A (toward Flagstaff) for 0.3 miles *0.5 km* to Jordan Road, in uptown Sedona **(1)**. Turn left (N) and drive Jordan Road to its end, at 1.1 miles *1.8 km* **(2)**. Turn left at the stop sign, onto W. Park Ridge Drive, a paved road, which goes through a subdivision ending at 1.3 miles *2.1 km*. Keep going on the unpaved road. At the 1.7 mile *2.7 km* point, you will come onto a bare redrock ledge at a curve **(3)**. Park here if there is space. If not, keep driving to the multi-trailhead parking lot **(P)**.

TRAILHEAD: At the 1.7 mile *2.7 km* point.

DESCRIPTION: This trail is a delight and connects to other trails in the area, permitting hikers to make a number of interesting combinations.
   At first, the trail goes uphill along an old road to a power line, then turns west and follows the line. At 0.25 miles *0.4 km* you look down on an electric power substation. You are quite near the base of the southern edge of Cibola Ridge, and will enjoy looking at its redrock cliffs.
   At 0.33 miles *0.5 km* you reach a high point on the ridge with good views. You round the toe of the ridge and then turn north, still hugging the base of the ridge, but getting into more interesting, wilder country.
   At the 1.1 mile *1.8 km* point the **Cibola Pass Trail** comes in from the right. Just beyond, the Jordan Trail turns and moves west along the bank of a deep gulch. At 1.25 miles *2.0 km* you reach another trail junction. Go straight here, NW, toward a redrock ledge. You will walk along the ledge until you find yourself on the brink of Devil's Kitchen, a natural sinkhole, the place where you intersect the Soldier Pass Trail.

Photo: We love this portion of this easy-to-reach trail, which gives you close views of beautiful redrock formations.

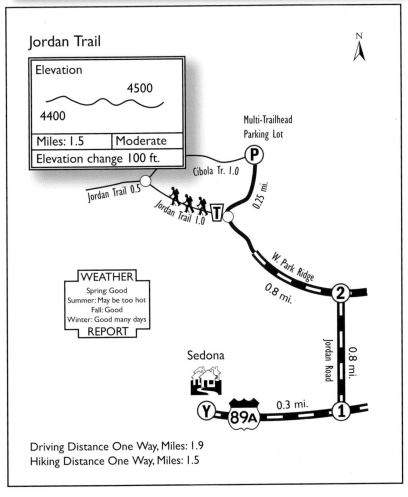

Jordan Trail

Elevation	
4400	4500

Miles: 1.5	Moderate
Elevation change 100 ft.	

Multi-Trailhead
Parking Lot
P

Cibola Tr. 1.0

Jordan Trail 0.5

Jordan Trail 1.0 **T**

0.25 mi.

W. Park Ridge

0.8 mi.

2

0.8 mi.

Jordan Road

WEATHER
Spring: Good
Summer: May be too hot
Fall: Good
Winter: Good many days
REPORT

Sedona

Y **89A** 0.3 mi. **1**

Driving Distance One Way, Miles: 1.9
Hiking Distance One Way, Miles: 1.5

Kel Fox Trail

General Information
Location Map G3
Lake Montezuma and Sedona USGS Maps
Coconino Forest Service Map

Driving Distance One Way: 12.6 miles *20.2 km* (Time 30 minutes)
Access Road: Last 1.4 miles *2.2 km* high clearance is a must
Hiking Distance One Way: 2.0 miles *3.2 km* (Time 1 hour)
How Strenuous: Moderate
Features: Interesting mesas and peaked hills, Views

NUTSHELL: You follow an old cattle trail from a pond up to Deer Pass from which you can see out over the Village of Oak Creek area, and then descend on the other side to the Rojo Estates subdivision.

DIRECTIONS:
From the Sedona Y (the intersection of Highways 179 and 89A) Go:
    Southeast on Highway 179 (toward Phoenix) for 10.4 miles *16.6 km* (MP 303), to Yavapai County Road 78 **(1)** where you take a right turn onto Highway 78). Follow the road to the 11.2 mile *18.0 km* point, where you will see the pipeline road to your right, with gray gravel surfacing, a stop sign and a cattle guard **(2)**. If you have a high clearance vehicle, you can drive all the way to Fuller Tank. If you are in a low slung car, drive as far as you are comfortable, then park and walk to the pond. It is an easy walk. Just follow the pipeline markers to the tank.

TRAILHEAD: The trail starts on top of the earth dam on the south end of Fuller Tank. A sign and steel poles mark the start of the trail.

DESCRIPTION: From the pond upward, this hike has a nice remote feeling. Pointy volcanic peaks surround you. There are a few places where redrock ledges are exposed, adding a welcome touch of color.
    As you near the top of the trail, at Deer Pass, you will see that you are heading to a saddle. At the saddle you will look down on the tremendous development that has taken place in the last few years in the Village of Oak Creek area.
    The trail ends at a neighborhood trailhead, on Arabian Drive in the Rancho Rojo Estates. Kel Fox was a rancher who had a winter range in the area of the trail and a summer range in Munds Park. The Foxboro Ranch School was named for his father.

Photo: The Kel Fox Trail starts at Fuller Tank, shown here. There is seldom water in the tank, but we were lucky to find it nearly full on the winter day when Sherry took this picture.

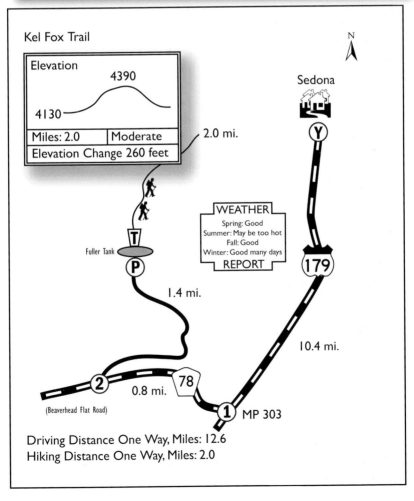

Kel Fox Trail

N

Sedona

Elevation

4390

4130

Miles: 2.0	Moderate
Elevation Change 260 feet	

2.0 mi.

WEATHER
Spring: Good
Summer: May be too hot
Fall: Good
Winter: Good many days
REPORT

Fuller Tank

T

P

Y

179

1.4 mi.

10.4 mi.

2

(Beaverhead Flat Road)

0.8 mi.

78

1 MP 303

Driving Distance One Way, Miles: 12.6
Hiking Distance One Way, Miles: 2.0

Lime Kiln Trail

General Information
Location Map F1
Clarkdale USGS Map
Coconino Forest Service Map

Driving Distance One Way: 22.4 miles *35.8 km* (Time 45 minutes)
Access Road*:* All cars, All paved
Hiking Distance One Way: 2.8 miles *4.5 km* (Time 1.5 hours)
How Strenuous*:* Moderate
Features*:* Easy to reach, Historic road

NUTSHELL: The Lime Kiln Trail starts inside the Dead Horse State Park in Cottonwood, passes a historic lime kiln, and heads toward Sedona.

DIRECTIONS:
From the Sedona Y (the intersection of Highways 179 and 89A) Go:
    Southwest on Highway 89A for 18.6 miles *29.8 km*, to the stoplight in Cottonwood at the junctions of Highways 279 and 89A. Go straight on Historic Highway 89A (Main Street) into Old Town Cottonwood. At 20.6 miles *33.0 km*, just past the cemetery, turn right on 10th Street. The entrance to the park is at 21.5 miles *34.4 km* **(1)**. Pay your fee and then drive back on the main road 0.9 miles *1.4 km*, parking at a Lagoon parking lot.

TRAILHEAD: Walk the main paved road for 0.1 miles *0.16 km*, through a gate. Turn left to the Lagoon trailhead with a 2-panel trailhead sign.

DESCRIPTION: Hike the Lagoon Trail for 0.2 miles *0.32 km* to intersect the Lime Kiln Trail, then turn right. Don't go down into the canyon. Almost immediately you will come to the site of the kiln—just a small enclosure made of pink native stone in a white cliff on the side of Rattlesnake Wash.
    Beyond the kiln the trail makes a steep climb up The Stairsteps to a ridge top. Once on top of the ridge you will be able to see out over the Verde Valley. The trail winds around ridges, then quits ridge running and moves fairly straight across country.
    At 1.8 miles *2.9 km* you reach a place where a road to the left runs 0.25 miles *0.4 km* to the Rattlesnake Wash Overlook (not recommended).
    At 2.0 miles *3.2 k*m you reach the Bill Ensign Trail to your right. At 2.2 miles *3.5 km* is the junction with the Thumper Trail, left. Just beyond you come to a gate. From the gate the trail continues across flat land, meeting with FR 9538 at Last Chance Tank, where the trail stops for now at 2.8 miles *4.5 km*. There are plans to take the trail all the way to the Red Rock State Park near Sedona, a distance of 14.0 miles *22.4 km*.

Photo: The Lime Kiln is in the center of this photo, but is hard to see. The door is the small dark rectangle in the middle of the photo.

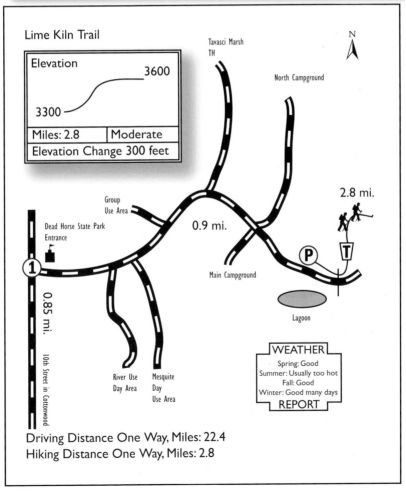

Lime Kiln Trail

Elevation
3600
3300
Miles: 2.8 | Moderate
Elevation Change 300 feet

N

Tavasci Marsh
TH

North Campground

2.8 mi.

Group
Use Area

0.9 mi.

Dead Horse State Park
Entrance

1

P

T

Main Campground

0.85 mi.

10th Street in Cottonwood

River Use
Day Area

Mesquite
Day
Use Area

Lagoon

WEATHER
Spring: Good
Summer: Usually too hot
Fall: Good
Winter: Good many days
REPORT

Driving Distance One Way, Miles: 22.4
Hiking Distance One Way, Miles: 2.8

Little Horse Trail #61

General Information
Location Map E5
Munds Mountain and Sedona USGS Maps
Coconino Forest Service Map

Driving Distance One Way: 3.6 miles *5.8 km* (Time 10 minutes)
Access Road: All cars, All paved
Hiking Distance One Way: 2.2 miles *3.5 km* (Time 1 hour)
How Strenuous: Moderate
Features: Views, Redrocks

NUTSHELL: Located near downtown Sedona, this hike takes you across relatively flat land to the top of Chicken Point, a well-known landmark.

DIRECTIONS:
From the Sedona Y (the intersection of Highways 179 and 89A) Go:
   South on Highway 179 (toward Phoenix) for a distance of 3.6 miles *5.8 km* (MP 309.8) **(1)**. You will see a large sign for the trailhead. Turn left into the trailhead parking lot. This is a major trailhead, with lots of parking and all facilities, including a toilet.

TRAILHEAD: At the parking lot, where you will find a map and signs.

DESCRIPTION: This trail is part of the Bell Rock Pathway system and is a very nice one, well posted, easy to follow and very scenic.
   You begin the hike by walking away from the highway and soon come up on top of a ridge. From here you can see the top of the Chapel of the Holy Cross in the distance. The trail moves you toward the Chapel and the beautiful redrock formation on which it is situated, Twin Buttes.
   The trail will bring you to the base of the redrocks of Twin Buttes, where you turn right. We love walking along here, so close to the majestic redrock. The erosion sculpting on the butte is quite fantastic. As you move along, you will come to a gate. This used to be a serious gate, closed at all times, but now it seems to be constantly open and neglected. Go through the gate. Just beyond the gate you will be at the foot of Chicken Point, which is at the top of the redrocks to your upper left. Chicken Point is a slickrock saddle between red buttes. The jeep tours drive there frequently, so don't be surprised if you hear people on top, towering above you.
   You will hike slightly past Chicken Point, and then the trail turns to the left, hooks back, and climbs to the top of the Chicken Point formation. Once up to the level of the point, you can walk over where the jeeps park. The passengers always seem startled to see hikers come out of the canyon.

Photo: This trail winds around a bit before breaking out into clear country and heading toward the colorful cliffs shown here.

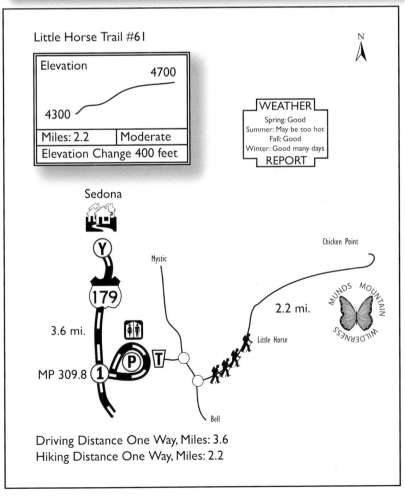

Little Horse Trail #61

Elevation
4700
4300

Miles: 2.2	Moderate
Elevation Change 400 feet	

N

WEATHER
Spring: Good
Summer: May be too hot
Fall: Good
Winter: Good many days
REPORT

Sedona

Mystic

Chicken Point

Y

179

3.6 mi.

2.2 mi.

MUNDS MOUNTAIN
WILDERNESS

MP 309.8 1

P T

Little Horse

Bell

Driving Distance One Way, Miles: 3.6
Hiking Distance One Way, Miles: 2.2

Llama Trail

General Information
Location Map F4
Munds Mountain and Sedona USGS Maps
Coconino Forest Service Map

Driving Distance One Way: 4.4 miles *7.0 km* (Time 15 minutes)
Access Road: All cars, All paved
Hiking Distance, Complete Loop: 2.75 miles *4.4 km* (Time 1.5 hours)
How Strenuous: Moderate
Features: Nice loop in the Lee Mountain-Courthouse Butte area

NUTSHELL: The Twin Buttes to the north, Lee Mountain on the east, and Courthouse Butte on the south enclose a backcountry bowl. This loop hike in that bowl brings you close to Lee Mountain, and then runs south along its base toward Courthouse Butte through interesting and scenic terrain.

DIRECTIONS:
From the Sedona Y (the intersection of Highways 179 and 89A) Go:
    South on Highway 179 (toward Phoenix) for a distance of 4.4 miles *7.0 km* (MP 308.9) **(1)**. There is a big parking apron on the left-hand side of the highway. Pull in there and park.

TRAILHEAD: The official trailhead has not yet been established, but our approach works fine.

DESCRIPTION: From the parking area walk north on the old jeep road and then jog to the right. In a few paces you will meet the **Bell Rock Pathway** (signed). Turn right and walk on the pathway uphill 50 paces from the sign and then turn left on a dim trail under the power line. The trail becomes more distinct as you go.
    You first hike north. At 0.5 miles *0.8 km* you reach the base of a little red knoll where the trail forks. Go right (E), walking along a redrock ledge toward Lee Mountain. Soon the trail will bend to the south, allowing you to walk along the base of Lee Mountain. It is pretty and remote feeling back here, even though you can hear the cars on Highway 179, which are never very far away.
    After a nice long walk parallel to Lee Mountain you near Courthouse Butte but then turn west, toward the highway. In this area beware of a trail going to the left, toward the butte. Do not take it. At about 2.5 miles *4.0 km* you will emerge onto the Bell Rock Pathway. Turn right on this path and walk back to your parking place.

Photo: The water holes are one of our favorite places on this trail, where it crosses by them at a slickrock shelf.

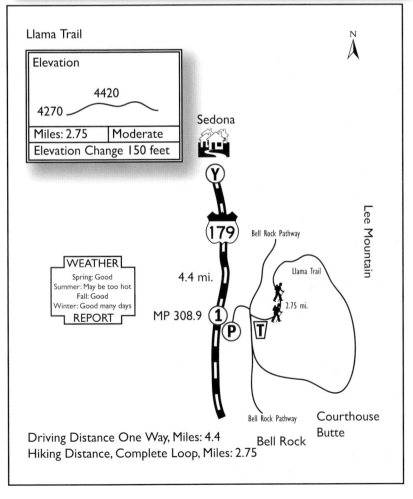

Llama Trail

Elevation

4420
4270

Miles: 2.75	Moderate
Elevation Change 150 feet	

N

Sedona

Y

179

Bell Rock Pathway

Lee Mountain

Llama Trail

WEATHER
Spring: Good
Summer: May be too hot
Fall: Good
Winter: Good many days
REPORT

4.4 mi.

2.75 mi.

MP 308.9   1   P   T

Bell Rock Pathway

Courthouse
Butte

Driving Distance One Way, Miles: 4.4
Hiking Distance, Complete Loop, Miles: 2.75

Bell Rock

Long Canyon Trail #63

General Information
Location Map G6
Casner Butte, Buckhorn Mtn. USGS Maps
Coconino Forest Service Map

Driving Distance One Way: 18.0 miles *28.8 km* (Time 30 minutes)
Access Road: All cars, Last 0.6 miles *1.0 km* good dirt road
Hiking Distance One Way: 2.5 miles *4.0 km* (Time 2 hours 30 minutes)
How Strenuous: Hard due to steep climb on first leg
Features: Views

NUTSHELL: Starting on the east bank of Wet Beaver Creek, this hike takes you along an old cattle trail, as you climb over one thousand feet.

DIRECTIONS:
From the Sedona Y (the intersection of Highways 179 and 89A) Go:
    South on Highway 179 (toward Phoenix) for 14.7 miles *23.5 km*, to the I-17 Interchange **(1)**. Instead of going onto I-17, go underneath it onto the paved country road FR 618. You will pass the Beaver Creek Ranger Station and the bridge over Beaver Creek, where the paving ends. Just after the paving ends, you will reach a three-way fork at 17.4 miles *27.8 km* **(2)**. Turn left here. At 18.0 miles *28.8 km* the parking area is to your left **(3)**.

TRAILHEAD: The trailhead is uphill to your right at a gate. The sign says, "Long Canyon Trail #63. Bell Trail #13—10 miles. Trail difficult to find after 2 miles." [We had no trouble finding the trail].

DESCRIPTION: This is an old cattle trail and climbs steeply, rising 700 feet in the first 0.4 miles *0.6 km*, but the trail zigzags and is well maintained. You climb to a ridge that is more level, and walk east along it. You can walk over to the rim of the ridge anywhere for fine views of the Verde Valley and some of the colored cliffs of Sedona. At 1.0 mile *1.6 km* you make another climb, but this one is not as steep or as long as the first climb.
    When you finish the second climb, you emerge onto the top of a mesa, where it is fairly flat but the ground is strewn with rocks everywhere, making for hard footing. The trail is marked by wire-cage cairns. In spite of the warning sign at the trailhead, we had no trouble seeing the trail.
    On top, we found the hike disappointing, as it passes through flat uninteresting country. The trail moves east, parallel to the south side of Long Canyon. The trail nears the edge of the canyon at about the 4.0 mile *6.4 km* point, and meets the Bell Trail, which skirts along the north side of Long Canyon, at the canyon's mouth. We stopped at the 2.5 mile point.

Photo: This trail is rocky and liberally studded with cactus, but offers fine views of the Beaver Creek area.

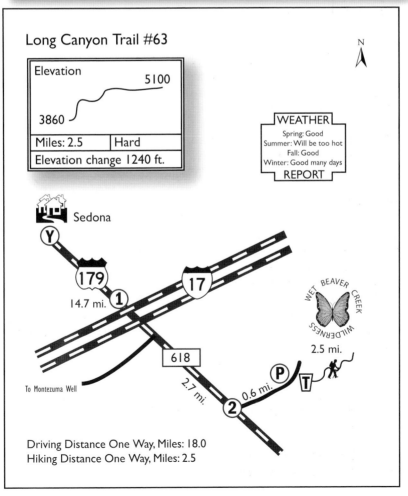

Long Canyon Trail #63

N

Elevation

5100

3860

Miles: 2.5	Hard
Elevation change 1240 ft.	

WEATHER
Spring: Good
Summer: Will be too hot
Fall: Good
Winter: Good many days
REPORT

Sedona

Y

179

14.7 mi.

(1)

17

WET BEAVER CREEK WILDERNESS

618

2.5 mi.

To Montezuma Well

2.7 mi.

0.6 mi.

P

T

(2)

Driving Distance One Way, Miles: 18.0
Hiking Distance One Way, Miles: 2.5

Long Canyon Trail #122

General Information
Location Map C3
Wilson Mt. USGS Map
Coconino Forest Service Map

Driving Distance One Way: 6.7 miles *10.7 km* (Time 15 minutes)
Access Road: All cars, All paved
Hiking Distance One Way: 3.0 miles *4.8 km* (Time 2 hours)
How Strenuous: Moderate
Features: Views, Great cliffs

NUTSHELL: This trail takes you right up against the base of gorgeous red cliffs. **A personal favorite.**

DIRECTIONS:
From the Sedona Y (the intersection of Highways 179 and 89A) Go:
    Southwest on Highway 89A (toward Cottonwood) for 3.2 miles *5.1 km* (MP 371) to the Dry Creek Road (stoplight) **(1).** Turn right onto Dry Creek Road and follow it to the 6.1 mile *9.8 km* point, where there is a stop sign **(2).** Turn right on Long Canyon Road. At the 6.7 miles *10.7 km* point **(3)** turn left into the parking area, an old road blocked with boulders.

TRAILHEAD: At the parking area.

DESCRIPTION: Walk the old road. At 0.3 miles *0.5 km* you will come to a 3-pronged fork. Take the left fork. At 0.6 miles *1.0 km* you will go through a gap in a fence, the boundary of the Redrock-Secret Mt. Wilderness Area. The trail is a footpath from this point as you skirt a golf course. At 1.0 miles *1.6 km* you will reach a fork. The left fork is the **Deadman Pass Trail.**
    Soon after that you will enter a shaded cypress forest fairly close to the magnificent red and white sculptured cliffs of Maroon Mountain to your right (north).
    Beyond the 2.5 mile *4.0 km* point the vegetation becomes more alpine, with many oaks and huge alligator bark junipers. At 3.0 miles *4.8 km* the trail turns straight north, climbing steeply. This is the stopping point. Here you will find genuine alpine conditions with pines and firs and a carpet of green on the forest floor. The canyon walls are nearer now and you have tremendous views.
    The trail dwindles. It plays out completely at 4.0 miles *6.4 km* in a side canyon, in a place that is one of the wildest in the Sedona area. It really feels remote. The path narrows there to a barely discernible game trail where you are totally out of sight of the works of man.

Photo: You hike toward the cliffs shown here, which form the north wall of Long Canyon, then turn left and hike along the canyon bottom.

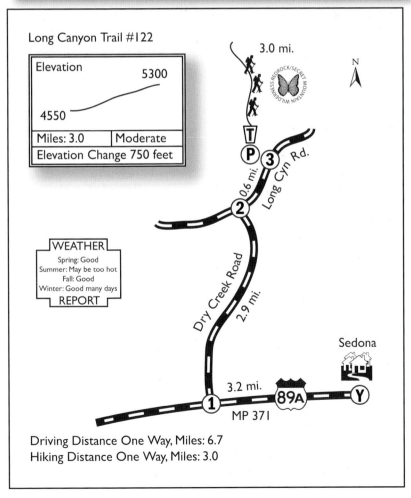

Long Canyon Trail #122

Elevation

5300

4550

Miles: 3.0	Moderate
Elevation Change 750 feet	

3.0 mi.

REDROCK/SECRET MOUNTAIN WILDERNESS

N

T
P 3

Long Cyn Rd.

0.6 mi.

2

Dry Creek Road

2.9 mi.

WEATHER
Spring: Good
Summer: May be too hot
Fall: Good
Winter: Good many days
REPORT

Sedona

3.2 mi.

1

89A
MP 371

Y

Driving Distance One Way, Miles: 6.7
Hiking Distance One Way, Miles: 3.0

Lost Canyon

General Information
Location Map C4
Wilson Mt. USGS Map
Coconino Forest Service Map

Driving Distance One Way: 7.7 miles *12.3 km* (Time 25 minutes)
Access Road: Most cars, Last 2.5 miles *4.0 km* bumpy dirt road
Hiking Distance One Way: 2.2 miles *3.5 km* (Time 1.5 hours)
How Strenuous: Moderate, but one short stretch is strenuous
Features: Scenic canyons, Indian ruins, Cave

NUTSHELL: You climb onto a ledge which you follow into two scenic canyons, enjoying Indian ruins and spectacular scenery on the way.

DIRECTIONS:
From the Sedona Y (the intersection of Highways 179 and 89A) Go:
SW on Highway 89 (toward Cottonwood) 3.2 miles *5.1 km* to Dry Creek Road **(1)**. Turn right and drive to the 5.2 mile *8.3 km* point **(2)**. Turn right on FR 152, the road to **Vultee Arch**, and follow it to the 7.7 mile *12.3 km* point **(3)**. Pull off to the right into the big **Brins Mesa Trail** parking area. Park.

TRAILHEAD: Use the Brins Mesa #119 trailhead.

DESCRIPTION: Start the hike by walking the Brins Mesa trail. From the rusty sign walk up the trail 210 feet (about 85 paces). Turn right (S) onto a footpath. There are no signs, as this is a non-system trail.

Once you are on the path, it is well-worn and easy to follow. You cross a sandy wash strewn with gray boulders then walk across country to a redrock-lined arroyo. Do not walk across the redrock ledge. Turn left (E) and hike up the arroyo. You soon reach a point where you must make a steep 450-foot climb to a ledge. From this point the trail becomes fairly level as it stays on the ledge. There are fine views from this area out over the Dry Creek area.

Hike south moving toward a giant red reef that marks the northern toe of Lost Canyon. The trail goes around the reef and into the canyon. Here the walls are tall, sheer and beautiful. At times the trail comes breathtakingly close to the edge of a cliff. This is not a trail for acrophobics.

At 0.75 miles *1.2 km* you will see above you a long shallow cave half way up the cliff. There is a ruin in the cave. Please treat it and any other ancient relic with respect. From here the trail goes to the head or apex of the canyon. In the canyon bottom at the apex and you will see a cliff house-type ruin. You can stop here, but the trail continues out to the canyon mouth and winds around another toe, then enters the canyon where **Devil's Bridge** is located.

Photo: Highly sculpted undercut cliffs protect an ancient Sinagua dwelling. Dick sits above it enjoying the surrounding soaring cliffs.

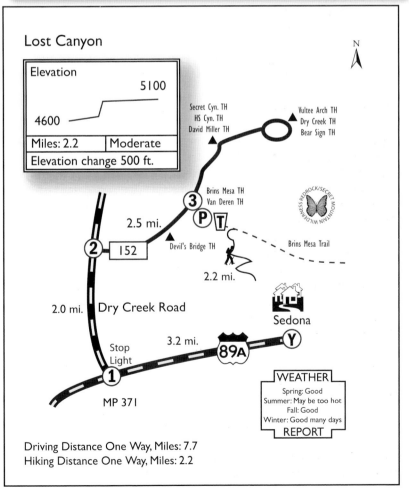

Lost Canyon

Elevation

5100

4600

Miles: 2.2	Moderate
Elevation change 500 ft.	

N

Secret Cyn. TH
HS Cyn. TH
David Miller TH

Vultee Arch TH
Dry Creek TH
Bear Sign TH

Brins Mesa TH
Van Deren TH

③

P T

2.5 mi.

② 152

Devil's Bridge TH

REDROCK/SECRET MOUNTAIN WILDERNESS

Brins Mesa Trail

2.2 mi.

2.0 mi. Dry Creek Road

Sedona

3.2 mi. 89A Y

Stop
Light

①

MP 371

WEATHER
Spring: Good
Summer: May be too hot
Fall: Good
Winter: Good many days
REPORT

Driving Distance One Way, Miles: 7.7
Hiking Distance One Way, Miles: 2.2

Lower Chimney Rock Trail

General Information
Location Map D4
Sedona USGS Map
Coconino Forest Service Map

Driving Distance One Way: 4.3 miles *6.9 km* (Time 10 minutes)
Access Road: All cars, All paved
Hiking Distance, Complete Loop: 1.5 miles *2.4 km* (Time 45 minutes)
How Strenuous: Easy
Features: Close to town, easy all-weather access

NUTSHELL: This is a dandy little hike that you can take when time is limited.

DIRECTIONS:
From the Sedona Y (the intersection of Highways 179 and 89A) Go:
Southwest on Highway 89A (toward Cottonwood) for 3.2 miles *5.1 km* (MP 371) to Dry Creek Road (stoplight) **(1)**. Turn right on Dry Creek Road and drive to the 3.7 mile *5.9 km* point **(2)**. Turn right on Thunder Mountain Road. Go to the 4.3 mile *6.9 km* point **(3)**, then turn left into the parking lot.

TRAILHEAD: At the parking area. There is a three-panel sign.

DESCRIPTION: Follow the main trail. At 0.1 miles *0.16 km* you will come to a trail junction marked by a signpost and a sign. The trail to the right is the **Thunder Mountain Trail**. Go straight ahead at this point.

At 0.35 miles *0.56 km* you will reach a second signposted trail junction at the top of a little pass, where you can see down into the Dry Creek Road area. The **Chimney Rock Loop Trail** takes off to the right at this junction. Walk straight ahead, down the north side of the ridge into the flat area below. You'll pass the **Summit Route Trail** to the left.

As you descend, the unmistakable Chimney Rock comes into view to your right. The big butte on your right has had several names: Thunder Mountain, Capitol Butte, Grey Mountain, and Shadow Mountain.

Down on the valley floor your views are restricted by a juniper forest. The Dry Creek Road is nearby, to your left, and the trail angles toward it. At 0.6 miles *1.0 km* you will come to a barbed wire fence around a housing area, where the trail turns left. At 0.75 miles *1.2 km* there is a confusing trail junction. Take the left fork.

You will return by hiking around the west and south faces of Little Sugarloaf. At 1.25 miles *2.0 km* you pass through a rusty wire fence and walk under a power line. At 1.5 miles *2.4 km* you're back at the parking lot.

Photo: This trail is wide and easy and loops around the redrock butte shown here. It is the same butte climbed by the Summit Route.

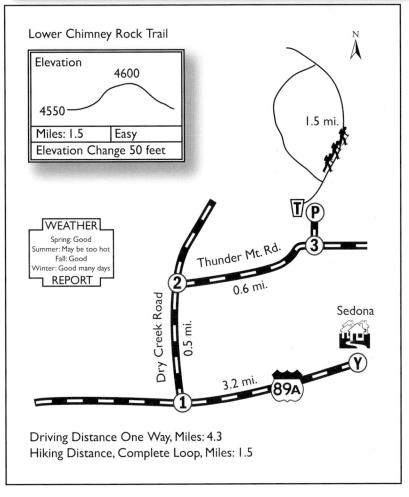

Lower Chimney Rock Trail

Elevation

4600

4550

Miles: 1.5	Easy
Elevation Change 50 feet	

1.5 mi.

WEATHER
Spring: Good
Summer: May be too hot
Fall: Good
Winter: Good many days
REPORT

Thunder Mt. Rd.

Dry Creek Road

0.6 mi.

0.5 mi.

Sedona

3.2 mi.

89A

Driving Distance One Way, Miles: 4.3
Hiking Distance, Complete Loop, Miles: 1.5

Loy Canyon Trail #5

General Information
Location Map C1
Loy Butte and Page Springs USGS Maps
Coconino Forest Service Map

Driving Distance One Way: 15.5 miles *24.8 km* (Time 40 minutes)
Access Road: All cars, Last 7.8 miles *12.5 km* bumpy dirt road
Hiking Distance One Way: 4.0 miles *6.4 km* (Time 4 hours)
How Strenuous: Hard
Features: Scenic canyon, Views

NUTSHELL: This trail goes through a pleasant canyon to the top of the Mogollon Rim.

DIRECTIONS:
From the Sedona Y (the intersection of Highways 179 and 89A) Go:
   Southwest on Highway 89A (toward Cottonwood) for 3.2 miles *5.1 km,* to a stoplight **(1)**, then turn right on Dry Creek Road. Drive to a stop sign at 6.1 miles *9.8 km* **(2)**. Turn left and drive to a second stop sign at 7.7 miles *12.3 km* **(3)**. Go left on unpaved road FR 152C. You will come to third stop sign at 11.7 miles *18.7 km* **(4)**, where you turn right on FR 525. At 11.8 miles *18.9 km* is a V-fork **(5)** where you go left on FR 525. At 15.5 miles *24.8 km,* where you come to a ranch fence **(6)**, turn left into the parking lot.

TRAILHEAD: On the other side of the road.

DESCRIPTION: The Loy Canyon trail was built in the 1890s to take cattle to the top of the Mogollon Rim. The first part of the trail goes through the Hancock Ranch, and you skirt a ranch fence. At 0.5 miles *0.8 km* you enter the canyon mouth and begin to walk up the sandy canyon bottom, leaving the ranch at about 0.75 miles *1.2 km.*
   As you hike the trail rises gradually through a forest for 4.0 miles *6.4 km,* and meanders across a creekbed a few times, so you don't want to make the hike when water is running high. Because the trail gains in elevation the vegetation along the trail also changes from desert-like growth to a pine forest. The trees block the views but there are places where you get glimpses of gorgeous redrock canyons topped with high white cliffs on both sides.
   At the end of 4.0 miles *6.4 km* you are at the base of the cliffs forming The Mogollon Rim, where we stop for a satisfying day hike. To go to the top requires some serious work. The trail becomes much steeper, requiring a strenuous climb of over 1,000 feet in 1.0 miles *1.6 km.*

Photo: Loy Canyon is well supplied with trees and shrubbery, but breaks in the vegetation give you superb views of magnificent cliffs.

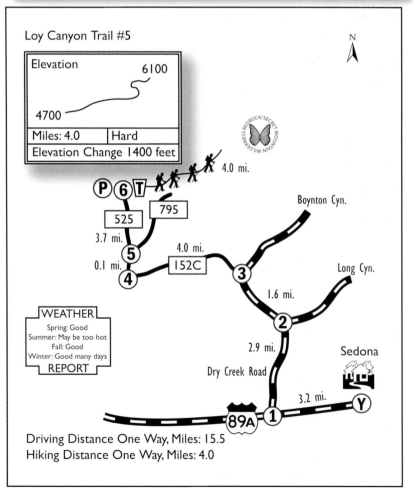

Loy Canyon Trail #5

Elevation
6100
4700

Miles: 4.0 | Hard

Elevation Change 1400 feet

REDROCK/SECRET MOUNTAIN WILDERNESS

N

4.0 mi.

P 6 T

525 | 795

3.7 mi.

5

0.1 mi.

4

4.0 mi.

152C

3

Boynton Cyn.

Long Cyn.

1.6 mi.

2

WEATHER
Spring: Good
Summer: May be too hot
Fall: Good
Winter: Good many days
REPORT

2.9 mi.

Dry Creek Road

Sedona

3.2 mi.

89A 1

Y

Driving Distance One Way, Miles: 15.5
Hiking Distance One Way, Miles: 4.0

Marg's Draw Trail

General Information
Location Map E5
Sedona USGS Map
Coconino Forest Service Map

Driving Distance One Way: 0.9 miles *1.4 km* (Time 5 minutes)
Access Road: All cars, All paved
Hiking Distance One Way: 1.4/2.0 miles *2.2/3.2 km* (Time 1/1.5 hour)
How Strenuous: Moderate
Features: Views, Easy access

NUTSHELL: Marg's Draw is a beautiful area in Sedona's backyard, a bowl surrounded by the Crimson Cliffs, Munds Mountain, Lee Mountain and Twin Buttes. This trail is a means of traversing it from north to south.

DIRECTIONS:
From the Sedona Y (the intersection of Highways 179 and 89A) Go:
    South on Highway 179 (toward Phoenix) for a distance of 0.7 miles *1.1 km* (MP 312.8) to Sombart Lane, which is at the Circle K store **(1)**. Turn left on Sombart Lane and follow it to the parking area at 0.9 miles *1.4 km*.

TRAILHEAD: At the parking lot. There is a map/sign.

DESCRIPTION: This trail has three access points. We have chosen the midpoint access but describe how to get to the others. The first leg of the trail, a connecting link to the Margs Draw Trail, is a brisk climb uphill, about 100 feet in 0.1 mile *0.16 km*. You then enter a relatively flat stretch. At 0.4 miles *0.6 km* you will come to a T-trail junction, the midpoint of the trail. You can go to the left (N) 1.0 mile *1.6 km* and hike around the Crimson Cliffs to the Schnebly Hill Road. If you turn to the right (S), you will hike 1.0 miles *1.6 km* to the **Broken Arrow** trailhead.
    Both sections of the trail are interesting. Even though you are very close to the settled areas of Sedona on this trail, you are screened by vegetation, so that you have a nice backcountry feeling. The views of the cliffs surrounding Marg's Draw are beautiful, whichever way you go.
    By starting from the midpoint trailhead, you have a 1.4 mile *2.2 km* hike (see map). If you start from either the south end at Broken Arrow trailhead or the north end off Schnebly Hill Road, you will have a 2.0 mile *3.2 km* hike (each way).
    Options: South trailhead—follow the directions for the **Broken Arrow Trail**. North trailhead—follow the directions for the **Huckaby Trail**.

Photo: Marg's Draw is a beautiful bowl surrounded by scenic cliffs.

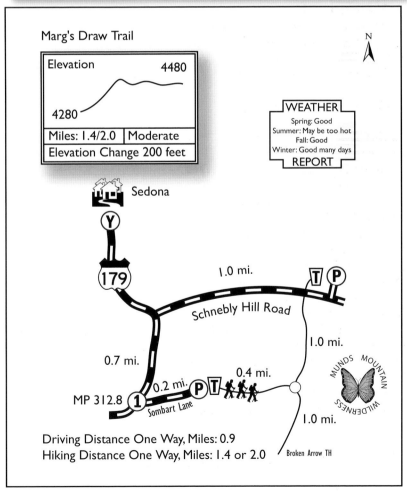

Marg's Draw Trail

N

Elevation
4480

4280

| Miles: 1.4/2.0 | Moderate |

Elevation Change 200 feet

WEATHER
Spring: Good
Summer: May be too hot
Fall: Good
Winter: Good many days
REPORT

Sedona

Y

179

1.0 mi.

T P

Schnebly Hill Road

1.0 mi.

0.7 mi.

0.2 mi.

0.4 mi.

MUNDS MOUNTAIN WILDERNESS

MP 312.8

1

P T

Sombart Lane

1.0 mi.

Driving Distance One Way, Miles: 0.9
Hiking Distance One Way, Miles: 1.4 or 2.0

Broken Arrow TH

Mescal Mountain

General Information
Location Map C3
Wilson Mt. USGS Map
Coconino Forest Service Map

Driving Distance One Way: 6.7 miles *10.7 km* (Time 15 minutes)
Access Road: All cars, All paved
Hiking Distance One Way: 2.5 miles *4.0 km* (Time 90 minutes)
How Strenuous: Moderate
Features: Views, Cave, Indian ruins

NUTSHELL: This non-system trail takes you to the top of Mescal Mountain, a mesa at the mouth of Boynton Canyon northwest of Sedona.

DIRECTIONS:
From the Sedona Y (the intersection of Highways 179 and 89A) Go:
Southwest on Highway 89A (toward Cottonwood) for 3.2 miles *5.1 km* (MP 371) to the Dry Creek Road (stoplight) **(1)**. Turn right and follow Dry Creek Rd. to the 6.1 mile *9.8 km* point, a stop sign, where you turn right on the paved Long Canyon Road **(2)**. Drive to the 6.7 miles *10.7 km* point, an unpaved road to your left **(3)**, where you pull in and park.

TRAILHEAD: At the parking area (signed for Long Canyon).

DESCRIPTION: Hike the **Long Canyon Trail #122** for 0.6 miles *1.0 km* to a gap in the fence at the entrance to the Redrock-Secret Mt. Wilderness Area. Stay outside the fence and walk the old road that parallels it. At the 1.0 mile *1.6 km* point you will reach the foot of a butte, where the trail climbs.

On the way up, you will see Grandma's Cave to your right with a large crack in the roof that allows water to pour into the cave when it rains. A side trail goes to this cave and it is worth a detour.

The main trail goes to a saddle. Just below the saddle, in a red ledge, you will see a shallow cave with an Indian ruin. On top of the saddle you will see a distinct footpath marked with cairns going up to the left (S). A few yards along this trail there is the ruin of a pit house. Beyond it the trail winds right up to a cliff face and then curves left, hugging the cliff at its base. It is fairly easy hiking, though steep, until you get to a point just below the top. There you will have to do some climbing if you want to go to the crest.

The small climb involved to reach the top is no worse than climbing a high ladder. Once you are on top, walk around and enjoy the view. The distance to the top is 1.5 miles *2.4 km*. Fully exploring the top can add another mile to the hike.

Photo: We enjoy the views from this saddle on the flank of Mescal Mountain. The Deadman Pass Trail is in the valley below.

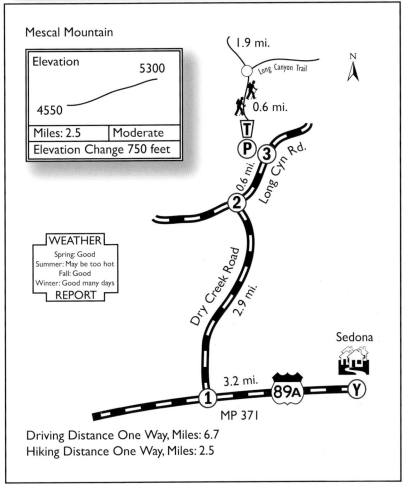

Mescal Mountain

Elevation
5300
4550

| Miles: 2.5 | Moderate |

Elevation Change 750 feet

1.9 mi.

Long Canyon Trail

N

0.6 mi.

T
P
3 Long Cyn Rd.

0.6 mi.

2

WEATHER
Spring: Good
Summer: May be too hot
Fall: Good
Winter: Good many days
REPORT

Dry Creek Road

2.9 mi.

Sedona

3.2 mi.
1
89A
Y

MP 371

Driving Distance One Way, Miles: 6.7
Hiking Distance One Way, Miles: 2.5

Mitten Ridge

General Information
Location Map E5
Munds Mt. and Munds Park USGS Maps
Coconino Forest Service Map

Driving Distance One Way: 3.8 miles *6.1 km* (Time 20 minutes)
Access Road: High clearance cars, Last 2.5 miles *4.0 km* rough dirt road
Hiking Distance One Way: 2.5 miles *4.0 km* (Time 2 hours)
How Strenuous: Moderate
Features: Views, Fascinating rock formations and sculptures

NUTSHELL: You explore the redrock buttes overlooking Sedona from the Schnebly Hill Road.

DIRECTIONS:
From the Sedona Y (the intersection of Highways 179 and 89A) Go:
South on Highway 179 (toward Phoenix) for a distance of 0.3 miles *0.5 km* (MP 313.1) to the Schnebly Hill Road. It is just across the bridge past Tlaquepaque **(1)**. Turn left onto the Schnebly Hill Road. It is paved for the first 1.0 mile *1.6 km* and then turns into a dirt road. At the 3.8 mile *6.1 km* point, turn into the signed parking area to the right **(2)**.

TRAILHEAD: Follow the trail sign for the Cow Pies Trail.

DESCRIPTION: As you drive up Schnebly Hill Road you will see a big butte between the road and Sedona. This is Mitten Ridge, one of the major Sedona landmarks, and it is your goal on this hike.

When you begin hiking you will dip into a streambed and then come up to a redrock shelf littered with small grey stones.

So far you are following the **Cow Pies** hike. At 0.5 miles *0.8 km*, the paths split. You will go straight instead of turning left as you would for the Cow Pies hike. You will walk toward ledges at the base of Mitten Ridge. You are on a system trail that is easy to follow and is rather exciting as it works its way out on the very edge of steep ledges. At 1.5 miles *2.4 km* you will break out onto clear slickrock. There are many marvelous viewpoints to enjoy from these ledges.

As you walk you will see a saddle above you to the right. The saddle is a great viewpoint. Look for cairns marking the way. It is easy and fun to walk up the sloping redrock face of the ridge to the saddle. We like to go to the saddle and then come down and continue walking out toward the toe of the butte. You can go pretty far, but the trail pinches out at the 2.5 miles *4.0 km* point.

Photo: The ridge is between Sedona and the Schnebly Hill Road, and the trail takes you along its base, walking on top of redrock ledges.

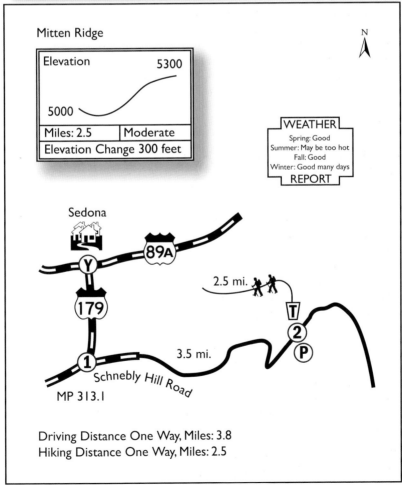

Mitten Ridge

N

Elevation   5300

5000

Miles: 2.5	Moderate
Elevation Change 300 feet	

WEATHER
Spring: Good
Summer: May be too hot
Fall: Good
Winter: Good many days
REPORT

Sedona

89A

Y

179

2.5 mi.

T
2
P

1

3.5 mi.

Schnebly Hill Road

MP 313.1

Driving Distance One Way, Miles: 3.8
Hiking Distance One Way, Miles: 2.5

Mooney Trail #12

General Information
Location Map C1
Loy Butte USGS Map
Coconino Forest Service Map

Driving Distance One Way: 20.9 miles *33.4 km* (Time 1 hour)
Access Road: All cars to Black Tank, High-clearance from there
Hiking Distance One Way: 4.5 miles *7.2 km* (Time 3.5 hours)
How Strenuous: Hard
Features: Views

NUTSHELL: This cattle trail starts at Black Tank southwest of Sedona, follows a ridge top with scenic views from both sides, then slips into Spring Creek's colorful canyon and finally makes a very strenuous climb to the top of Buck Ridge near the top of the Mogollon Rim.

DIRECTIONS:
From the Sedona Y (the intersection of Highways 179 and 89A) Go:
Southwest on Highway 89A (toward Cottonwood) for 9.6 miles *15.4 km* (MP 364.5) to the Red Canyon Road, FR 525 **(1)**. Turn right on FR 525 and follow it to the 12.4 miles *19.8 km* point where FR 525C branches to the left **(2)**. Turn left onto FR 525C. Drive it to the 18.1 miles *29 km* point **(3)** at high-walled Black Tank. Set your odometer to zero here. Drive straight back through the open area to the gate in back, at 0.2 miles *0.32 km*. Careful: the roads are badly eroded. At the gate turn right. At 0.8 miles *1.3 km* turn left on 9551A **(4)**. At 1.6 miles *2.6 km* is a critical turn **(5)**. Go left onto a narrow deeply cut unmarked road. This is the Mooney Trail, a primitive jeep road. Zero out again. We were able to drive in 1.2 miles *1.9 km* on this jeep road. Drive no farther; the road is terrible beyond and will damage your vehicle.

TRAILHEAD: Deceptive: officially it is at the junction of FR 525C and the road going into Black Tank, where the metal sign is planted, but for practical purposes it is as we describe . You don't want to walk it from Black Tank

DESCRIPTION: We found no signs, cairns or markers on this trail. Just stay on the jeep road. It soon takes you to the top of a narrow ridge where you will walk about 2.0 miles *3.2 km*. Great views along this ridge. Near the end of the ridge is a little ranch down to the right. The trail splits here. Take the right turn. It changes from a jeep road to a path. The trail hugs the side of the ridge, gradually descending into the canyon of Spring Creek, where the water's erosion has exposed some sculptured redrock. At the head of the canyon the trail takes on a new aspect, a steep hard climb. Many hikers happily stop here.

Photo: This shot shows the first part of the Mooney Trail, where you hike along the top of a ridge on an old road, with great views off to the sides.

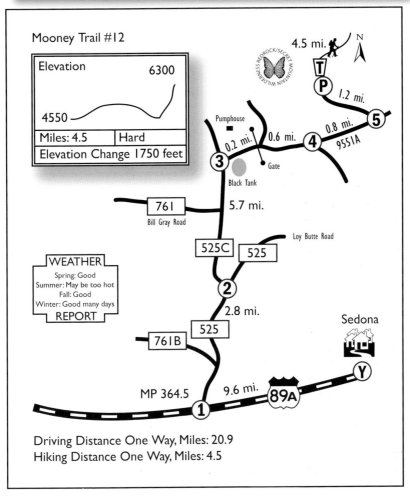

Mooney Trail #12

Elevation		6300
4550		
Miles: 4.5		Hard
Elevation Change 1750 feet		

REDROCK/SECRET MOUNTAIN WILDERNESS

4.5 mi.

N

T P

1.2 mi.

Pumphouse

0.6 mi.

4

0.8 mi.

5

0.2 mi.

3

9551A

Gate

Black Tank

761

Bill Gray Road

5.7 mi.

Loy Butte Road

525C 525

WEATHER
Spring: Good
Summer: May be too hot
Fall: Good
Winter: Good many days
REPORT

2

2.8 mi.

Sedona

761B

525

Y

MP 364.5

9.6 mi.

89A

1

Driving Distance One Way, Miles: 20.9
Hiking Distance One Way, Miles: 4.5

Munds Mountain Trail #77

General Information
Location Map E5
Munds Mt. and Munds Park USGS Maps
Coconino Forest Service Map

Driving Distance One Way: 6.6 miles *10.6 km* (Time 30 minutes)
Access Road: High clearance cars, Last 5.3 miles *8.5 km* rough dirt road
Hiking Distance One Way: 2.9 miles *4.6 km* (Time 2.5 hours)
How Strenuous: Hard
Features: Views

NUTSHELL: This hike takes you to the top of the north end of Munds Mountain for superb views.

DIRECTIONS:
From the Sedona Y (the intersection of Highways 179 and 89A) Go:
   South on Highway 179 (toward Phoenix) for 0.3 miles *0.5 km* (MP 313.1) to the Schnebly Hill Road, just across the bridge past Tlaquepaque **(1)**. Turn left on the Schnebly Hill Road, which is paved for the first 1.0 mile *1.6 km* and then turns into a dirt road that is sometimes very rough. Drive to the top, 6.6 miles *10.6 km* from the Y and park at the big parking lot at the Schnebly Hill Vista.

TRAILHEAD: From the parking area go back out to the main road, turn left and walk up the main road 100 paces, and then take the dirt road to your right (it is what is left of the original Schnebly Hill Road). This road is closed to cars from December 15-April 1, but even if it is open we would not drive it because of big exposed rocks. At 1.0 miles *1.6 km* you come to a fork. Go left. At 1.5 miles *2.4 km* you will see a small microwave tower and then come to a fork. Go right and at 1.7 miles *2.7 km* where the road makes a hairpin curve to your right take a footpath to the left marked by a cairn and a rusty sign reading "Munds Jacks Hot Loop." (It's part of the **Schnebly Hill Trail**). From here the trail follows the edge of the rim, with superb views. You pass through two gates, the second at Committee Tank. The trail then goes out on a thin ridge connected to Munds Mt. At 2.4 miles *3.8 km* you will find the trailhead, with a sign, "Munds Mt. Trail 77," just beyond the point where the **Jacks Canyon Trail** comes up and meets the ridge.

DESCRIPTION: At the trailhead the trail splits. Take the right fork, a sandy groove uphill. As you make the steep climb to the top you will get thrilling glimpses into the Mitten Ridge area. At the top you emerge onto a rather bare park. Move around its edge for unsurpassed views.

Photo: Views, views, views. They start on the access road on the way to the trailhead, where this shot was taken.

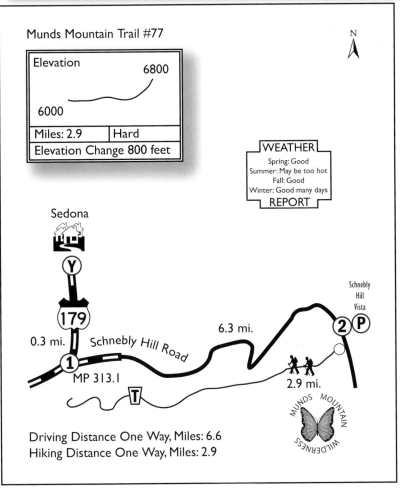

Munds Mountain Trail #77

N

Elevation
6800
6000

| Miles: 2.9 | Hard |
| Elevation Change 800 feet | |

WEATHER
Spring: Good
Summer: May be too hot
Fall: Good
Winter: Good many days
REPORT

Sedona

Y

179

0.3 mi.   Schnebly Hill Road   6.3 mi.

MP 313.1

1

T

2 P

Schnebly
Hill
Vista

2.9 mi.

MUNDS MOUNTAIN WILDERNESS

Driving Distance One Way, Miles: 6.6
Hiking Distance One Way, Miles: 2.9

Munds Wagon Trail

General Information
Location Map E5
Munds Mt. and Munds Park USGS Maps
Coconino Forest Service Map

Driving Distance One Way: 1.3 miles *2.1 km* (Time 10 minutes)
Access Road: All vehicles, All paved
Hiking Distance One Way: 4.5 miles *7.2 km* (Time 3 hours)
How Strenuous: Hard
Features: Historic road, Redrocks, Views

NUTSHELL: This hike takes you up Schnebly Hill the hard way, following portions of the old wagon road. It is very interesting and very scenic.

DIRECTIONS:
From the Sedona Y (the intersection of Highways 179 and 89A) Go:
    South on Highway 179 (toward Phoenix) for a distance of 0.3 miles *0.5 km* (MP 313.1) just over the bridge by Tlaquepaque and then turn left on the Schnebly Hill Road **(1)**. Drive to the 1.3 mile *2.1 km* point, where you turn left into a multi-trail parking lot **(2)**.

TRAILHEAD: At the parking lot. There is a three-panel map/sign and toilet

DESCRIPTION: The trail runs east from the parking lot, parallel to the modern road. You cross the road, go above it for a time and then cross it again. At 0.8 miles *1.3 km* you reach an area where it is clear that you are hiking the wagon road. It goes downhill and crosses the creek. You will find and lose the old road from time to time. You will reach a pair of concrete picnic tables at 1.25 miles *2.0 km*.
    The section from the picnic tables to the next road crossing is the middle part of the trail, with immensely high, sheer white cliffs to the right and red cliffs on the left.
    At 3.0 miles *4.8 km* you cross today's road and cross it again at 3.25 miles *5.2 km*—the final crossing. From here there is no question that you are on the wagon road, going straight up to the 4.0 mile *6.4 km* point, where it does a very interesting thing, winding halfway around the Merry-Go-Round, using a flat rock-free shelf of limestone as a natural roadway. This is a super part of the trail, great fun, with great views.
    From here you follow the old road to the end of the trail, at 4.5 miles *7.2 km* where the trail meets the modern road. Across the road is the trailhead for the **Schnebly Hill Trail** going on up to the top of the rim.

Photo: Parts of this trail are footpaths, but the most interesting portions are clearly old road segments, such as the one shown here.

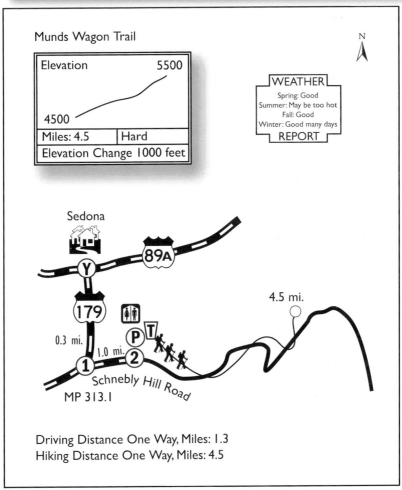

Munds Wagon Trail

N

Elevation 5500

4500

| Miles: 4.5 | Hard |

Elevation Change 1000 feet

WEATHER
Spring: Good
Summer: May be too hot
Fall: Good
Winter: Good many days
REPORT

Sedona

89A

Y

179

4.5 mi.

0.3 mi.

P T

1 1.0 mi. 2

Schnebly Hill Road

MP 313.1

Driving Distance One Way, Miles: 1.3
Hiking Distance One Way, Miles: 4.5

Mystic Trail

General Information
Location Map E5
Sedona USGS Map
Coconino Forest Service Map

Driving Distance One Way: 3.1 miles *5.0 km* (Time 10 minutes)
Access Road: All cars, All paved
Hiking Distance One Way: 1.0 miles *1.6 km* (Time 30 minutes)
How Strenuous: Easy
Features: Views, Easy to reach, All weather

NUTSHELL: This trail takes you from the road to the Chapel of the Holy Cross to the Sedona Cemetery.

DIRECTIONS:
From the Sedona Y (the intersection of Highways 179 and 89A) Go:
   South on Highway 179 (toward Phoenix) for a distance of 2.8 miles *4.5 km* (MP 310.6) to Chapel Road **(1)**. Turn left (E) onto Chapel Road and follow it until you are just east of Antelope Drive, the 3.1 mile *5.0 km* point, where you will see the trailhead to your left (N), at a gate in the fence **(2)**. Park on the shoulder by the gate.

TRAILHEAD: At the gate. There is a one-panel sign/map.

DESCRIPTION: This trail starts at the base of Twin Buttes, a lovely redrock formation. The Chapel of the Holy Cross is built on the south face of this butte "around the corner" from the trailhead.
   From the starting point, the trail heads north, hugging the base of the beautiful Twin Buttes. The trail feels almost level, though it does slope downward as you walk, taking a pronounced dip near the end. As you hike, you will enjoy looking at the red cliffs of Twin Buttes to your right. You are also unfortunately all too aware of many nearby homes. This is not a trail for someone seeking a wilderness experience, but it is just the ticket for someone who wants a nice little walk near town.
   At the halfway point you come around the buttes to a point where you can see into Sedona and enjoy pleasant views to the north. Then you move more noticeably downhill, toward Battlement Mesa, finally ending at the north end of the trail, at a cul-de-sac in a little subdivision adjacent to the Sedona Cemetery.
   The trail gets its name—not because it is a vortex site—from the nearby Mystic Hills Subdivision.

Photo: The Mystic Trail is short but gives you fine views of beautiful redrock buttes.

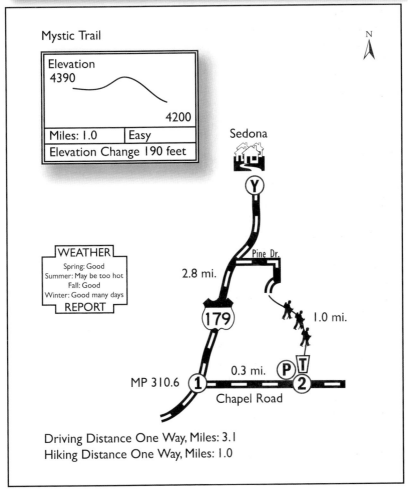

Mystic Trail

N

Elevation
4390

4200

Miles: 1.0	Easy
Elevation Change 190 feet	

Sedona

Y

WEATHER
Spring: Good
Summer: May be too hot
Fall: Good
Winter: Good many days
REPORT

Pine Dr.

2.8 mi.

1.0 mi.

179

P T

0.3 mi.

MP 310.6   1

2

Chapel Road

Driving Distance One Way, Miles: 3.1
Hiking Distance One Way, Miles: 1.0

Old Post Trail

General Information
Location Map E4
Sedona USGS Map
Coconino Forest Service Map

Driving Distance One Way: 6.2 miles *9.9 km* (Time 20 minutes)
Access Road: All cars, All paved
Hiking Distance One Way: 3.0 miles *4.8 km* (Time 1.5 hours)
How Strenuous: Moderate
Features: Easy to reach, Historic road, Views

NUTSHELL: Part of this trail is a historic road used for mail delivery.

DIRECTIONS:
From the Sedona Y (the intersection of Highways 179 and 89A) Go:
    Southwest on Highway 89A (toward Cottonwood) a distance of 4.2 miles *6.8 km* (MP 368.9) then turn left onto the Upper Red Rock Loop Road **(1)**. Follow it to the 6.0 mile *9.6 km* point, where you turn left on a paved road **(2)**. At the 6.2 mile *9.9 km* point **(3)** turn left into a parking apron.

TRAILHEAD: At the two-panel trail sign.

DESCRIPTION: You begin this hike by walking along an old road. At the 0.7 mile *1.1 km* point you reach a V-fork where the **Herkenham Trail** branches to the left. Keep going straight.
    The trail begins to climb into the hills. You can see that it was once an important road because sections of it show a lot of work. This road was vital, the mail route back in the horse-and-buggy days, used by the post office, hence the name, Old Post Trail. There are some nice views from these high sections, the most interesting part of the trail. At 1.5 miles *2.4 km* you will meet the **Carroll Canyon Trail** coming in from your left. The Old Post and Carroll trails are blended together for the next 1.0 mile *1.6 km*, separating at the 2.5 mile *4.0 km* point, where the Carroll Canyon Trail forks to the right.
    From this point, the Old Post Trail is a footpath taking off over a rise, running behind a subdivision, ending at the Shelby Drive parking area at 3.0 miles *4.8 km*. See the entries for the **Bandit, Ridge**, and Carroll Canyon Trails in this book. This last half-mile is not very interesting, and we recommend that unless you have a second car at the Shelby Drive parking area, you turn back at the Carroll Canyon Trail junction and retrace your steps.
    By looking at the map you can see how the Old Post Trail ties into other trails around Airport Mesa. It is easy and fun to hook into one of the other trails to make a loop instead of simply backtracking.

Photo: This trail began its life as a wagon road, and there are parts of it where the old road is clearly visible.

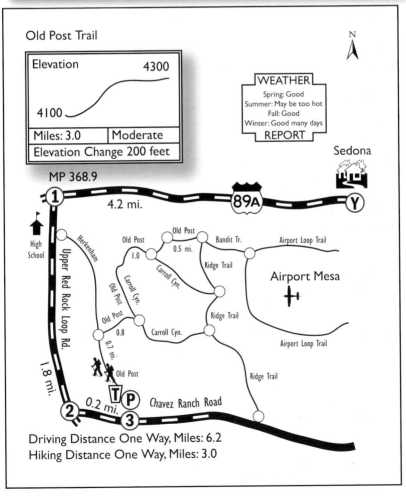

Old Post Trail

Elevation 4300

4100

Miles: 3.0 | Moderate

Elevation Change 200 feet

N

WEATHER
Spring: Good
Summer: May be too hot
Fall: Good
Winter: Good many days
REPORT

Sedona

MP 368.9

① 4.2 mi. 89A Ⓨ

High School

Upper Red Rock Loop Rd.

Herkenham

Old Post

Old Post
1.0

Carroll Cyn.

Carroll Cyn.

Old Post
0.5 mi.

Bandit Tr.

Ridge Trail

Airport Loop Trail

Airport Mesa

Ridge Trail

Old Post
0.8

Carroll Cyn.

Ridge Trail

Airport Loop Trail

Old Post
0.7 mi.

Old Post

T P

Ridge Trail

1.8 mi.

② 0.2 mi. ③ Chavez Ranch Road

Driving Distance One Way, Miles: 6.2
Hiking Distance One Way, Miles: 3.0

Overlook Point Trails #126

General Information
Location Map E4
Sedona USGS Map
Coconino Forest Service Map

Vortex

Driving Distance One Way: 1.5 miles *2.4 km* (Time 10 minutes)
Access Road: All cars, Paved all the way
Hiking Distance, Complete Loop: 0.7 miles *1.1 km* (Time 45 minutes)
How Strenuous: Easy to Hard
Features: Vortex Spot, Views

NUTSHELL: This is the easiest and most accessible Sedona Vortex spot.

DIRECTIONS:
From the Sedona Y (the intersection of Highways 179 and 89A) Go:
    Southwest on Highway 89A for 1.0 mile *1.6 km,* to Airport Road **(1)**. Turn left onto Airport Road and drive uphill half a mile, to the 1.5 miles *2.4 km* point **(2)**. Turn left into the parking lot.

TRAILHEAD: At the cable fence on the east side of the parking lot.

DESCRIPTION: There are several trails here:
    Yavapai Route: Take one step through the cable fence and turn left on a narrow footpath. You will move north toward a bald red knob. In 0.1 mile *0.16 km* you will see a path going to your right. This is a connector that can be used as a shortcut.
    Coconino Loop: Keep going ahead from the place where the Yavapai Route meets the connector. As you reach the red knob, the trail turns to the right (E). You make a short climb to a gap and then go down to a red ledge at 0.3 miles *0.5 km.* You will probably find a medicine wheel here, for this is regarded as one of Sedona's vortex spots. You will see a path going off to the north here, but don't take it. It is not one of the loop trails. Instead head back south on a path that you will see well-worn into the redrocks. In 0.4 miles *0.6 km* you will meet the connector trail that you saw on the other side of the ridge. Keep going forward and in a few yards you will come to a place where the Overlook Trail goes uphill.
    Overlook Trail: This trail is very short, taking off from the Coconino Loop. It makes a steep climb to the top of a red knob, and is worth doing if you have the energy. It climbs 70 feet in 0.05 miles *0.08 km.* From the top, known as Overlook Point, you will enjoy the views. You can climb down the front face of the rock, but it is pretty scary for some people, as you must scale down bare rock. Some people like to go back down the way they came up and take a path that is unnamed, parallel to the Yavapai Route but a few feet higher. It is well worn and takes you back to the top of the "stairs." If you do this, you will have hiked about 0.6 miles *1.0 km.* It's about another 0.1 mile

0.16 km back down to the parking lot.

If you go down the front of Overlook Point, you come to a point at the top of the "stairs," a natural walkway up from the parking lot. Here you have a chance to take the last of the loop trail, to Courthouse Butte Vista.

Courthouse Butte Vista: This is a very short trail to the south, which climbs about 25 feet in less than 0.1 miles *0.16 km* to a viewpoint.

You will also see a distinct trail running SW along Airport Mesa. This is not a part of the Airport Saddle Loop Trails, despite its appearance. It is much harder and longer than the little loop trails, dropping 500 feet over 1.5 miles *2.4 km* to a point overlooking Oak Creek.

Photo: There is a photo from this trail system on page 252.

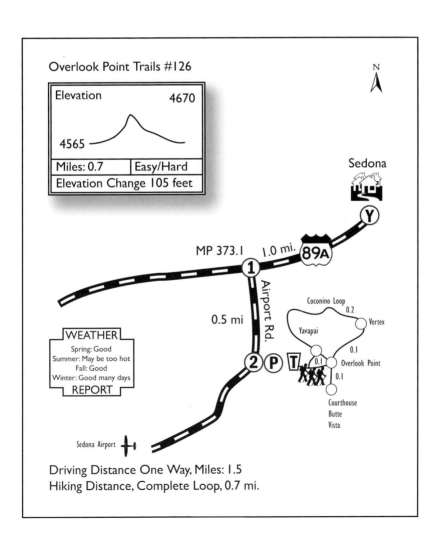

Palatki

General Information
Location Map C2
Loy Butte and Page Springs USGS Maps
Coconino Forest Service Map

Driving Distance One Way: 13.5 miles *21.6 km* (Time 25 minutes)
Access Road: All cars, Last 5.8 miles *9.3 km* bumpy dirt road
Hiking Distance: Trail #1 is a 0.6 mile *1.0 km* loop; **Trail #2** is 0.3 miles *0.5 km* one way
How Strenuous: Both hikes are Easy
Features: Indian ruins, Pictographs, Caves

NUTSHELL: Cliff dwellings and caves full of rock art. Reservations must be made a week in advance and a fee is charged. Call 928-282-4119 for info.

DIRECTIONS:
From the Sedona Y (the intersection of Highways 179 and 89A) Go:
SW on Highway 89A for 3.2 miles *5.1 km,* then turn right on Dry Creek Road (stoplight) **(1)**. Drive to a stop sign at 6.1 miles *9.8 km* **(2)**. Turn left and drive to a second stop sign at 7.7 miles *12.3 km* **(3)**. Go left on unpaved road FR 152C. You will come to third stop sign at 11.7 miles *18.7 km,* where you turn right on FR 525 **(4)**. At 11.8 miles *18.9 km* is a V-fork **(5)**. Turn right on FR 795 and travel to the parking lot at 13.5 miles *21.6 km.*

TRAILHEAD: In spite of the trailhead map there are two hikes here.

DESCRIPTION:
Palatki Ruins Trail, 0.6 miles *1.0 km*, for the complete loop. Walk to the Visitor Center and go to the right. After 0.2 miles *0.3 km* of level walking you will make a short climb, helped by stone stairs, to the ruins. The trail takes you to the larger ruin, a two-story structure with eight rooms. The second ruin is smaller and also had eight chambers, but its walls have collapsed and you cannot enter the area. Retrace your path to the Visitor Center and take the Rock Art path.
Rock Art Trail, 0.3 miles *0.5 km*, one way. This trail makes a easy climb to the base of tall red cliffs where there are a number of undercut caves containing the largest collection of rock art in the Verde Valley, ranging from art of the ancient Sinagua to the more modern tribes.
Both the ruins and the caves are staffed by volunteers. They are friendly, well-informed and happy to share their knowledge. We really appreciate their devotion and service.

Photo: These fine ruins and a wealth of ancient rock art make a visit to Palatki a special experience.

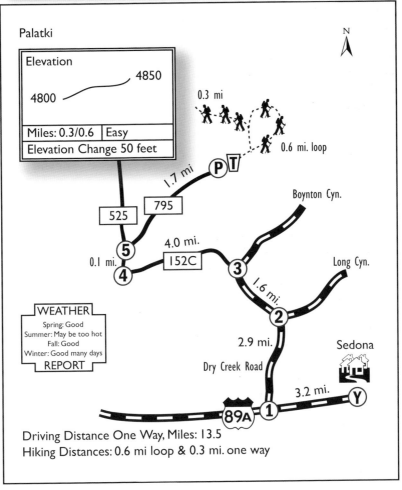

Palatki

N

Elevation

4850

4800

Miles: 0.3/0.6 | Easy

Elevation Change 50 feet

0.3 mi

0.6 mi. loop

1.7 mi

P T

795

Boynton Cyn.

525

4.0 mi.

152C

3

Long Cyn.

0.1 mi.

5

4

1.6 mi.

2

WEATHER
Spring: Good
Summer: May be too hot
Fall: Good
Winter: Good many days
REPORT

2.9 mi.

Sedona

Dry Creek Road

3.2 mi.

89A

1

Y

Driving Distance One Way, Miles: 13.5
Hiking Distances: 0.6 mi loop & 0.3 mi. one way

Parsons Trail #65

General Information
Location Map F1
Clarkdale and Sycamore Basin USGS Maps
Coconino Forest Service Map

Driving Distance One Way: 34.3 miles *54.9 km* (Time 1 hour)
Access Road: All cars, Last 9.0 miles *14.4 km* good dirt road
Hiking Distance One Way: 3.7 miles *5.9 km* (Time 2 hours)
How Strenuous: Moderate
Features: Tremendous colorful canyon, Year-around stream

NUTSHELL: This trail enters the south end of huge Sycamore Canyon and allows you to walk along the canyon bottom next to a flowing stream.

DIRECTIONS:
From the Sedona Y (the intersection of Highways 179 and 89A) Go:
Southwest on Highway 89A for 19.4 miles *31 km*, into the town of Cottonwood. Go straight through Cottonwood on Main Street and then on Broadway, headed toward Tuzigoot National Monument. At 23.4 miles *37.4 km* turn right on the road to Tuzigoot **(1)**. Follow it to the 23.8 mile *38.1 km* point, just over the bridge **(2)**. Turn left on the paved (for 1.5 miles *2.4 km*) Sycamore Canyon Road, FR 131. Stay on FR 131 to the 34.3 mile *54.9 km* point, a parking area at the top of Sycamore Canyon.

TRAILHEAD: There is a one-panel sign.

DESCRIPTION: You hike down into the south end of Sycamore Canyon, where it is not as deep as it is upstream. The trail follows along Sycamore Creek, usually on the right bank, though it does cross the creek twice. It is fairly level. In all but extremely dry years, water runs year around.
At 1.3 miles *2.1 km* you reach Summers Spring where water seeps across the trail. Don't drink it unless you treat it because giardia is a threat. Upstream from Summers Spring the trail gets rough. A heavy flood in 1980 tore out a lot of the trail. In spots you must scramble over boulders. Stay near the streambed and you will pick up the surviving parts of the trail every time you pass one of the washouts. In places there are large pools that hold fish.
Before it received Wilderness Area protection some mining occurred in this canyon. You will pass the entrance to an agate mine at 2.7 miles *4.3 km*. It has been plugged but bits of hardware are still around.
The canyon narrows and the walls get steeper as you work your way upstream. You will reach Parsons Spring at 3.7 miles *5.9 km*. Above this point the stream is only intermittent. The spring is the place to stop.

Photo: Dick is standing at the beginning of the trail, which slopes down to the long canyon below.

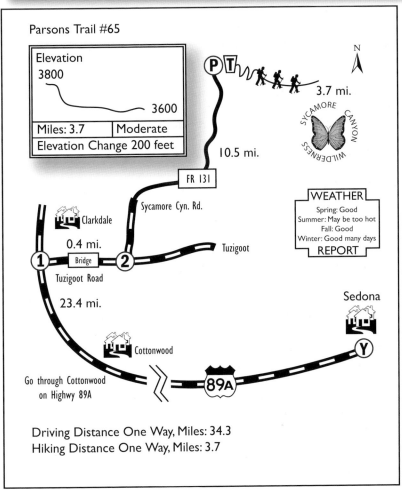

Parsons Trail #65

Elevation
3800

3600

| Miles: 3.7 | Moderate |
| Elevation Change 200 feet | |

N

P T

3.7 mi.

SYCAMORE CANYON WILDERNESS

10.5 mi.

FR 131

Sycamore Cyn. Rd.

Clarkdale

WEATHER
Spring: Good
Summer: May be too hot
Fall: Good
Winter: Good many days
REPORT

0.4 mi.

1 Bridge 2

Tuzigoot

Tuzigoot Road

23.4 mi.

Sedona

Y

Cottonwood

Go through Cottonwood
on Highway 89A

89A

Driving Distance One Way, Miles: 34.3
Hiking Distance One Way, Miles: 3.7

Pumphouse Wash

General Information
Location Map B5
Mountainaire USGS Map
Coconino Forest Service Map

Driving Distance One Way: 13.5 miles *21.6 km* (Time 20 minutes)
Access Road: All vehicles, All paved
Hiking Distance One Way: 1.5 miles *2.4 km* (Time 1.5 hours)
How Strenuous: Moderate
Features: Steep-walled scenic canyon ramble

NUTSHELL: Pumphouse Wash is a tributary canyon meeting Oak Creek at the bottom of the Highway 89A switchbacks. There is no trail. You rock hop along the canyon bottom enjoying the sight of immense towering cliffs, redrock sculptures and a get-away-from-it-all feeling.

DIRECTIONS:
From the Sedona Y (the intersection of Highways 179 and 89A) Go:
   North on Highway 89A (toward Flagstaff) for 13.5 miles *21.6 km* (MP 387.7) to the Pumphouse Wash bridge. Drive over the bridge and make an immediate left turn onto a parking apron, where you park.

TRAILHEAD: There is no marking or official trail. However, you will see a clear footpath going from the parking place to the canyon bottom.

DESCRIPTION: Once you reach bottom turn left, walk under the bridge and keep going up the canyon. The bottom is strewn with large boulders so you have to hop from rock to rock. This makes the trail harder than the mileage and elevation change would seem to indicate.
   Pumphouse Wash is normally dry. The trick is to make the hike when there is enough water in the wash to add to the hiking enjoyment but not so much that the canyon is impassable. Try mid-May. If you see water running high under the bridge, there is too much for the hike to be fun.
   Soon after you enter the canyon you will begin looking upward at the soaring high cliff walls that engulf you. At about 0.3 miles *0.5 km* you will reach the first of a chain of pools. If the water is high you would have to swim them. If the water is low you can wade or hop across. We like to bring a pair of old canvas shoes, allowing them to get wet if need be.
   You leave the area of the pools at 0.6 miles *1.0 km* where the cliffs change from white to red, a gorgeous unspoiled area. This is what the entire Oak Creek Canyon must have looked like before it was commercialized. Stop where you wish. We think the 1.5 mile *2.4 km* point makes a good ending.

Photo: There are always towering scenic cliffs to enjoy on this hike. If you are lucky, as we were in mid-April 2004, there is also water.

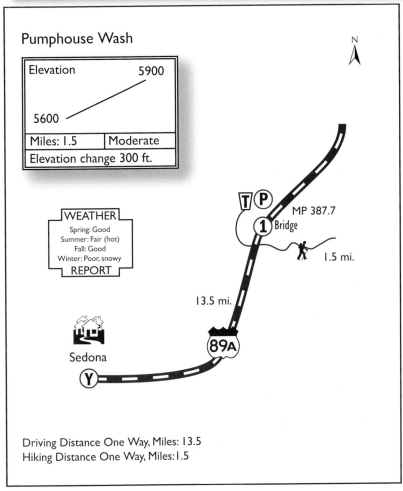

Pumphouse Wash

Elevation
5900
5600

| Miles: 1.5 | Moderate |

Elevation change 300 ft.

WEATHER
Spring: Good
Summer: Fair (hot)
Fall: Good
Winter: Poor, snowy
REPORT

N

T P

MP 387.7

1 Bridge

1.5 mi.

13.5 mi.

89A

Sedona

Y

Driving Distance One Way, Miles: 13.5
Hiking Distance One Way, Miles: 1.5

Purtymun Trail

General Information
Location Map B5
Munds Park and Wilson Mt. USGS Maps
Coconino Forest Service Map

Driving Distance One Way: 8.5 miles *13.6 km* (Time 20 minutes)
Access Road: All cars, All paved
Hiking Distance One Way: 1.0 miles *1.6 km* (Time 1 hour)
How Strenuous: Hard
Features: Views

NUTSHELL: A hard hike up the east wall of Oak Creek Canyon directly across Highway 89A from the Junipine Resort.

DIRECTIONS:
From the Sedona Y (the intersection of Highways 179 and 89A) Go:
   North on Highway 89A (toward Flagstaff) for 8.4 miles *13.4 km* (MP 382.6) to the entrance to the Junipine Resort, which is on your left **(1)**. Go past it 0.1 mile *0.16 km* and park on the wide apron **(2)** on the right.

TRAILHEAD: Across the highway from Junipine at the yellow fire plug.

DESCRIPTION: The trail starts at the side of a two-car garage where you will see a yellow fire plug. Go up between the garage and the fence.
   This trail was built by the Purtymun family, which homesteaded Junipine in 1896, in order go to Flagstaff. They would leave a wagon at the top. When they wanted to go to town they would walk a horse to the rim, hitch it to the wagon and then drive to Flagstaff, a very laborious process.
   The alternative was worse. There was no convenient wagon road from Sedona to Flagstaff until the Schnebly Hill Road was built in 1902. Before that the only wagon road was the old **Beaverhead** route several miles farther south. Highway 89A did not come onto the scene until much later. It was built in phases starting in the early 1920s, and took a decade to complete.
   For years this old trail was in such poor condition that it was almost useless. We are pleased to report, however, that the Forest Service has come to the rescue. As this book goes to press in the Spring of 2004, the Forest Service has rebuilt about two-thirds of the trail and will probably have it all finished in the summer or fall of 2004. It is steep and zigzags endlessly, but rewards hikers with breathtaking views that make the effort worthwhile.
   When it is finished, it will be on a par with other hikes up the east rim of upper Oak Creek Canyon such as **Cookstove**, **Harding Spring**, **Telephone** and **Thomas Point**.

Photo: Just above the midway point of the trail hikers can begin to enjoy open views.

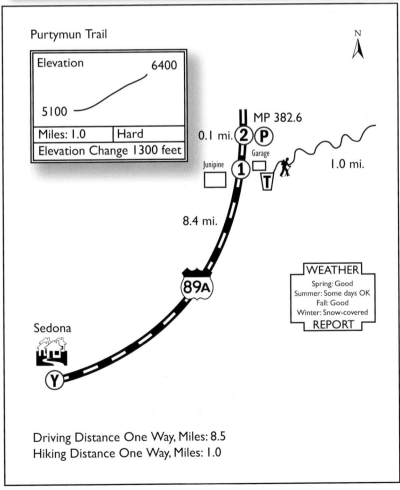

Purtymun Trail

N

Elevation 6400

5100

Miles: 1.0	Hard
Elevation Change 1300 feet	

MP 382.6

0.1 mi. ②Ⓟ

Garage

Junipine ①

Ⓣ

1.0 mi.

8.4 mi.

89A

WEATHER
Spring: Good
Summer: Some days OK
Fall: Good
Winter: Snow-covered
REPORT

Sedona

Ⓨ

Driving Distance One Way, Miles: 8.5
Hiking Distance One Way, Miles: 1.0

Rabbit Ears

General Information
Location Map F5
Munds Mountain and Sedona USGS Maps
Coconino Forest Service Map

Driving Distance One Way: 9.4 miles *15.0 km* (Time 15 minutes)
Access Road: All cars, Last 0.1 mile *0.16 km* good dirt road
Hiking Distance One Way: 2.75 miles *4.4 km* (Time 1.5 hours)
How Strenuous: Moderate
Features: Uncrowded scenic hike

NUTSHELL: This trail follows a curved ridge from the **Jacks Canyon** trailhead to the **Courthouse Butte Loop Trail.**

DIRECTIONS:
From the Sedona Y (the intersection of Highways 179 and 89A) Go:
   South on Highway 179 (toward Phoenix) for a distance of 7.2 miles *11.5 km* (MP 306.2) to Jack's Canyon Road (stoplight) **(1)**. Turn left (E) onto Jack's Canyon Road and follow it to the 9.3 miles *14.9 km* point, where you turn right onto an unpaved road **(2)** into a corral area. Drive in and park at the 9.4 mile *15.0 km* point, next to a brown metal horse gate.

TRAILHEAD: You will see a pole gate and rusty sign, "Jack's Canyon #55." This is the starting point.

DESCRIPTION: Do not go through the horse gate. Instead, walk back down to the paved road following the fence and staying outside it, along a primitive path. At the paved road, go through a horse gate, cross the paved road and go through the second horse gate on the other side.
   You make a gradual climb to the top of a curved ridge. At 0.35 miles *0.6 km* you will see where the trail strayed over onto private land which has since been fenced. The trail makes a little detour to avoid the fence and then gets back on track. At 0.4 miles *0.6 km* you will reach the third and final horse gate. Here you look down to the left into a grassy bowl dotted with houses.
   The highest point on the trail is at 1.5 miles *2.4 km*, a wonderful place, where the developed areas are out of sight. You look out at Rabbit Ears to the NE, about 0.25 miles *0.4 km* away.
   From this high point, you descend the ridge to the west, hiking toward Courthouse Butte. At the bottom of the ridge is another horse trail. Turn right here and in a few yards you will emerge into a slickrock wash. The Courthouse Butte Loop Trail enters this wash from the west. It is 1.5 miles *2.4 km* from here to its trailhead, or you can hike back the way you came.

Photo: The Rabbit Ears are one of those formations that are aptly named, as they look like rabbit ears. This trail gives you a good look at them.

Rabbit Ears

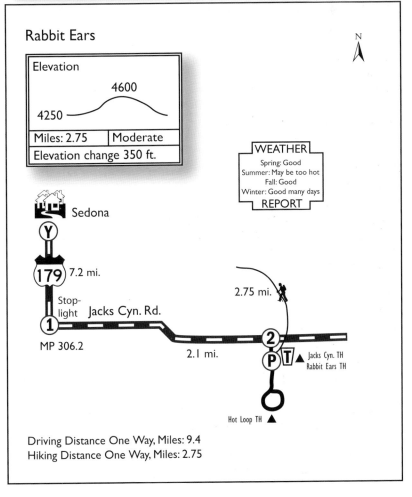

Elevation

4600

4250

| Miles: 2.75 | Moderate |

Elevation change 350 ft.

WEATHER
Spring: Good
Summer: May be too hot
Fall: Good
Winter: Good many days
REPORT

Sedona

Y

179 7.2 mi.

Stop-light Jacks Cyn. Rd.

1

MP 306.2

2.1 mi.

2.75 mi.

2

P T ▲ Jacks Cyn. TH
Rabbit Ears TH

Hot Loop TH ▲

N

Driving Distance One Way, Miles: 9.4
Hiking Distance One Way, Miles: 2.75

Raptor Hill Trail

General Information
Location Map F1
Clarkdale USGS Map
Coconino Forest Service Map

Driving Distance One Way: 21.5 miles *34.4 km* (Time 45 minutes)
Access Road: All cars, All paved
Hiking Distance One Way: 2.8 miles *4.5 km*
How Strenuous: Moderate
Features: Views of Verde Valley, Tuzigoot and Jerome

NUTSHELL: Originating in Dead Horse State Park at Cottonwood, this trail follows an old jeep road out of the park and up onto high flatlands.

DIRECTIONS:

From the Sedona Y (the intersection of Highways 179 and 89A) Go:
   SW on Hwy 89A for 18.6 miles *29.8 km*, to the stoplight in Cottonwood at the junction of Highways 279 and 89A. Go straight on Historic Hwy 89A (Main Street). At 20.6 miles *33.0 km*, past the cemetery, turn right on 10th Street **(1)**. The entrance to the park is at 21.5 miles *34.4 km* (fee required). Once inside the park follow the main road, taking the second turn to the left, which is marked "Tavasci Marsh." **(2)** Drive to the end of the paved road, and park in the parking area there.

TRAILHEAD: The parking area is a joint trailhead for the Raptor Hill and **Tavasci Marsh** trails.

DESCRIPTION: Go through the gate, turn right, and walk up the wide dirt road. At 0.1 mile *0.16 km* the Raptor Hill Trail peels away from the Tavasci Marsh Trail, going to the right (E) uphill. Be sure to take this turn.
   You will now make a steep but brief climb, passing an old cabin on a knoll to your right. At 0.7 miles *1.1 km* you will pass through a gate in the park boundary fence. From the gate, the trail follows an old jeep road.
   You continue to climb, although the climb is gradual, and the higher you rise, the better views you have (behind you) of the Verde Valley. You look down on Tuzigoot National Monument from an aspect that is just right for photos. The area up to the top looks like a pink and white layer cake.
   At 1.4 miles *2.2 km* you will pass through another fence. There is a high horse gate for riders and a stile for walkers here. Another landmark is reached at 2.6 miles *4.2 km*, when you pass under a power line. The area here is quite flat and there is a veritable forest of chaparral. At 2.8 miles *4.5 km* you reach a multi-trail junction, which is where this trail stops.

Photo: On the early part of the trail hikers see this old cabin to their right. The photo gives a good sense of the wide open countryside crossed by this trail.

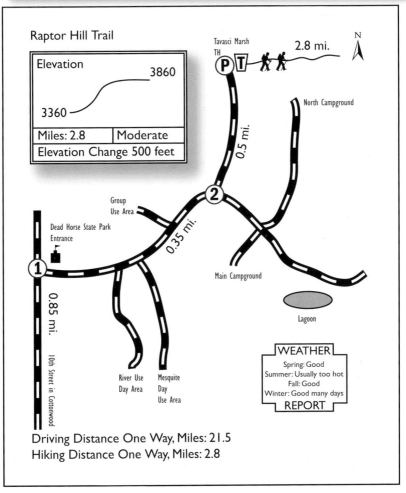

Raptor Hill Trail

Elevation

3860

3360

Miles: 2.8	Moderate
Elevation Change 500 feet	

Tavasci Marsh
TH
P T   2.8 mi.   N

North Campground

0.5 mi.

2

Group
Use Area

0.35 mi.

Dead Horse State Park
Entrance

1

Main Campground

0.85 mi.

10th Street in Cottonwood

River Use
Day Area

Mesquite
Day
Use Area

Lagoon

WEATHER
Spring: Good
Summer: Usually too hot
Fall: Good
Winter: Good many days
REPORT

Driving Distance One Way, Miles: 21.5
Hiking Distance One Way, Miles: 2.8

Rattlesnake Canyon

General Information
Location Map G5
Munds Mt. USGS Map
Coconino Forest Service Map

Driving Distance One Way: 23.0 miles *36.8 km* (Time 45 minutes)
Access Road: High-clearance needed for the last 1.0 mile *1.6 km*
Hiking Distance One Way: 1.0 miles *1.6 km* (Time 40 minutes)
How Strenuous: Moderate
Features: Remote scenic canyon

NUTSHELL: This trail takes you to a little known beautiful spot.

DIRECTIONS:
From the Sedona Y (the intersection of Highways 179 and 89A) Go:
   South on Highway 179 (toward Phoenix) for 14.7 miles *23.5 km*, to the I-17 Interchange **(1)**. Turn north and head toward Flagstaff on I-17. At the 22.0 mile *35.2 km* spot take Exit 306 "Stoneman Lake" **(2)**. From the stop sign **(3)** go under I-17 into the lane marked south, to Phoenix, and turn right onto a dirt road, FR 647, just beyond the underpass **(3)**. The road has an eroding gray gravel surface. Almost immediately there is a bad spot where it crosses a wash. Drive to the 22.8 mile *36.5 km* point where the gravel ends **(4)** and turn right on a dirt road. Drive to the 23.0 mile *36.8 km* point and park—it's too rough beyond.

TRAILHEAD: No official trailhead.

DESCRIPTION: Walk the road 0.5 miles *0.8 km* to the canyon rim. Rattlesnake Canyon is deep and interesting. The walls are sheer and composed of successive layers of columnar-jointed basalt.
   At the canyon rim you will see a road going down into the canyon. Walk down the road to a big clear landing at 0.25 miles *0.4 km*. Everything has been easy to follow up to this point. Now you have to do a bit of looking for the footpath that goes from here to the bottom of the canyon. It is not a recreational trail, but is used to provide access to the gaging station that you will find at the bottom.
   The trail is well-constructed and takes you down to the canyon floor. At the base you will come to a cable strung across the canyon and beyond that the gaging station, which is a sort of tall corrugated tube with a box on top.
   At the gaging station there is a pool and a waterfall with a 30-foot drop. It seems dangerous to climb. This is a beautiful and tranquil spot with varied plant and bird life.

Photo: The trail takes you to the bottom of Rattlesnake Canyon at a thirty-foot waterfall. If you are lucky, as we were when Sherry shot this photo in mid-April 2004, water will be running over the falls.

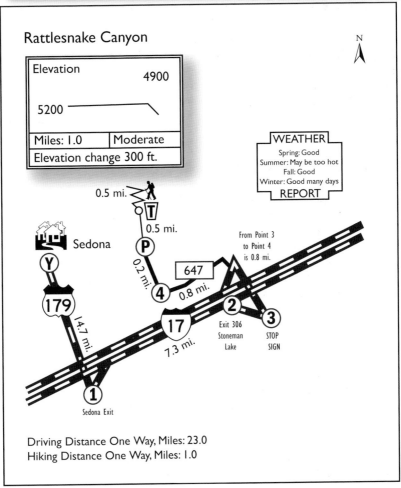

Rattlesnake Canyon

Elevation	4900
5200	

Miles: 1.0	Moderate
Elevation change 300 ft.	

N

0.5 mi.

0.5 mi.

Sedona

From Point 3
to Point 4
is 0.8 mi.

WEATHER
Spring: Good
Summer: May be too hot
Fall: Good
Winter: Good many days
REPORT

0.2 mi.

647

0.8 mi.

14.7 mi.

17

7.3 mi.

Exit 306
Stoneman
Lake

STOP
SIGN

1

Sedona Exit

Driving Distance One Way, Miles: 23.0
Hiking Distance One Way, Miles: 1.0

Red Rock Loop Trail #118

General Information
Location Map E3
Sedona USGS Map
Coconino Forest Service Map

Driving Distance One Way: 5.9 miles *9.4 km* (Time 15 minutes)
Access Road: All vehicles, Last 0.1 mi. *0.16 km* good gravel road
Hiking Distance One Way: 1.8 miles *2.9 km* (Time 1.0 hours)
How Strenuous: Moderate
Features: Part of Arizona Pathways trails, Easy to reach, Views

NUTSHELL: This trail offers fine views from a high redrock ledge.

DIRECTIONS:
From the Sedona Y (the intersection of Highways 179 and 89A) Go:
 Southwest on Highway 89 (toward Cottonwood) for 5.5 miles *8.8 km* (MP 368.6) then turn left on the Lower Red Rock Loop Road **(1)** and follow it to the 5.8 miles *9.3 km* point, where you turn left on a gravel road, FR 9853 **(2)**. Drive in on this road to the 5.9 mile *9.4 km* point, the parking lot.

TRAILHEAD: At the parking lot.

DESCRIPTION: You first climb onto the shoulder of Schuerman Mountain where redrock cliffs are exposed. There is a bench on which to rest as you make this climb. You will walk right on the redrocks and for about the first 0.5 miles *0.8 km* follow a ledge along the base of beautiful high red cliffs. There is a bench at the end of this ledge so that hikers may pause and enjoy the scenery. From the trailhead up to this bench is the best part of the trail, and if you don't have much time, you might want to stop here.

 From the bench the trail rounds the toe of the mountain and then heads toward Sedona. Here the views are not good because you enter into an area covered with brush. The trail is also uncomfortably close to busy Highway 89—definitely not a wilderness experience. The red cliffs disappear here, covered by lava.

 Farther on you walk next to the playing fields of the Sedona Red Rock High School, and soon after this, will reach the end of the trail, where it meets the Upper Red Rock Loop Road.

 This trail fills a need for many people, who don't have the time to get out into the country, or who face a situation where they want to hike but the weather has made the backcountry roads impassable. One should be able to make this hike almost any day of the year. We believe that short trails such as this fill a much-needed niche in the repertoire of Sedona trails.

Photo: The first part of this trail—the best part—takes you along a redrock ledge.

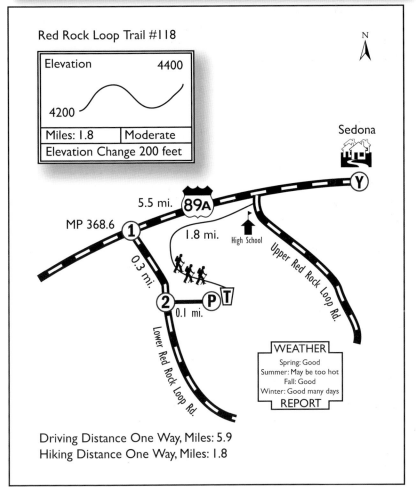

Red Rock Loop Trail #118

Elevation

4400

4200

Miles: 1.8 | Moderate

Elevation Change 200 feet

N

Sedona

5.5 mi.
89A

MP 368.6
1

1.8 mi.
High School

0.3 mi.

2
P T
0.1 mi.

Upper Red Rock Loop Rd.

Lower Red Rock Loop Rd.

Y

WEATHER
Spring: Good
Summer: May be too hot
Fall: Good
Winter: Good many days
REPORT

Driving Distance One Way, Miles: 5.9
Hiking Distance One Way, Miles: 1.8

Red Rock State Park Trails

General Information
Location Map F3
Sedona USGS Map
Coconino Forest Service Map

Drive Distance One Way: 8.8 miles *14.1 km* (Time 15 minutes)
Access Road: All vehicles, All paved
Hiking Distance: 8 hikes of various distances, see map
How Strenuous: Easy-Moderate, except Eagles' Nest, which is Hard
Features: Oak Creek, Red Rock State Park, Views

NUTSHELL: Eight trails located in Red Rock State Park 8.8 miles *14.1 km* SW of Sedona. They range from easy to hard and offer a variety of features. This is a good place to take the family.

DIRECTIONS:
From the Sedona Y (the intersection of Highways 179 and 89A) Go:
    Southwest on Highway 89A (toward Cottonwood) for 5.5 miles *8.8 km* (MP 368.6) then turn left on the Lower Red Rock Loop Road and follow it to the 8.5 miles 13.6 *km* point, where you turn right into Red Rock State Park. An admission is charged at an information center. After paying the fee, drive to the Visitor Center and park, at 8.8 miles *14.1 km*.

TRAILHEAD: The Visitor Center. Drinking water and toilet available.

DESCRIPTION: Go through the Visitor Center and turn right on the paved trail. At 0.08 miles *0.13 km* you will come to the first junction. (Note: our mileage includes connections to the trails.)
    (1) **Smoke Trail.** 0.4 miles *0.6 km*. Walk down to the water and turn right for a creekside stroll. Easy.
    (2) **Black Hawk Trail.** 0.6 mi. *1.0 km*. From the end of Smoke Trail, cross the creek to join the end of the Kisva Trail. Easy.
    (3) **Coyote Ridge Trail.** 1.7 mi. *2.7 km*. Connects the Eagle's Nest and Apache Fire trails, running along a ridge between them. Moderate.
    (4) **Kisva Trail.** 1.0 miles *1.6 km*. Walk to Kingfisher Crossing bridge. Cross the creek and walk to the trail junction for the Apache Fire Trail and the Eagles' Nest Trail. Turn right. The Kisva Trail follows an old ranch road along the banks of the creek. Easy.
    (5) **Eagles' Nest Trail.** 3.23 miles *5.2 km* for a complete loop, requiring a 200 ft. climb. Take the Kisva Trail to its end, where you will see the Eagles' Nest Trail going uphill to the left. Make the steep climb to the top, where you will enjoy great views. Then loop around to join the Kisva Trail at its

midsection; though you could take the Coyote Ridge connector over to Apache Fire. Hard.

(6) **Apache Fire Trail.** 1.7 mi. *2.7 km* loop. Cross Kingfisher bridge. At the trail junction where the Kisva and Eagles' Nest trails go to the right, go left instead and walk to the base of the knoll on which the house is located. There you find the Apache Fire trail. Moderate.

(7) **Javelina Trail.** 2.0 mile *3.2 km* loop. Follow directions to the Apache Fire Trail and begin to hike it. Just before the Apache Fire trail begins climbing out of the creek bed, the Javelina Trail goes left. Moderate

(8) **Yavapai Trail.** 1.58 miles *2.5 km* loop. Walk across Kingfisher bridge to the Apache Fire Trail. Here you take the left fork, on the unpaved East Gate Road. Soon you will reach the Yavapai Trail, going to the left (N). The Javelina Trail joins the road here. Moderate.

Photo: There is a photo from Red Rock State Park on page 253.

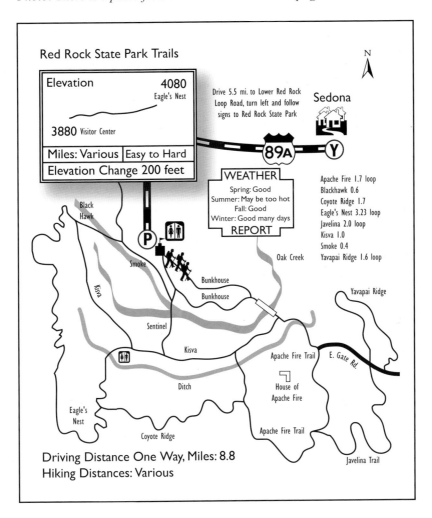

Ridge Trail

General Information
Location Map E4
Sedona USGS Map
Coconino Forest Service Map

Driving Distance One Way: 2.6 miles *4.2 km* (Time 10 minutes)
Access Road: All vehicles, All paved
Hiking Distance One Way: 2.3 miles *3.7 km* (Time 1.5 hours)
How Strenuous: Hard
Features: Nice views and variety, Connects to other trails

NUTSHELL: This fine trail climbs up to the top of a ridge on Airport Mesa, then descends along the crest of a narrow spine on the other side.

DIRECTIONS:
From the Sedona Y (the intersection of Highways 179 and 89A) Go:
    Southwest on Highway 89A for 2.1 miles *3.4 km,* to a stoplight **(1)**. Turn left on Shelby Drive. Take Shelby for 0.5 miles *0.8 km* (just past Stanley Steamer) and turn right into the parking lot of La Entrada, at 2155 Shelby Drive **(2)**. Park at the back of the paved parking lot at the trailhead signs.

TRAILHEAD: At the parking area.

DESCRIPTION: Take the footpath going into the trees from the parking area. When you see a sign for the **Old Post Trail** go past it; do not turn. Next you will come to the junction for the **Bandit Trail**. Again, ignore the Bandit Trail and go straight. You will curve along the base of Airport Mesa.
    At 0.6 miles *1.0 km* you reach the trail junction where the **Carroll Canyon Trail** comes in from your right. Go straight, as the Carroll Canyon and Ridge Trails merge. At 0.8 miles *1.3 km* the Carroll Canyon Trail splits off to the right. Go straight ahead here.
    You will now begin to climb. At first you ascend the east side of Carroll Canyon, which is deep here, with high rock cliffs. Soon you leave the canyon. You climb to the toe of a ridge, the high point on the trail, at 1.6 miles *2.6 km*. There are nice views from here. You will see a trail going off to your left, making a steep climb to join the **Table Top Trail**. Ignore this, as it is an illegal hiker-made trail. From this point, you will begin a steep descent.
    The exciting last segment of the trail goes down on the spine of a narrow ridge, with wonderful views. At 2.2 miles *3.5 km* you reach an old blocked road, where there is a trail sign. Turn to the right and you will come to a point on the Chavez Ranch Road at 2.3 miles *3.7 km*.

Photo: This trail takes you up high on a ridge on the side of Airport Mesa, giving good views of the redrocks that make Sedona famous.

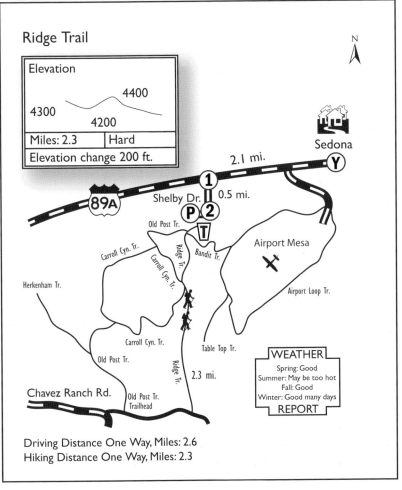

Ridge Trail

N

Elevation

4400

4300

4200

| Miles: 2.3 | Hard |
| Elevation change 200 ft. | |

Sedona

Y

2.1 mi.

89A

Shelby Dr. — 1

0.5 mi. — 2

P

T

Old Post Tr.

Carroll Cyn. Tr.

Ridge Tr.

Carroll Cyn. Tr.

Bandit Tr.

Airport Mesa

Herkenham Tr.

Carroll Cyn. Tr.

Airport Loop Tr.

Carroll Cyn. Tr.

Old Post Tr.

Table Top Tr.

Ridge Tr.

2.3 mi.

WEATHER
Spring: Good
Summer: May be too hot
Fall: Good
Winter: Good many days
REPORT

Chavez Ranch Rd.

Old Post Tr.
Trailhead

Driving Distance One Way, Miles: 2.6
Hiking Distance One Way, Miles: 2.3

Robbers Roost

General Information
Location Map C1
Loy Butte and Page Springs USGS Maps
Coconino Forest Service Map

Driving Distance One Way: 18.8 miles *30.0 km* (Time 40 minutes)
Access Road: All cars, Last 9.4 miles *15.0 km* good dirt road
Hiking Distance One Way: 1.5 miles *2.4 km* (Time 45 minutes)
How Strenuous: Easy
Features: Fascinating cave with unique window, Redrock butte to explore

NUTSHELL: On the side of a redrock butte is a cave with a window, reputed to have been used by rustlers, robbers and bootleggers.

DIRECTIONS:
From the Sedona Y (the intersection of Highways 179 and 89A) Go:
Southwest on Highway 89A for 9.4 miles *15.0 km* (MP 364.2) then turn right on FR 525 **(1)**. Follow FR 525 to the 12.2 mile *19.5 km* point, then turn left on FR 525C **(2)**. Follow FR 525C to the 18.8 miles *30.0 km* point, then turn right on FR 9530 **(3)** but drive it only a few yards, then park off the road. If you have high clearance you can drive another 0.8 miles *1.28 km.*

TRAILHEAD: At a point that is 1.1 miles *1.8 km* from the beginning of FR 9530. There you will see the trail going down into a ravine to your right. This is an unofficial trail and it is not signed.

DESCRIPTION: As you walk up the road to the trailhead you approach Casner Mountain. Your target is the loaf-shaped red butte just in front of you on the right. Robbers Roost is located on the far side of that butte. At the trailhead is an area to your left where tire tracks make an arc and the vegetation is matted down because of cars parking. Look for the trail to your right. Usually there are cairns marking it. The trail goes straight downhill into the bottom of a ravine, then up the other side.

The trail curls around to the north side of the red butte and climbs it. At 0.35 miles *0.6 km* when it seems that you are about to reach the top, the trail forks. The right fork goes to the top. Ignore it for now and go left. You walk out on the face of the butte. You will see the cave after you have walked a few yards. There is a retaining wall at the mouth of the cave and a short flight of steps.

There is a circular window in the cave. It gets its name, Robbers Roost, from the legend that it was a hideout for outlaws, who used the window as a lookout.

Photo: This cave with its unique circular window is a favorite for young and old alike.

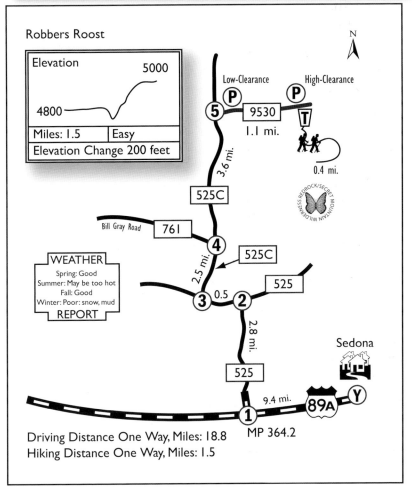

Robbers Roost

N

Elevation

5000

4800

Miles: 1.5 | Easy
Elevation Change 200 feet

Low-Clearance | High-Clearance

P | P

5 | 9530 | T
1.1 mi.

0.4 mi.

3.6 mi.

525C

WILDERNESS REDROCK/SECRET MOUNTAIN

Bill Gray Road | 761

4

525C

2.5 mi.

WEATHER
Spring: Good
Summer: May be too hot
Fall: Good
Winter: Poor: snow, mud
REPORT

3 | 0.5 | 2 | 525

2.8 mi.

Sedona

525

1 | 9.4 mi. | 89A | Y

MP 364.2

Driving Distance One Way, Miles: 18.8
Hiking Distance One Way, Miles: 1.5

Rupp Trail

General Information
Location Map D3
Wilson Mountain USGS Map
Coconino Forest Service Map

Driving Distance One Way: 10.7 miles *17.1 km* (Time 20 minutes)
Access Road: All cars, Last 3.0 miles bumpy dirt roads
Hiking Distance One Way: 2.0 miles *3.2 km* (Time 1.0 hour)
How Strenuous: Moderate
Features: Views

NUTSHELL: This trail starts near Doe Mountain, goes to the Cockscomb, then turns to follow a ranch fence until it meets a jeep road. It then follows the jeep road to Dry Creek, where it joins the **Girdner Trail**.

DIRECTIONS:
From the Sedona Y (the intersection of Highways 179 and 89A) Go:
Southwest on Highway 89A for 3.2 miles *5.1 km* (MP 371) to Dry Creek Road **(1)**. Turn right and follow Dry Creek Road to the stop sign at 6.1 miles *9.8 km* **(2)**. Turn left. At 7.7 miles *12.3 km* turn left on FR 152C, a dirt road **(3)**. At the 9.7 mile *15.5 km* point, turn left on FR 9583 **(4)** and follow it to the 10.7 mile *17.1 km* point, where you will find a locked gate. There is no real parking lot. Park on the shoulder of the road.

TRAILHEAD: At the gate: follow the sign marked "Public Trail."

DESCRIPTION: The public trail follows a fence. At 0.5 miles *0.8 km* you reach a fence corner where you turn left, continuing along the fence line. At 0.75 miles *1.2 km* you reach a gate where an old jeep road went inside the fence. Don't take the jeep road; stay on the footpath. The fence disappears. At 1.0 miles *1.6 km* you start down a long downhill grade at the foot of which you meet the fence again where an old road went inside. Follow the trail along the fence until you come to an open gate blocked by boulders. Go inside and you will find the Rupp Trail marker on a signpost at the 1.1 mile *1.8 km* point.

The Rupp Trail is a jeep road, easy to follow and easy to walk. It slopes downhill all the way and gives some good views. At 1.7 miles *2.7 km* you will find a Rupp Trail signpost where another jeep road comes in from the right. Turn left, going downhill. The trail ends on the bank of Dry Creek where you join the **Girdner Trail**. The Rupp family owned the property inside the fence, where they operated the Tree Farm, fondly remembered by Sedona old-timers.

Photo: Thunder Mountain, Chimney Rock and Brins Mesa are spread out for the hiker's delight.

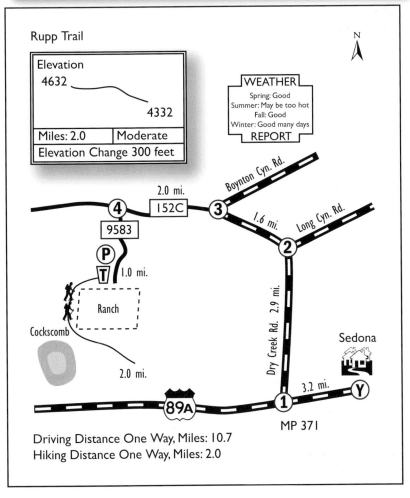

Rupp Trail

Elevation
4632
                    4332

| Miles: 2.0 | Moderate |
| Elevation Change 300 feet | |

WEATHER
Spring: Good
Summer: May be too hot
Fall: Good
Winter: Good many days
REPORT

Boynton Cyn. Rd.

2.0 mi.

④ 152C ③

9583

1.6 mi.

Long Cyn. Rd.

②

P
T   1.0 mi.

Ranch

Dry Creek Rd. 2.9 mi.

Cockscomb

Sedona

2.0 mi.

89A

① 3.2 mi. Ⓨ

MP 371

N

Driving Distance One Way, Miles: 10.7
Hiking Distance One Way, Miles: 2.0

Sacred Mountain

General Information
Location Map G6
Casner Butte USGS Map
Coconino Forest Service Map

Driving Distance One Way: 18.1 miles *29.0 km* (Time 30 minutes)
Access Road: All cars, Last 0.8 miles *1.3 km* good dirt road
Hiking Distance One Way: 0.5 miles *0.8 km* (Time 30 minutes)
How Strenuous: Moderate
Features: Indian ruins, Views

NUTSHELL: Located 18.1 miles *29.0 km* southeast of Sedona, this special mountain takes moderate effort to climb. At the top are located some significant pueblo ruins and the views are fine.

DIRECTIONS:
From the Sedona Y (the intersection of Highways 179 and 89A) Go:
    South on Highway 179 (toward Phoenix) for 14.7 miles *23.5 km*, to the I-17 Interchange **(1)**. Instead of going onto I-17, go underneath it onto a paved road, FR 618. Stay on FR 618. The paving ends at the bridges at the Beaver Creek Campground. Half a mile beyond, at 17.9 miles *28.6 km*, as the road is curving around a hill, turn left on an unmarked dirt road **(2)**. It's the first road to the left after the V—V Heritage Site. It leads to a fence. The road gets very rough, so try to get as close to the fence as you can (it's about 0.2 miles *0.3 km*) and park.

TRAILHEAD: No trail signs. At the gate, where you will see a small sign about protecting antiquities.

DESCRIPTION: Sacred Mountain is to your right sitting out by itself and set apart by its color—white—against the darker colors of the background, which are gray, black and red.
    Go through the gate walk forward a few paces and pick up the trail, which curves right, looking like a dim jeep track that runs parallel to the fence. You approach a gully where the trail becomes much more distinct and you will see the trail—on red soil—going up the toe of the mountain that faces the road. About half way up you will find a visitors' register to which you should add your name. The trail then winds around the side of the mountain and comes out on top where you will find extensive ruins. Unfortunately, these fine ruins were thoroughly pothunted before scientists could conduct a scientific excavation, greatly diminishing their archaeological value. Please do not disturb them.

Photo: The white cliffs of this special mountain make it stand out. Once on top you will find extensive ruins and fine views.

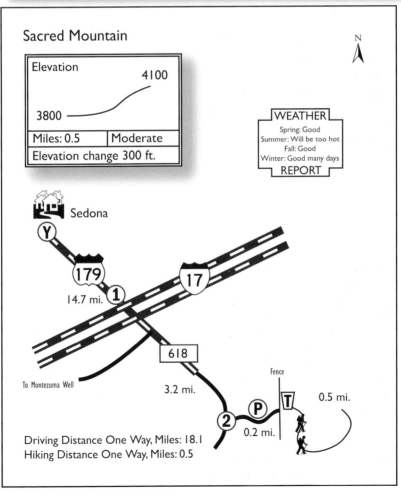

Sacred Mountain

N

Elevation

4100

3800

| Miles: 0.5 | Moderate |

Elevation change 300 ft.

WEATHER
Spring: Good
Summer: Will be too hot
Fall: Good
Winter: Good many days
REPORT

Sedona

Y

179

14.7 mi. 1

17

618

To Montezuma Well

3.2 mi.

Fence

0.5 mi.

2 P T

0.2 mi.

Driving Distance One Way, Miles: 18.1
Hiking Distance One Way, Miles: 0.5

Schuerman Mountain Trail #56

General Information
Location Map E3
Sedona USGS Map
Coconino Forest Service Map

Driving Distance One Way: 4.5 miles *7.2 km* (Time 10 minutes)
Access Road: All vehicles, All paved
Hiking Distance One Way: 1.1 miles *1.8 km* (Time 1 hour)
How Strenuous: Moderate
Features: Views

NUTSHELL: This sprawling mountain southwest of Sedona is rather drab but is a platform for great views.

DIRECTIONS:
From the Sedona Y (the intersection of Highways 179 and 89A) Go:
    Southwest on Highway 89 (toward Cottonwood) for 4.2 miles *6.7 km* (MP 368.9) and then turn left on the Upper Red Rock Loop Road, the road to the high school **(1)**. Follow it to the 4.45 miles *7.1 km* point, where you turn right on Scorpion Way **(2)**. (You will pass Scorpion Drive first, then come to Scorpion Way.) There's a trailhead sign at the turn. Follow it, turning left into the parking area.

TRAILHEAD: At the parking lot.

DESCRIPTION: The beginning of the trail is marked by cairns in wire cages. At 0.15 miles *0.24 km*, you will come to a gate. Beyond the gate the trail climbs up to a saddle, winding its way uphill so that the climb is gradual. Almost immediately you are rewarded with good views. After a steep but short climb of 0.5 miles *0.8 km*, you will reach the top, a good place to catch your breath and enjoy the scenery.
    At the top the trail has two branches. Each is worthwhile and is about 0.3 miles *0.5 km* long. The one we enjoy the most is the trail to the left, going to an overlook from where you will enjoy good views of Cathedral Rock and Oak Creek. The viewpoint is about 0.3 miles *0.5 km* from the fork. (About 30 paces from the beginning you will intersect a trail going to the right. It goes about 2.0 miles *3.2 km* SW to join the Lower Red Rock Loop Road. We find this part of the trail to be colorless and not very interesting. For these reasons we do not recommend it.)
    After enjoying the views, return to the main trail junction and take the trail that goes westerly out into another lookout point. You have to pick your way out to the edge, but navigating is easy.

Photo: After an invigorating climb, this trail takes you to the edge of the mountain where one can sit and drink in the views.

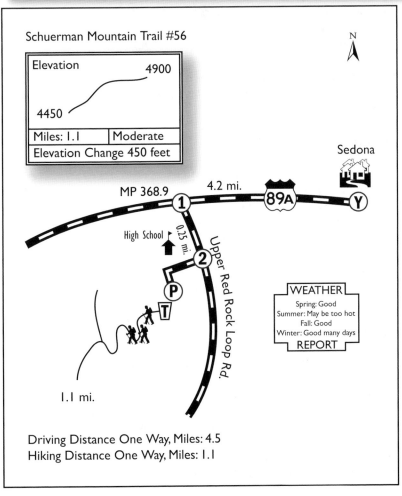

Schuerman Mountain Trail #56

N

Elevation	4900
4450	

Miles: 1.1	Moderate
Elevation Change 450 feet	

Sedona

MP 368.9   4.2 mi.   89A   Y

High School   0.25 mi.

1

2

Upper Red Rock Loop Rd.

P
T

WEATHER
Spring: Good
Summer: May be too hot
Fall: Good
Winter: Good many days
REPORT

1.1 mi.

Driving Distance One Way, Miles: 4.5
Hiking Distance One Way, Miles: 1.1

Schnebly Hill Trail #158

General Information
Location Map E5
Munds Mt. and Munds Park USGS Maps
Coconino Forest Service Map

Driving Distance One Way: 5.5 miles *8.8 km* (Time 30 minutes)
Access Road: High clearance cars, Last 4.2 miles *6.7 km* rough dirt road
Hiking Distance One Way: 2.4 miles *3.8 km* (Time 1.5 hours)
How Strenuous: Hard
Features: Historic road, Views

NUTSHELL: This trail starts where the **Munds Wagon Trail** ends, climbing to the top of Schnebly Hill, on an old road, then swinging south and following the edge of the rim to join the **Munds Mountain Trail**.

DIRECTIONS:
From the Sedona Y (the intersection of Highways 179 and 89A) Go:
    South on Highway 179 (toward Phoenix) for 0.3 miles *0.5 km* (MP 313.1) to the Schnebly Hill Road—across the bridge past Tlaquepaque **(1)**. Turn left onto the Schnebly Hill Road. It's paved for the first 1.0 miles *1.6 km* and then turns into a rough dirt road. At 5.5 miles *8.8 km*, you will see a low redrock butte to your left with a parking area in front of it. Park there.

TRAILHEAD: Walk down the road about twenty yards from the parking place. The trailhead marker is to your left, on the uphill side of the road.

DESCRIPTION: This trail starts where the **Munds Wagon Trail** ends. It is steep but there are many superb vista points. At 1.2 miles *1.9 km* look to your right just as you come to the top of the grade, at a hairpin curve. Here you will see a footpath going to your right (S), into the trees. Follow it. This is the new leg of the trail. It is marked by cairns and takes you south along the rim. In some places you are right on the rim and have choice views into colorful country. You will pass through two gates. The second gate is at Committee Tank, located to your left (E), a favorite spot for wildlife.
    Soon after, the trail reaches a knife-thin ridge connecting to Munds Mountain. From the ridge you can see to the north into the Schnebly Hill area and south into Jacks Canyon, a great double-header. You are high enough to have sweeping views out over the landscape on top of the Mogollon Rim. The ridge then dips down to join the **Munds Mountain Trail** at the 2.4 miles *3.8 km* point, a place marked by a giant cairn. The **Jacks Canyon Trail** ends here, coming up from the bottom of Jacks Canyon. The Munds Mt. Trail is steep, climbing 500 feet in 0.5 mile *0.8 km* to the top.

Photo: This shot was taken near the top of this steep trail. Dick is resting and enjoying the tremendous views of Mitten Ridge and the Cow Pies.

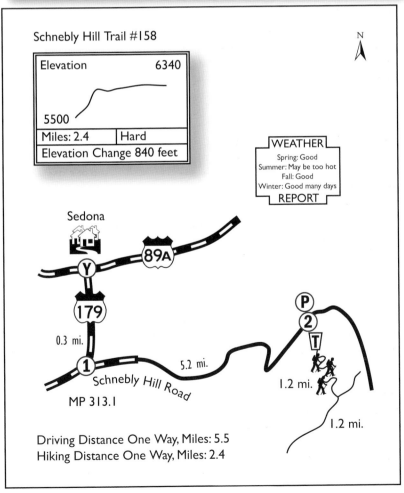

Schnebly Hill Trail #158

N

Elevation	6340
5500	
Miles: 2.4	Hard
Elevation Change 840 feet	

WEATHER
Spring: Good
Summer: May be too hot
Fall: Good
Winter: Good many days
REPORT

Sedona

89A

Y

179

0.3 mi.

1

Schnebly Hill Road

5.2 mi.

MP 313.1

P

2

T

1.2 mi.

1.2 mi.

Driving Distance One Way, Miles: 5.5
Hiking Distance One Way, Miles: 2.4

Secret Canyon Trail #121

General Information
Location Map C4
Loy Butte and Wilson Mt. USGS Maps
Coconino Forest Service Map

Driving Distance One Way: 8.6 miles *13.8 km* (Time 30 minutes)
Access Road: Most cars, Last 3.4 miles *5.4 km* rough dirt road
Hiking Distance One Way: 5.5 miles *8.8 km* (Time 3 hours)
How Strenuous: Hard
Features: Views, Remote canyon

NUTSHELL: This beautiful canyon, 8.6 miles *13.8 km* northwest of uptown Sedona, provides a delightful hike along a streambed through the redrocks. **A personal favorite.**

DIRECTIONS:

From the Sedona Y (the intersection of Highways 179 and 89A) Go:

Southwest on Highway 89A (toward Cottonwood) for 3.2 miles *5.1 km* (MP 371) to Dry Creek Road **(1)**. Turn right on Dry Creek Road and proceed to the 5.2 mile *8.3 km* point, where you turn right on FR 152, the Vultee Arch Road **(2)**, and follow it to the 8.6 mile *13.8 km* point. You will see a road sign pointing to the trail turnoff **(3)**. Turn left into the parking area. The driveway into the parking space is rough and the area holds only about five cars.

TRAILHEAD: There is a signboard with map, and a bronze plaque in memory of David Miller.

DESCRIPTION: From the parking area the trail goes immediately to Dry Creek and then turns right (N) and runs along the creek bottom. If water is running in Dry Creek you may not be able to make this hike, as the trail winds back and forth across the creek several times.

The trail takes you through some beautiful back country, passing through impressive redrocks. At 0.6 miles *1.0 km* you will see the **H S Canyon** trail taking off to the left. We like this redrock part of the Secret Canyon hike the best. At about 2.0 miles *3.2 km* you come up out of the canyon bottom and walk along the side, on the redrocks. At 2.1 miles *3.4 km* you will meet the **David Miller Trail**, which goes to the right.

Just beyond this trail junction the trail enters a pine forest. For the purposes of this book, which features day hikes, we recommend that you stop in the cool pines at 2.5 miles *4.0 km*, in which case this is a moderate hike. The trail goes 3.0 miles *4.8 km* farther, following the course of the canyon as it winds its way to the base of the rim.

Photo: Once you get into the canyon, you are treated to an endless display of redrock beauty.

Secret Canyon Trail #121

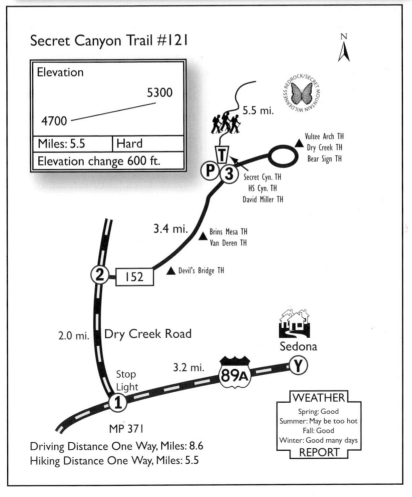

N

Elevation	
4700	5300
Miles: 5.5	Hard
Elevation change 600 ft.	

5.5 mi.

WILDERNESS REDROCK/SECRET MOUNTAIN

Vultee Arch TH
Dry Creek TH
Bear Sign TH

P T 3
Secret Cyn. TH
HS Cyn. TH
David Miller TH

3.4 mi.   Brins Mesa TH
Van Deren TH

2 152   ▲ Devil's Bridge TH

2.0 mi.   Dry Creek Road

Sedona

Stop
Light   3.2 mi.   89A   Y

1

MP 371

Driving Distance One Way, Miles: 8.6
Hiking Distance One Way, Miles: 5.5

WEATHER
Spring: Good
Summer: May be too hot
Fall: Good
Winter: Good many days
REPORT

Sedona Centennial Trail

General Information
Location Map E3
Sedona USGS Map
Coconino Forest Service Map

Driving Distance One Way: 4.4 miles *7.0 km* (Time 10 minutes)
Access Road: All vehicles, All paved
Hiking Distance One Way: 0.5 miles 0.8 *km* (Time 20 minutes)
How Strenuous: Easy
Features: Views

NUTSHELL: This simple trail, built in 2002 for Sedona's Centennial celebration (the town was named in 1902), provides an easy walk to a viewpoint.

DIRECTIONS:
From the Sedona Y (the intersection of Highways 179 and 89A) Go:
    Southwest on Highway 89 (toward Cottonwood) for 4.1 miles *6.6 km* (MP 369.9) **(1)**; then turn right onto Cultural Park Place. As you drive in, there is a series of parking lots to your right. Go to the farthest lot on your right, Red J, where you see a picnic table under a big roof with massive pillars. There is a 3-panel trailhead sign here **(2)**. Pull in and park.

TRAILHEAD: The trail starts at the sign.

DESCRIPTION: At the start there is a trail fork where the **Girdner Trail** goes straight (NW) and the Sedona Centennial Trail goes to the right (E).
    You will notice as you stroll along that trailside signs identify many of the plants. You will soon come to a bench built in honor of Norm Herkenham, after whom the **Herkenham Trail** was named. This is a fine roost where you can sit for a while and enjoy sweeping views over a vast stretch of the Sedona backcountry.
    After the bench you will soon cross the Girdner trail (the crossing is well marked with signs) and go through a barbed wire fence, heading westerly to a knoll.
    You will cross a road and begin making the gentle ascent to the top of the knoll. All through the area where you have hiked up to this point you may see glittering shards of broken glass, evidence of the fact that this area was once the Sedona dump.
    Near the top of the knoll you reach a loop. You can go in either direction here and come back to this point. We usually go to the right. As you walk around the loop, enjoy the views, for they are the point of this trail.

Photo: These interpretive signs at the trailhead give you some interesting information about the area. The trail itself is short but has some fine views.

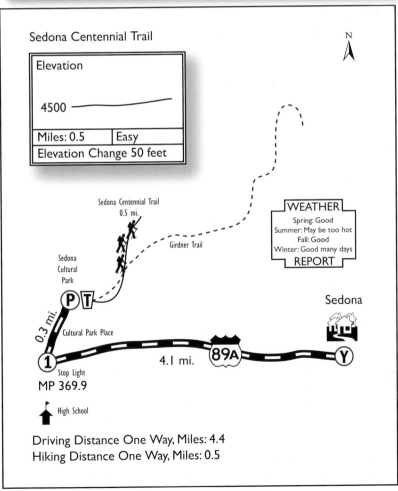

Sedona Centennial Trail

Elevation	
4500	
Miles: 0.5	Easy
Elevation Change 50 feet	

N

Sedona Centennial Trail
0.5 mi.

Girdner Trail

Sedona
Cultural
Park

WEATHER
Spring: Good
Summer: May be too hot
Fall: Good
Winter: Good many days
REPORT

Sedona

P T

0.3 mi.

Cultural Park Place

1

Stop Light

MP 369.9

4.1 mi.

89A

Y

High School

Driving Distance One Way, Miles: 4.4
Hiking Distance One Way, Miles: 0.5

Slide Rock Trails

General Information
Location Map C5
Wilson Mt. USGS Map
Coconino Forest Service Map

Driving Distance One Way: 6.9 miles *11.0 km* (Time 15 minutes)
Access Road: All cars, All paved
Hiking Distance One Way: Each trail 0.5 miles *0.8 km* (Time 30 minutes)
How Strenuous: Easy
Features: Slide Rock State Park

NUTSHELL: You enjoy two hiking trails in Slide Rock State Park 6.9 miles *11.0 km* north of Sedona, one at water's edge and the other on the cliffs above Oak Creek.

DIRECTIONS:
From the Sedona Y (the intersection of Highways 179 and 89A) Go:
    North on Highway 89A (toward Flagstaff) a distance of 6.9 miles *11.0 km* (MP 381.1) to the entrance to Slide Rock State Park. The park is well marked and signed and you will have no trouble finding it. Pull in to Slide Rock State Park (there is an entry fee) and park on the large lot.

TRAILHEAD: From the parking lot, walk upstream along a paved walkway, the Pendley Homestead Trail about 0.1 mile *0.16 km*. When you get to the Apple Packing Shed, you will be at the place where the Cliff Top and Creekside trails start. Drinking water and toilets are on site.

DESCRIPTION: (1) **Creekside Trail**: At the Packing Shed you will see a flight of steps going down to Oak Creek. Take the steps. You will emerge onto a long redrock ledge going upstream. It is easy and fun to walk along the ledge, enjoying the water and the redrock cliffs on either side. This is a favorite place for visitors and is likely to be crowded. You will see a place in the creek where the water has cut a channel into the bedrock. This is the *slide* of Slide Rock and you will probably see people using it, as they sit in the water at the beginning of the channel and let the current sweep them down to its end in a deep pool.
    There are well-worn trails at the base of the cliffs and also at the edge of the water. When the water is low, you can walk across the creek on a duckboard bridge, but we think the best sights are on the west bank, the side you start on. The trails end at an interesting old shed built of rock in front of an irrigation flume at about 0.5 miles *0.8 km*. From there you can rock hop upstream for a considerable distance depending on the depth of the water and your desire to explore.
    (2) **Clifftop Trail**: Now go back to the top of the stairs. There you will see a sign for the Cliff Top Trail. The trail runs along the top of the cliffs

parallel to the creek, providing several places where you can step off the trail and go over to the cliff tops to look down on Slide Rock. The Cliff Top Trail is rated as being 3/8 mile *0.6 km* long but you must add the distance from the parking lot to the trailhead, making it an easy 0.5 miles *0.8 km* each way. Park literature describes this as a nature trail but on our most recent hike in April 2004 the plant signs were missing. There were a few concrete pads with animal footprints alongside the trail, however, and these are fun to explore.

Slide Rock has been a popular spot for years, but its use soared when the state bought it and turned it into a park in 1987. In the height of the tourist season, it can be so crowded as to be annoying. We like to visit it in the off season in order to avoid the throngs.

Photo: There is a photo of Slide Rock on page 253.

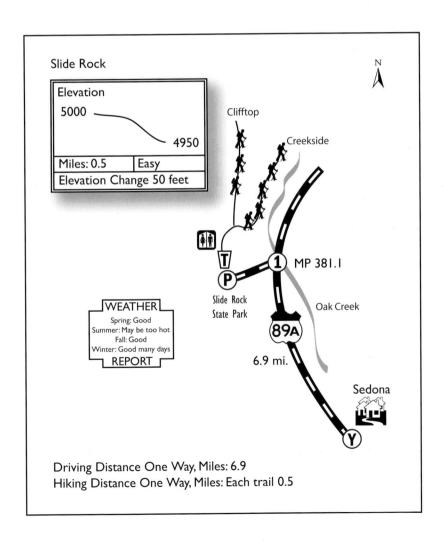

Driving Distance One Way, Miles: 6.9
Hiking Distance One Way, Miles: Each trail 0.5

Soldier Pass Arches

General Information
Location Map D4
Sedona and Wilson Mt. USGS Maps
Coconino Forest Service Map

Driving Distance One Way: 3.0 miles *4.8 km* (Time 10 minutes)
Access Road: All cars, All paved
Hiking Distance One Way: 1.5 miles *2.4 km* (Time 60 minutes)
How Strenuous: Moderate
Features: Views, Arches

NUTSHELL: Near town, this fine hike takes you to 3 interesting arches.

DIRECTIONS:
From the Sedona Y (the intersection of Highways 179 and 89A) Go:
　　Southwest on Highway 89A (toward Cottonwood) for 1.25 miles *2.0 km* (MP 372.8) then turn right onto Soldier Pass Road **(1)** and follow it to the 2.75 mile *4.4 km* point, then turn right on Rim Shadows Drive **(2)**. Follow trail signs to the 3.0 miles *4.8 km* point **(3)** and turn left into the parking area. The parking area is controlled by a locked gate, open from 8 am—6 pm. Be sure to return on time; don't get locked in.

TRAILHEAD: At the three-panel map/sign in the parking area.

DESCRIPTION: You will reach Devil's Kitchen, the area's biggest sinkhole, in 0.15 miles *0.2 km*. At 0.55 miles *0.9 km* you will walk onto bare redrock, where the Seven Sacred Pools are located in a little canyon to your left. These natural scoops, though small, hold water even in dry periods and are important to birds and animals.
　　From here, you hike to the 1.25 mile *2.0 km* point, the Wilderness Boundary, marked by a two-strand cable fence. Walk along the fence and then turn right through the gate, across a stony creek bottom. On the other side of the creek you come to a trail sign. The **Soldier Pass Trail** goes straight ahead, while the trail to the arches goes uphill, right, on a primitive road.
　　You emerge onto a large slickrock ledge in a box canyon, with good views all around. Walk across the ledge to its far edge and then turn right. Look up at the cliffs to your left from this spot and you will see one arch.
　　Soon the trail turns narrow and is steep (180 feet climb), but is short (0.2 miles *0.3 km*). At the end are two arches (really alcoves). The main-traveled trail goes to the largest one. A lesser trail branches to the left to the next biggest. There is a third arch that you can't see. You reach it by walking along the cliff face on a faint trail. The third arch is hardly worth the effort.

Photo: Sherry was standing under one of the arches looking out across the canyon when she made this picture.

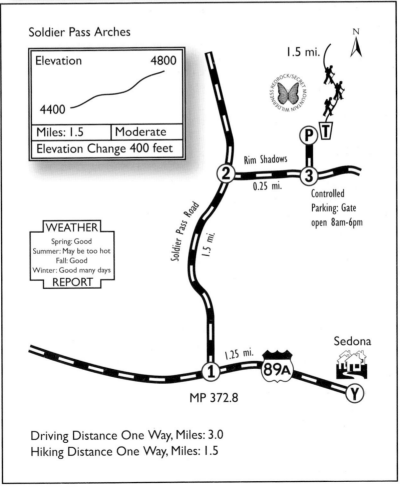

Soldier Pass Arches

Elevation	4800
4400	
Miles: 1.5	Moderate
Elevation Change 400 feet	

1.5 mi.

N

REDROCK/SECRET MOUNTAIN WILDERNESS

P T

Rim Shadows

2 ——— 3
0.25 mi.

Controlled
Parking: Gate
open 8am-6pm

Soldier Pass Road

1.5 mi.

1.25 mi.

Sedona

1 ——— 89A ——— Y

MP 372.8

Driving Distance One Way, Miles: 3.0
Hiking Distance One Way, Miles: 1.5

Soldier Pass Trail #66

General Information
Location Map D4
Sedona and Wilson Mt. USGS Maps
Coconino Forest Service Map

Driving Distance One Way: 3.0 miles *4.8 km* (Time 10 minutes)
Access Road: All cars, All paved
Hiking Distance One Way: 2.2 miles *3.5 km* (Time 1 hour)
How Strenuous: Moderate
Features: Views

NUTSHELL: Near town this trail takes you through colorful redrock country to the top of Brins Mesa, a Sedona landmark.

DIRECTIONS:
From the Sedona Y (the intersection of Highways 179 and 89A) Go:
   Southwest on Highway 89A (toward Cottonwood) for 1.25 miles *2.0 km* (MP 372.8) then turn right onto Soldier Pass Road **(1)**, go to the 2.75 mile *4.4 km* point, and turn right on Rim Shadows Drive **(2)**. Follow trail signs to the 3.0 mile *4.8 km* point **(3)** and turn left into the parking area where there is a locked gate, open from 8 am—6 pm. Exit on time; don't get locked in.

TRAILHEAD: At the parking area where there is a three-panel map/sign.

DESCRIPTION: You'll reach Devil's Kitchen, the area's biggest sinkhole, in 0.15 miles *0.2 km*. From the Kitchen you hike around the rim of the sinkhole, don't go down onto the jeep road.
   At 0.55 miles *0.9 km* you will walk onto bare redrock where the Seven Sacred Pools are located in a little canyon to your left. These natural scoops, though small, hold water even in dry periods and are important to wildlife.
   From here, you will hike to the 1.25 mile *2.0 km* point, the end of the marked trail, at the Wilderness Boundary, marked by a two-strand cable fence. Walk a short distance along the fence, then turn right through the gate and go across a stony creek bed. On the other side is a sign. Go straight. The trail uphill to the right goes to **Soldier Pass Arches**.
   The trail moves along a streambed and then climbs 370 feet in 0.4 miles *0.6 km*, following the crest of a ridge that rises gently to the top of Brins Mesa. As it climbs, the trail rewards your effort with great views.
   The trail tops out on a redrock shelf at 2.2 miles *3.5 km*. To the right is a little connector going 0.25 miles *0.4 km* to link up with the **Brins Mesa Trail**. The final leg of the Soldier Pass Trail going downhill to join the Vultee Arch Road at the Brins Mesa Trailhead is now blocked, so the trail ends here.

Photo: The Devil's Kitchen, the area's largest known sinkhole, is a special attraction that you reach on the early part of this trail.

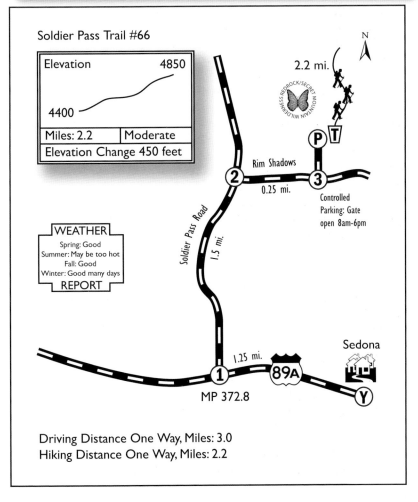

Soldier Pass Trail #66

Elevation	4850
4400	

Miles: 2.2	Moderate
Elevation Change 450 feet	

2.2 mi.

REDROCK/SECRET MOUNTAIN WILDERNESS

N

P T

Rim Shadows

2 ————— 3
0.25 mi.

Controlled
Parking: Gate
open 8am-6pm

WEATHER
Spring: Good
Summer: May be too hot
Fall: Good
Winter: Good many days
REPORT

Soldier Pass Road

1.5 mi.

Sedona

1.25 mi.
1 —— 89A
MP 372.8
Y

Driving Distance One Way, Miles: 3.0
Hiking Distance One Way, Miles: 2.2

Sterling Pass Trail #46

General Information
Location Map C5
Munds Park and Wilson Mt. USGS Maps
Coconino Forest Service Map

Driving Distance One Way: 6.2 miles *9.9 km* (Time 10 minutes)
Access Road: All cars, All paved
Hiking Distance One Way: 1.65 miles *2.6 km* (Time 60 minutes)
How Strenuous: Hard
Features: Views, Great rock formations

NUTSHELL: This steep hike in upper Oak Creek Canyon climbs through a heavy forest to a mountain pass with scenic views along the way.

DIRECTIONS:
From the Sedona Y (the intersection of Highways 179 and 89A) Go:
   North on Highway 89A (toward Flagstaff) for a distance of 6.2 miles *9.9 km* (MP 380.4) **(1)**. Park anywhere you can along the roadside in this area.

TRAILHEAD: There is a rusty sign in a little alcove.

DESCRIPTION: This trail rises steeply, climbing all the way. At first you parallel a little side canyon, which may contain running water during spring thaw. The trail wanders back and forth over the streambed four times.
   The trail goes through a cool pine forest and you will also see Douglas fir and a few spruces. The soil underfoot is a rich brown loam. Soon you are far enough away from the road so that you can no longer hear its sounds and can see no signs of human activity. The area feels primeval and is truly delightful.
   Views are restricted until you have gone about 1.25 miles *2.0 km*. Then you rise above the trees for great views across Oak Creek Canyon and nearby. The cliffs here are a treat to the eye, highly sculptured, with many interesting lines and angles. At a bend of the trail you can look into an adjacent canyon to your left for views of soaring white cliffs.
   The crest is at 1.65 miles *2.6 km*, where you come onto a saddle. There is a heavy stand of oaks and maples here so the views are not as good at the top as they are just below it. This is a true mountain pass, where there is a gap in the cliffs.
   The trail continues down the other side, another 0.75 miles *1.2 km*, to intersect the **Vultee Arch Trail.** If you go down the west side you might as well see Vultee Arch, which is only 0.2 miles *0.3 km* from the trail junction. Many hikers will stop at the saddle.

Photo: Near the top of this trail the views of immense towering white cliffs are stunning, reminding us of the cliffs of Zion National Park.

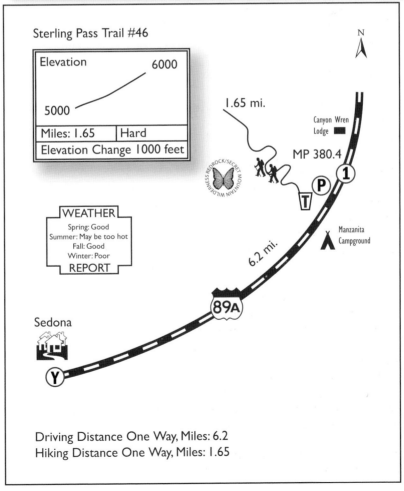

Sterling Pass Trail #46

Elevation
6000
5000

| Miles: 1.65 | Hard |
| Elevation Change 1000 feet | |

1.65 mi.

Canyon Wren
Lodge

MP 380.4

REDROCK/SECRET MOUNTAIN WILDERNESS

1

P

T

Manzanita
Campground

WEATHER
Spring: Good
Summer: May be too hot
Fall: Good
Winter: Poor
REPORT

6.2 mi.

89A

Sedona

Y

Driving Distance One Way, Miles: 6.2
Hiking Distance One Way, Miles: 1.65

Submarine Rock Trail

General Information
Location Map E5
Sedona USGS Map
Coconino Forest Service Map

Driving Distance One Way: 2.1 miles *3.4 km* (Time 10 minutes)
Access Road: All cars, Last 0.1 mile *0.16 km* good dirt road
Hiking Distance One Way: 1.0 miles *1.6 km* (Time 30 minutes)
How Strenuous: Easy
Features: Interesting rock formation, Views

NUTSHELL: Located only a couple of miles southeast of uptown Sedona, this interesting rock formation is fun to climb and explore.

DIRECTIONS:
From the Sedona Y (the intersection of Highways 179 and 89A) Go:
    South on Highway 179 (toward Phoenix) for 1.4 miles *2.2 km* (MP 312.1) to Morgan Road in the Broken Arrow Subdivision **(1)**. Turn left (east) on Morgan Road and follow it to its end, at 2.0 miles *3.2 km*, then proceed another 0.1 mile *0.16 km* to the parking lot.

TRAILHEAD: The trailhead for the **Broken Arrow Trail**, which is marked by a three-panel map/sign.

DESCRIPTION: The Broken Arrow Trail is well marked and you will have no trouble finding and following it. At first it takes you close to Battlement Mesa, where you will enjoy looking at the red cliffs. You will also have expansive views out over the area to your left, including the town of Sedona.
    At 0.5 miles *0.8 km* you will come downhill to the fence enclosing a sinkhole, the Devil's Dining Room. At 0.75 miles *1.2 km* you will come to a trail junction. The trail to the right goes to Chicken Point. Take the left fork, going downhill to Submarine Rock. The trail crosses the road and then works its way to the north end of the rock.
    This is the highest end of the formation. We found no distinct trail going up to the top of the rock, but that is not a problem because it is easy to pick your way up by trial and error. Once you are on top of the butte you can have great fun walking around, getting the views from the top of the "conning tower."
    Submarine Rock is located at the south end of **Marg's Draw**, a scenic bowl. This is a beautiful natural area and the home of several good hikes. You will enjoy the views from this Sedona favorite.

Photo: This shot is taken from a distance in order to show the entire "submarine", the low rounded slickrock formation in the foreground. The trail takes you up on top of the submarine.

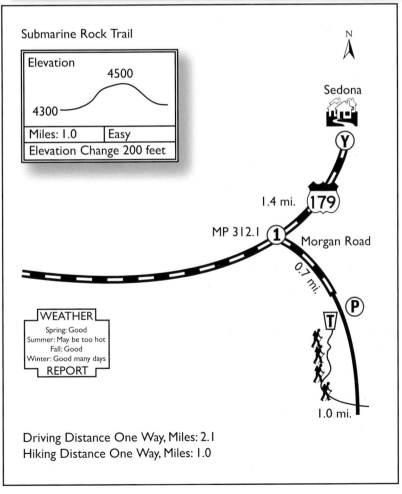

Submarine Rock Trail

N

Elevation

4500

4300

Miles: 1.0	Easy
Elevation Change 200 feet	

Sedona

Y

1.4 mi. 179

MP 312.1 1 Morgan Road

0.7 mi.

P

T

WEATHER
Spring: Good
Summer: May be too hot
Fall: Good
Winter: Good many days
REPORT

1.0 mi.

Driving Distance One Way, Miles: 2.1
Hiking Distance One Way, Miles: 1.0

Sugarloaf Loop Trail

General Information
Location Map D4
Sedona and Wilson Mountain USGS Maps
Coconino Forest Service Map

Driving Distance One Way: 2.85 miles *4.6 km* (Time 10 minutes)
Access Road: All cars, All paved
Hiking Distance, Complete Loop: 2.2 miles *3.5 km* (Time: 1 hour)
How Strenuous: Moderate
Features: Easy access, Gorgeous views

NUTSHELL: You climb up the back of a ramp-shaped butte to enjoy wonderful views from its top, and then loop around back to your starting point.

DIRECTIONS:
From the Sedona Y (the intersection of Highways 179 and 89A) Go:
Southwest on Highway 89A for 1.9 miles *3.0 km* (MP 372.7) then turn right on Coffee Pot Drive **(1)**. Follow it to the 2.5 mile *4.0 km* point and turn left on Sanborn **(2)**. Go west to the 2.65 mile *4.2 km* point, and turn right on Little Elf Drive **(3)**. At 2.85 miles *4.6 km*, the end of Little Elf, turn right on Buena Vista **(4)**, drive a few yards **(5)** and turn left into the parking lot.

TRAILHEAD: At the parking area. There is a signboard with maps.

DESCRIPTION: From the parking area walk north. The trail splits and you take the right fork. Keep moving north and heading toward Sugarloaf. You reach a power line at 0.3 miles *0.5 km* and go just beyond it to a T-intersection where there is a sign, for the **Thunder Mountain Trail** (left), Sugarloaf and the **Teacup Trail** (right). Go right.

You rise up on the flank of Sugarloaf and at the 0.5 mile *0.8 km,* point reach a posted trail junction. Turn right and make a steep climb. As you rise above the tree line, you begin to enjoy the views. When you reach the top, at 0.75 mile *1.2 km* you will find that you are on a perfect viewing platform. There are no tall trees and you are able to see out in all directions. This is a great place to come in the evening to watch the sunset.

On the way down, when you come to the trail junction, turn right and follow the signs and cairns, as there are many false trails in the area. You will be treated to magnificent views of a Sedona landmark, Coffeepot Rock. The Sugarloaf Loop officially ends where it joins the Teacup Trail. Turn left here and hike the Teacup back to the starting point.

Photo: Sugarloaf, a familiar Sedona landmark, gives you great views as you climb to its bare top. Coffeepot Rock is visible in the background.

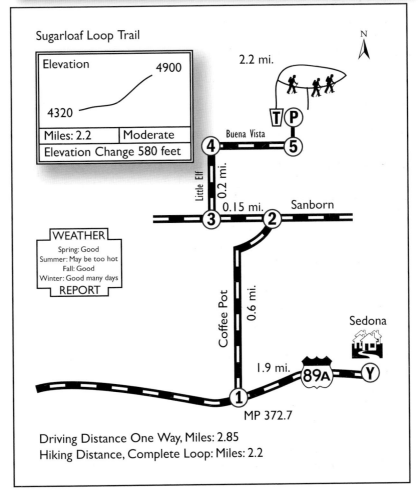

Sugarloaf Loop Trail

Elevation
4900
4320

Miles: 2.2 | Moderate
Elevation Change 580 feet

2.2 mi.

N

Buena Vista

T P

4 — 5

Little Elf
0.2 mi.

0.15 mi. | Sanborn
3 — 2

WEATHER
Spring: Good
Summer: May be too hot
Fall: Good
Winter: Good many days
REPORT

Coffee Pot
0.6 mi.

Sedona

1.9 mi.
89A
Y

1
MP 372.7

Driving Distance One Way, Miles: 2.85
Hiking Distance, Complete Loop: Miles: 2.2

Summit Route Trail

General Information
Location Map D4
Sedona USGS Map
Coconino Forest Service Map

Driving Distance One Way: 4.3 miles *6.9 km* (Time 10 minutes)
Access Road: All cars, All paved
Hiking Distance One Way: 0.7 miles *1.1 km* (Time 40 minutes)
How Strenuous: Moderate
Features: Close to town, easy all-weather access, Views

NUTSHELL: This is a small hike that you can make in a hurry, but it will give you a good workout and great views.

DIRECTIONS:
From the Sedona Y (the intersection of Highways 179 and 89A) Go:
Southwest on Highway 89A (toward Cottonwood) for 3.2 miles *5.1 km* (MP 371) then turn right on Dry Creek Road **(1)** and proceed to the 3.7 mile *5.9 km* point **(2)**. Turn right Thunder Mountain Road. Drive to the 4.3 miles *6.9 km* point **(3)**, then turn left into the trail parking lot.

TRAILHEAD: At the parking area. There is a sign with a map of the trails in the area, but this hike is not on it.

DESCRIPTION: Follow the main trail. At 0.1 miles *0.16 km* you will come to a trail junction. The trail to the right is the Thunder Mountain Trail. Go straight ahead.

At 0.35 miles *0.6 km* you will reach a second trail junction at the top of a little pass, where you can see down into the Dry Creek Road area. The **Chimney Rock Loop Trail** takes off to the right here, while the **Lower Chimney Rock Trail** goes straight ahead.

Walk straight ahead just a few feet. At 0.5 miles *0.8 km,* just as the trail begins to go downhill, turn left (S). There is a small sign here. There is a six-foot tall juniper stump—looking like a fencepost—at the place where you turn.

Almost immediately you will approach Little Sugarloaf and begin to climb its north face. There are several trails going up. Take the most-used one. At the top, you emerge onto bare slickrock with unobstructed views, very fine for enjoying the Sedona landscape.

Photo: The top of this butte is bare, so hikers can sit—as Dick is doing here—and enjoy terrific views.

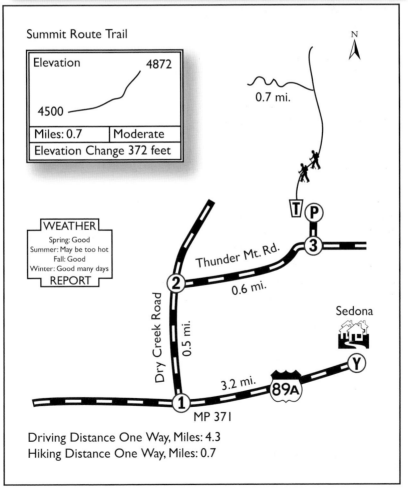

Summit Route Trail

Elevation	4872
4500	
Miles: 0.7	Moderate
Elevation Change 372 feet	

0.7 mi.

N

WEATHER
Spring: Good
Summer: May be too hot
Fall: Good
Winter: Good many days
REPORT

T P

3

Thunder Mt. Rd.

0.6 mi.

2

Dry Creek Road

0.5 mi.

Sedona

Y

3.2 mi.

89A

1

MP 371

Driving Distance One Way, Miles: 4.3
Hiking Distance One Way, Miles: 0.7

Sunrise Trail

General Information
Location Map D4
Sedona and Wilson Mt. USGS Maps
Coconino Forest Service Map

Driving Distance One Way: 1.5 miles *2.4 km* (Time 5 minutes)
Access Road: All cars, All paved
Hiking Distance One Way: 1.2 miles *1.9 km* (Time 45 minutes)
How Strenuous: Easy
Features: Convenience, all-weather surface, nature trail features, connections to other trails

NUTSHELL: This urban trail is perfect for walking the dog in the evening or just stretching your legs after a day at the office.

DIRECTIONS:
From the Sedona Y (the intersection of Highways 179 and 89A) Go:
Southwest on Highway 89A (toward Cottonwood) for 1.25 miles *2.0 km* (MP 372.8) then turn right on Soldier Pass Road **(1)** and follow it to the 1.5 mile *2.4 km* point, just past Calle Contenta **(2)**. On the left side of the road you will see the Sunrise Trail joining the road, at a parking apron.

TRAILHEAD: At the parking apron.

DESCRIPTION: The trail runs along in a generally northward direction parallel to the Soldier Pass Road. It is wide, well surfaced and marked with trail signs. It also serves as a modest nature trail, as there are signs identifying some of the plants that grow along the side of the trail.

At the 0.15 mile *0.24 km* point, you will find a side trail to your left with a sign for the upper level. We recommend that you take this little detour, as you get away from the Soldier Pass Road and have better views. You will climb about 50 feet to the top of a hill. Turn right (NE) at the top and walk past an elevated open stage. Keep going until you meet the paved Carruth Road at the 0.5 mile *0.8 km* point. Across the street you will see the **Carruth Trail**, another part of this trail system.

Turn right at Carruth Road (E) and walk downhill. You will rejoin the Sunrise Trail at Soldier Pass Road at the 0.6 mile *1.0 km* point. Turn left (NNE), walk across Carruth Road, and pick up the Sunrise Trail again.

At the 1.1 mile *1.8 km* point you will find the Carruth Trail joining the Sunrise Trail to your left, creating a loop possibility if you leave the Sunrise Trail and take the Carruth Trail at this point. At the 1.2 mile *1.9 km* point the Sunrise Trail ends, bumping into the Soldier Pass Road.

Photo: Most of the time hikers on Sedona trails are looking up or off in the distance at the scenery. This trail gives you reason to look down, to see the signs identifying the plants.

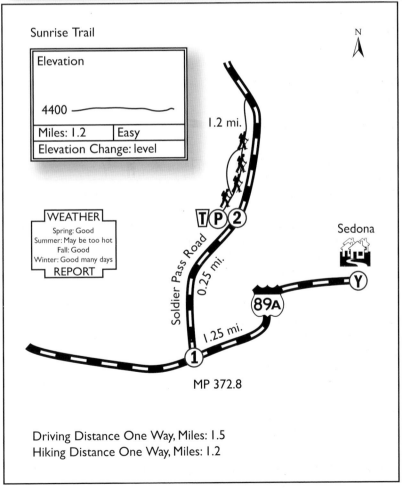

Sunrise Trail

N

Elevation	
4400	
Miles: 1.2	Easy
Elevation Change: level	

1.2 mi.

WEATHER
Spring: Good
Summer: May be too hot
Fall: Good
Winter: Good many days
REPORT

T P 2

Sedona

Soldier Pass Road

0.25 mi.

89A

Y

1.25 mi.

1

MP 372.8

Driving Distance One Way, Miles: 1.5
Hiking Distance One Way, Miles: 1.2

Table Top Trail

General Information
Location Map E4
Sedona USGS Map
Coconino Forest Service Map

Driving Distance One Way: 2.6 miles *4.2 km* (Time 10 minutes)
Access Road: All cars, Paved all the way
Hiking Distance One Way: 1.9 miles *3.0 km* (Time 1.25 hours)
How Strenuous: Moderate
Features: 360-degree views

NUTSHELL: This trail takes you onto Airport Mesa and out to a knob.

DIRECTIONS:
From the Sedona Y (the intersection of Highways 179 and 89A) Go:
　　Southwest on Hwy 89A for 2.1 miles *3.4 km* (stoplight **(1)**. Turn left on Shelby Drive. Stay on it for 0.5 miles *0.8 km* (just past Stanley Steamer) then right into the parking lot of the La Entrada building **(2)**, at 2155 Shelby Drive. Park at the back of the lot at the trailhead parking signs.

TRAILHEAD: Access is via the **Bandit Trail**. There is a trailhead sign just outside the bushes at the parking lot.

DESCRIPTION: Almost immediately you will come to the **Old Post Trail** fork. Pass by. Soon after this you will reach the junction where you turn left onto the Bandit Trail which skirts the private property, bringing you up very close to the fence that surrounds a storage yard. Then you begin to climb, making a steep ascent up the shoulder of Airport Mesa. At 0.6 miles *1.0 km* you will intersect the **Airport Loop Trail**.
　　Turn to the right, still climbing, on the joint Airport Loop-Bandit trails. At 0.9 miles *1.4 km* at the side of the trail is Bandit's grave (a well-loved pet). You keep climbing the side of the mesa, topping out at 1.2 miles *1.9 km*. You will walk a bit farther, going around the toe of the mesa until at 1.4 miles *2.2 km* you meet the junction with the **Table Top Trail**.
　　Turn right for a short easy walk out to the top of the knob. Some psychics regard the knob as a vortex site. As you hike you will see another trail veering off to the left, descending steeply. This is an illegally constructed social trail that goes down to join the **Ridge Trail**. Bypass it and go to the tippy top of the knob at the end of the Table Top Trail. We like the sensation of being able to stand on the very pinnacle of a formation, which is possible on this knob. Great unobstructed views! Airport Mesa is officially called Table Top Mesa on the Sedona 7.5 topo map, giving this trail its name.

Photo: A thin ridge joins this hilltop to Airport Mesa. It's an easy walk out to the peak.

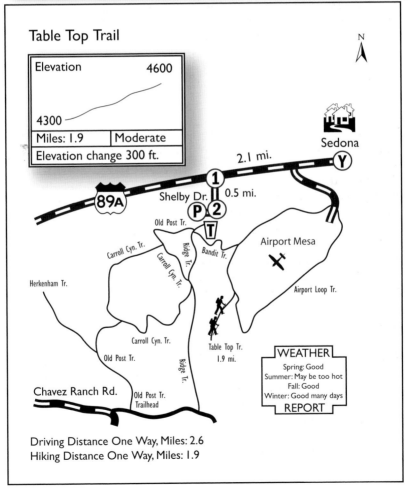

Table Top Trail

Elevation   4600

4300

Miles: 1.9	Moderate
Elevation change 300 ft.	

N

Sedona

2.1 mi.

89A

Shelby Dr.   0.5 mi.

P

Old Post Tr.

Airport Mesa

Carroll Cyn. Tr.

Ridge Tr.

Carroll Cyn. Tr.

Bandit Tr.

Herkenham Tr.

Airport Loop Tr.

Carroll Cyn. Tr.

Old Post Tr.

Ridge Tr.

Table Top Tr.
1.9 mi.

WEATHER
Spring: Good
Summer: May be too hot
Fall: Good
Winter: Good many days
REPORT

Chavez Ranch Rd.

Old Post Tr.
Trailhead

Driving Distance One Way, Miles: 2.6
Hiking Distance One Way, Miles: 1.9

Teacup Trail

General Information
Location Map D4
Sedona and Wilson Mt. USGS Maps
Coconino Forest Service Map

Driving Distance One Way: 3.0 miles *4.8 km* (Time 10 minutes)
Access Road: All cars, All paved
Hiking Distance One Way: 1.6 miles *2.6 km* (Time 1 hour)
How Strenuous: Moderate
Features: Views, Connects to other system trails, Easy to reach

NUTSHELL: Starting at the Soldier Pass TH, you pass under Coffeepot Rock, then drop south to join Thunder Mtn. Trail behind Sugarloaf.

DIRECTIONS:
From the Sedona Y (the intersection of Highways 179 and 89A) Go:
SW on Highway 89A for 1.25 miles *2.0 km* (MP 372.8) to Soldier Pass Road **(1)**. Turn right onto Soldier Pass Road and drive to the 2.75 mile *4.4 km* point, then turn right on Rim Shadows Drive **(2)**. You will see trailhead signs. Drive to the 3.0 miles *4.8 km* point. Go left into the parking area **(3)**. Entry is controlled by a gate open from 8 am to 6 pm. Mind the closing time.

TRAILHEAD: Use the "Soldier Pass Trail #66."

DESCRIPTION: From the trailhead, follow the Soldier Pass Trail to Devil's Kitchen, a big sinkhole, about 0.2 mile *0.3 km* away. From here, go west, taking the jeep road downhill until you get to the main road, at the 0.4 mile *0.6 km* point. Turn to the right and walk up the road a few feet, to a point where you will see a sign for the Teacup Trail to your left.

You will hike west, climbing, toward famous Coffee Pot Rock through an Arizona cypress forest. At the 0.8 mile *1.3 km* point the forest thins and you find a jarring view onto an area of extensively developed homesites. From this point to the end of the hike, you will enjoy looking at the massive cliffs of which Coffeepot Rock is the tip. The trail skirts along the base of these cliffs, undulating a bit, though there are no great changes in grade. West of Coffeepot Rock, you will notice a prominent spire. The top of this spire has been undercut so that it is tulip-shaped. This top is the "teacup."

Once around the base of Coffeepot Rock, you come to a point where you cannot see the housing developments and you feel as it you are out in the country again, and the trail begins to move southerly, toward **Sugarloaf**. At the 1.6 mile *2.6 km* point, the Teacup Trail joins the **Thunder Mountain Trail** just north of Sugarloaf.

Photo: The "Teacup" is seen here on top of the butte to the farthest left. It is an undercut spire.

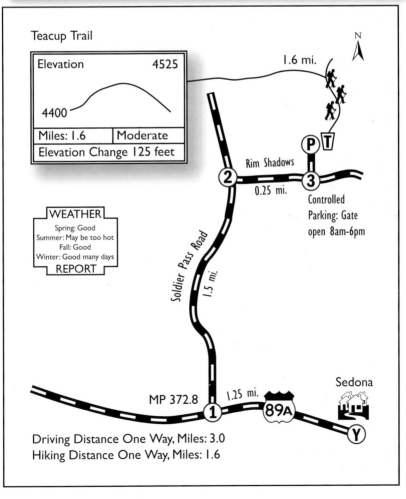

Teacup Trail

Elevation	4525
4400	

Miles: 1.6	Moderate
Elevation Change 125 feet	

1.6 mi.

N

P T

Rim Shadows

2 ——0.25 mi.—— 3

Controlled
Parking: Gate
open 8am-6pm

WEATHER
Spring: Good
Summer: May be too hot
Fall: Good
Winter: Good many days
REPORT

Soldier Pass Road

1.5 mi.

Sedona

MP 372.8   1.25 mi.   89A

1   Y

Driving Distance One Way, Miles: 3.0
Hiking Distance One Way, Miles: 1.6

Telephone Trail #72

General Information
Location Map B5
Munds Park USGS Map
Coconino Forest Service Map

Driving Distance One Way: 10.9 miles *17.4 km* (Time 20 minutes)
Access Road: All cars, All paved
Hiking Distance One Way: 1.25 miles *2.0 km* (Time 2.0 Hours)
How Strenuous: Hard (Very steep)
Features: Interesting rock formations, Views

NUTSHELL: This trail in upper Oak Creek makes a steep climb to the rim. For experienced hikers only, as the trail is rough and hard to follow.

DIRECTIONS:
From the Sedona Y (the intersection of Highways 179 and 89A) Go:
   North on Highway 89A for 10.9 miles *17.4 km* (MP 385.1) **(1)**. Park on a wide apron on the right side of the road under a 20-foot high cliff.

TRAILHEAD: Walk up Highway 89A on the right shoulder for about one hundred yards. Uphill from the road, you will see the rusty metal trailhead sign off the highway a few feet to your right.

DESCRIPTION: From the sign cairns mark the trail. It runs parallel to the highway for about 0.05 mile *0.08 km*, then swings to the right, where you will walk on an old road bed. At 0.1 miles *0.16 km* you will walk under the present phone line. The trail up to here is obvious and easy to follow. From this point on, the trail is difficult to find, and is *for experienced hikers only.*
   The next leg of the hike takes you sharply uphill, to your left (N). You zigzag your way to the top of a finger ridge that runs west from the East Rim, reaching the first top at about 0.5 miles *0.8 km*. Turn right (E). You are in a zone of white sandstone studded with fossils. You stay on top of the ridge for a while and then dip below it. At 0.6 miles *1.0 km*, you will be on top again, and will come to a fascinating little reef about thirty feet long and sixteen feet high that contains several windows, called the Peep Holes.
   Beyond is a rough spot where the trail dips again and is difficult. Follow the flags and cairns. You will find one of the old pole stubs, with guy wire and support sleeve where the trail turns back to the top.
   When you get back to the ridge top, the trail becomes more obvious. At about 0.75 miles *1.2 km*, you move along another intermediate top. Soon after that, you begin the very steep climb to the top of the rim. This is in a beautiful fir forest. Along the way here you will see the remains of several old phone poles. The trail ends at 1.25 miles *2.0 km*, at a large cairn.

Photo: This shot shows a couple of the Peep Holes, a favorite spot on this rugged trail. The big hole here is about two feet high and five feet wide.

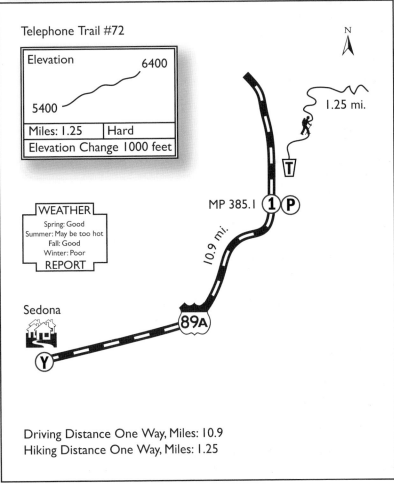

Telephone Trail #72

Elevation
6400
5400

Miles: 1.25 | Hard

Elevation Change 1000 feet

N

1.25 mi.

T

MP 385.1 ① P

10.9 mi.

WEATHER
Spring: Good
Summer: May be too hot
Fall: Good
Winter: Poor
REPORT

Sedona

89A

Y

Driving Distance One Way, Miles: 10.9
Hiking Distance One Way, Miles: 1.25

Templeton Trail

General Information
Location Map F4
Munds Mountain and Sedona USGS Maps
Coconino Forest Service Map

Driving Distance One Way: 4.7 miles *7.5 km* (Time 10 minutes)
Access Road: All cars, All paved
Hiking Distance One Way: 3.5 miles *5.6 km* (Time 2 hours)
How Strenuous: Moderate
Features: Views, Redrocks, Creekside, Variety

NUTSHELL: This trail leaves the Bell Rock Pathway, crosses under Hwy. 179, meanders to Cathedral Rock, rounds it on a high redrock shelf, and then drops down to Oak Creek on the other side. We shortcut it, omitting part.

DIRECTIONS:
From the Sedona Y (the intersection of Highways 179 and 89A) Go:
   South on Highway 179 (toward Phoenix) for 4.7 miles *7.5 km* MP 308.7, then turn right onto a wide unsigned parking apron and park **(1)**.

TRAILHEAD: Start the hike from the parking place.

DESCRIPTION: From the parking area walk down into the arroyo on the south side. Here you will see a sign marked "Trail" with arrows to the left and right. Turn right, crossing the arroyo and coming out on the other bank.
   You next hike a fairly level area moving away from the highway and entering some nice remote-feeling areas, where you have good views.
   At 1.0 miles *1.6 km* you meet the **H. T. Trail**, coming in from your right. From this point you make a beeline toward Cathedral Rock. As you near its base, the trail undulates, and at about 1.7 miles *2.7 km* you will see some old metal roofing, all that remains of a couple of shacks. Then you climb up onto a redrock ledge, which makes a natural pathway.
   At 2.5 miles *4.0 km* the **Cathedral Rock Trail** comes up from your right from the trailhead at Back O' Beyond. Continue hiking along the ledge. At the 3.0 miles *4.8 km* point, as you round the north tip, the trail starts down, winding its way to creek level at 3.25 miles *5.2 km*. There is a heavy screen of trees which blocks your view of Oak Creek, though you can hear the waters running. There is a break in the screen on trees on the banks of Oak Creek shortly and you can see the water and go down to creekside to sit on boulders and meditate—one of the nicest parts of the trail.
   Then the trail moves away from the stream though you can still hear it. The trail ends at the 3.5 mile *5.6 km* point where it joins the **Baldwin Trail**.

Photo: The Templeton Trail takes you along the base of Cathedral Rock, perhaps the most famous Sedona landmark.

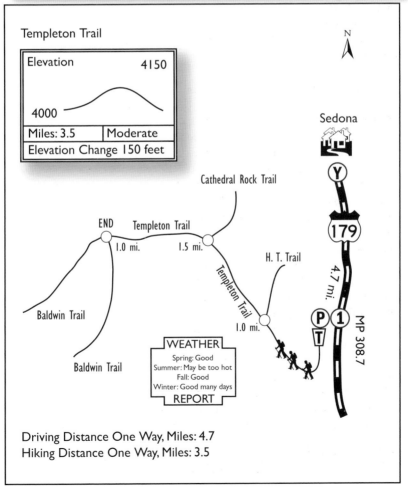

Templeton Trail

Elevation	4150
4000	
Miles: 3.5	Moderate
Elevation Change 150 feet	

N

Sedona

Cathedral Rock Trail

Y

179

END   Templeton Trail
1.0 mi.   1.5 mi.

H. T. Trail

Templeton Trail

Baldwin Trail

Templeton Trail
1.0 mi.

4.7 mi.

P
T   1

MP 308.7

Baldwin Trail

WEATHER
Spring: Good
Summer: May be too hot
Fall: Good
Winter: Good many days
REPORT

Driving Distance One Way, Miles: 4.7
Hiking Distance One Way, Miles: 3.5

Thomas Point Trail #142

General Information
Location Map B5
Munds Park USGS Map
Coconino Forest Service Map

Driving Distance One Way: 10.5 miles *16.8 km* (Time 20 minutes)
Access Road: All cars, All paved
Hiking Distance One Way: 1.5 miles *2.4 km* (Time 1.5 hours)
How Strenuous: Hard
Features: Views

NUTSHELL: This historic trail climbs the east wall of upper Oak Creek Canyon for superb views.

DIRECTIONS:
From the Sedona Y (the intersection of Highways 179 and 89A) Go:
   North on Highway 89A (toward Flagstaff) for 10.5 miles *16.8 km* MP 384.7 **(1)** and then turn left into the West Fork parking area. There is a fee to park there. There is a toilet.

TRAILHEAD: Walk over to the big signboard with map. You will see the trail depicted. Walk toward the picnic tables and keep going. The trail is rather dim past the tables. You angle toward Highway 89A, which you must cross. Turn right and walk along the highway about 100 yards to the trailhead.

DESCRIPTION: This trail was built in 1890 by the Thomas family so that they could get from their place in West Fork to Flagstaff. They did a marvelous job of following the terrain.
   After hiking a short distance you are high enough for stirring views of the sheer white cliffs across the canyon, and can see the path of Oak Creek and glimpse bits of the highway. At about 0.5 miles *0.8 km* the pines disappear and you enter the chaparral and juniper life zone. These plants are small compared to the pines so you have better views along this part of the trail but no shade. Near the top you come back into the pine and spruce forest.
   The trail ends at the top, at Thomas Point, which is a peninsula or tongue pointing west. Standing at the tip of the point you have terrific views. The point was named after J. L. V. "Dad" Thomas, who bought the West Fork Ranch in 1888. Before today's road through the canyon was finished, Flagstaff people who wanted to visit Oak Creek used the Thomas Point Trail. Getting from town to Thomas Point was a 4-5 hour wagon drive, and then they unhitched the wagon and walked the horses down this trail. Thomas built a lodge in 1900. It eventually became Mayhews Lodge.

Photo: This photo gives a sense of how steep this historic trail is. Fortunately there is tree cover most of the way, so it is shady and cool.

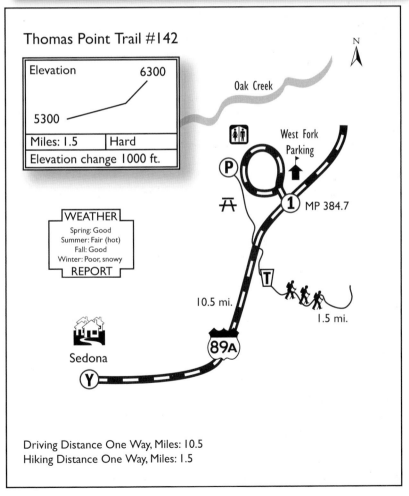

Thomas Point Trail #142

Elevation	6300
5300	
Miles: 1.5	Hard
Elevation change 1000 ft.	

Oak Creek

West Fork Parking

P

MP 384.7

WEATHER
Spring: Good
Summer: Fair (hot)
Fall: Good
Winter: Poor, snowy
REPORT

T

10.5 mi.

1.5 mi.

Sedona

89A

Y

Driving Distance One Way, Miles: 10.5
Hiking Distance One Way, Miles: 1.5

Thunder Mountain Trail

General Information
Location Map D4
Sedona and Wilson Mountain USGS Maps
Coconino Forest Service Map

Driving Distance One Way: 4.3 miles *6.9 km* (Time 15 minutes)
Access Road: All cars, All paved
Hiking Distance One Way: 2.0 miles *3.2 km*
How Strenuous: Easy
Features: Rock formations, Views

NUTSHELL: Near town, this trail provides a nice hike, and connects to other good trails.

DIRECTIONS:
From the Sedona Y (the intersection of Highways 179 and 89A) Go:
Southwest on Highway 89A (toward Cottonwood) for 3.2 miles *5.1 km* (MP 371) then turn right on Dry Creek Road (stoplight) **(1)** and drive it to the 3.7 mile *5.9 km* point **(2)**. Turn right on Thunder Mountain Road and drive to the 4.3 miles *6.9 km* point **(3)**, then turn left into the trail parking lot.

TRAILHEAD: At the three-panel map/sign.

DESCRIPTION: From the parking area, you walk north, toward the redrock buttes. At 0.1 miles *0.16 km* you reach a trail junction. Turn right here. This is the beginning of the Thunder Mountain Trail. The trail moves easily to the east, holding to one contour with only a few dips and rises.

At 0.6 miles *1.0 km* you reach another trail junction. The trail to the right goes downhill. Go straight ahead. At 0.75 miles *1.2 km* you come to another trail junction. The trail to the left goes up to Chimney Rock. Keep going straight.

As you continue you will see a large number of social trails. Many of these come up from the subdivision to your right so you are not likely to go off in the wrong direction on them. Others are not so easy to distinguish. So keep alert.

You are very close to habitation to your right as you walk along this trail, but there is enough of a screen between you and the subdivisions to create a feeling of being out in the country. The views to your left are wonderful.

At 2.0 miles *3.2 km* you are under a powerline at a wash, where you find another trail junction. To your right is a connection coming north from the Little Elf parking lot (see **Sugarloaf Loop**). The Thunder Mountain Trail ends and the Teacup Trail begins at this trail junction.

Photo: Thunder Mountain's edges are composed of weathered spires and this trail takes you along the base of the mountain to enjoy looking at them.

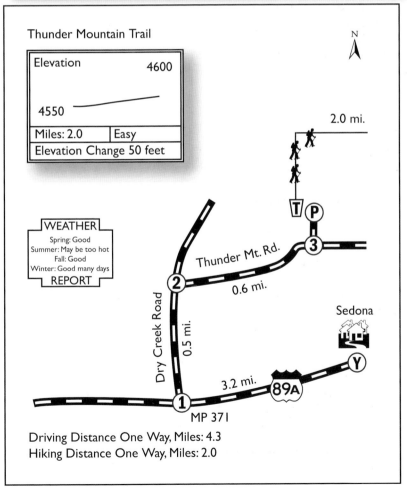

Thunder Mountain Trail

N

Elevation   4600

4550

Miles: 2.0	Easy
Elevation Change 50 feet	

2.0 mi.

WEATHER
Spring: Good
Summer: May be too hot
Fall: Good
Winter: Good many days
REPORT

T P
3

Thunder Mt. Rd.

0.6 mi.

2

Dry Creek Road

0.5 mi.

Sedona

3.2 mi.   89A   Y

1

MP 371

Driving Distance One Way, Miles: 4.3
Hiking Distance One Way, Miles: 2.0

Turkey Creek Trail #92

General Information
Location Map F3
Sedona USGS Map
Coconino Forest Service Map

Driving Distance One Way: 11.9 miles *19.0 km* (Time 30 minutes)
Access Road: All cars, Last 1.7 miles *2.7 km* good dirt roads
Hiking Distance One Way: 3.5 miles *5.6 km* (Time 2.0 hours)
How Strenuous: Hard
Features: Rock formations, Views, Backcountry solitude

NUTSHELL: This hard hike takes you through interesting redrocks to the top of House Mountain.

DIRECTIONS:
From the Sedona Y (the intersection of Highways 179 and 89A) Go:
   South on Highway 179 (toward Phoenix) for 7.2 miles *11.5 km* (MP 306.1), then turn right on the Verde Valley School Road (stoplight) **(1)**. Follow it to the 11.3 mile *18.1 km* point where you will see a sign for the **Turkey Creek Trail**. Turn left onto FR 9216B, a dirt road **(2)**. Any vehicle with medium clearance can handle the dirt road. At 11.9 miles *19.0 km* is a parking area.

TRAILHEAD: From the parking area you have to walk 1.5 miles *2.4 km* to get to the trailhead, which is located at Turkey Creek Tank.

DESCRIPTION: At the parking place, you will see an old road to the south that is closed by a barrier of stones. Walk this road for 0.25 miles *0.4 km*, to a V-junction. The fork to your right (SW) is the trail to Turkey Creek and it is marked with wired cairns. The fork to the left (SE) goes to **Twin Pillars**.
   Keep going down the road. At 1.5 miles *2.4 km* you reach Turkey Creek Tank flanked by cottonwood trees. The hiking trail starts at its farthest edge and follows a former jeep road. It changes to a footpath at 2.0 miles *3.2 km,* which winds through a hidden backcountry wonderland of superb redrocks.
   In this colorful remote basin you climb House Mountain on an old steep livestock trail that zigzags to a saddle on the top, where you crest out on the rim of an extinct volcanic crater, a rather flat and shallow one. From that point you can take the trail down into the bowl of the crater, though there isn't much to see there. We prefer to bushwhack along the rim to the north for the fine views of Sedona, which are magnificent from there. The mountain's high point is to the north, a basalt hump worth scaling. Old-timers say that there was a stone pillar on top of the hump which looked like a chimney on a house, giving the name House Mountain. Lightning brought down the pillar.

Photo: Portions of this trail are highly scenic and the area through which it passes is remote, giving a great sense of being "out there."

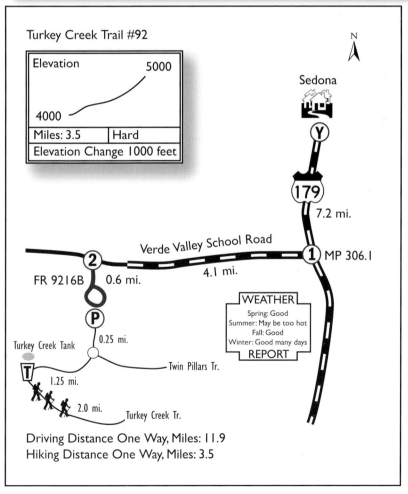

Turkey Creek Trail #92

Elevation	5000
4000	

Miles: 3.5	Hard
Elevation Change 1000 feet	

N

Sedona

Y

179

7.2 mi.

Verde Valley School Road

2

FR 9216B   0.6 mi.

1   MP 306.1

4.1 mi.

P

WEATHER

Spring: Good
Summer: May be too hot
Fall: Good
Winter: Good many days

REPORT

Turkey Creek Tank

0.25 mi.

T

Twin Pillars Tr.

1.25 mi.

2.0 mi.   Turkey Creek Tr.

Driving Distance One Way, Miles: 11.9
Hiking Distance One Way, Miles: 3.5

Twin Pillars

General Information
Location Map F4
Sedona USGS Map
Coconino Forest Service Map

Driving Distance One Way: 11.9 miles *19.0 km* (Time 30 minutes)
Access Road: All cars, Last 1.7 miles *2.7 km* good dirt roads
Hiking Distance One Way: 1.0 miles *1.6 km* (Time 45 minutes)
How Strenuous: Moderate
Features: Rock formations, Views

NUTSHELL: You climb to a redrock saddle overlooking the Verde Valley School.

DIRECTIONS:
From the Sedona Y (the intersection of Highways 179 and 89A) Go:
South on Highway 179 (toward Phoenix) for 7.2 miles *11.5 km* (MP 306.1), then turn right on the Verde Valley School Road (stoplight) **(1)**. Follow it to the 11.3 mile *18.1 km* point where you will see a sign for the **Turkey Creek Trail**. Turn left onto FR 9216B, a dirt road **(2)**. Any vehicle with medium clearance can handle the road. At 11.9 miles *19.0 km* is a parking area.

TRAILHEAD: Not marked. The trail begins where you park.

DESCRIPTION: At the parking place, you will see an old road to the south that is closed by a barrier of stones. Walk down this road for 0.25 miles *0.4 km*, where you will find a V-junction. The fork to your right (SW) is the fork for the **Turkey Creek Trail**. Take the fork to the left (SE).
You will continue to walk down a closed road that takes you ever closer to a redrock butte. The road ends at the foot of the butte, 0.5 miles *0.8 km* from the parking place, against a red wall, where you will see a foot trail going uphill.
Though the trail is not marked, you will have no trouble following it. The path winds around in such a fashion that it makes good use of the terrain to climb the butte gradually. It is not very steep, rising 200 feet in 0.35 miles *0.6 km*. As you climb you rise high enough to get views of pretty country.
At the top you come onto the saddle. The Twin Pillars for which we named the hike are to your right (S). We could find no name for this place on any map, so we christened it after these prominent redrock pillars. From the saddle you look down onto the Verde Valley School, where there are white buildings with red roofs in a beautiful setting.

Photo: Dick is headed toward the twin pillars, which are clearly seen here.

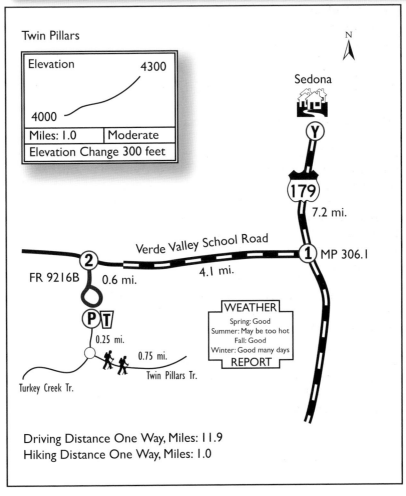

Twin Pillars

Elevation 4300
4000
Miles: 1.0 | Moderate
Elevation Change 300 feet

N

Sedona

Y

179

7.2 mi.

Verde Valley School Road

2 FR 9216B 0.6 mi.

1 MP 306.1

4.1 mi.

P T

0.25 mi.

0.75 mi.

Twin Pillars Tr.

Turkey Creek Tr.

WEATHER
Spring: Good
Summer: May be too hot
Fall: Good
Winter: Good many days
REPORT

Driving Distance One Way, Miles: 11.9
Hiking Distance One Way, Miles: 1.0

Two Fences Trail

General Information
Location Map D3
Loy Butte and Wilson Mt. USGS Maps
Coconino Forest Service Map

Driving Distance One Way: 5.2 miles *8.3 km* (Time 15 minutes)
Access Road: All paved
Hiking Distance One Way: 2.1 miles *3.4 km* (Time 1 hour and 15 minutes)
How Strenuous: Easy
Features: Easy little diversion close to town and easy to reach.

NUTSHELL: This trail is designed to give access to the backcountry to residents of subdivisions along the Dry Creek Road. It's not a major trail but is pleasant and adds something new to the system.

DIRECTIONS:
From the Sedona Y (the intersection of Highways 179 and 89A) Go:
   Southwest on Highway 89A (toward Cottonwood) for 3.2 miles *5.1 km* (MP 371) then turn right on Dry Creek Road (stoplight) **(1)** and proceed to the 5.2 mile *8.3 km* point, where FR 152, the Vultee Arch Road, goes right **(2)**. Don't take the Vultee Arch Road. Instead, look to your left, below the road, and you will see a small trail sign on a post. Park on the apron as near to this sign as you can get. There is no designated parking.

TRAILHEAD: An orphan. Start at the trail sign mentioned above. It marks the Girdner Trail.

DESCRIPTION: Start by hiking the Girdner Trail. At 1.1 miles *1.8 km* you will reach the trailhead for the Two Fences Trail. From this starting point, the Two Fences Trail moves easterly along the bank of an unnamed wash. It runs parallel to the Girdner Trail at first but you can't see the Girdner because of the vegetation. Soon it veers away from the Girdner.
   At 1.5 miles *2.4 km* you will see how the trail got its name, when you reach the two fences. The barbed wire fence on your right marks the boundary of private property, an upscale subdivision in which there are huge homes. The fence on your left marks public land. There is a lane between the two fences about ten feet wide (3 meters), and this trail uses that lane.
   The trail meets the Dry Creek Road. As you get very close to the road, the trail's end becomes ambiguous. It has been very easy to follow up to this point. No matter. We suggest that you end it by turning around when you are close to the paving and retracing your footsteps back to your car, although you could turn left and walk down the road instead.

Photo: The Two Fences trail crosses a little wash that has been worn down to the bedrock over time.

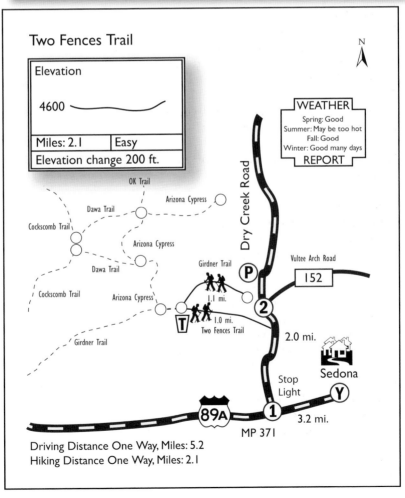

Two Fences Trail

Elevation

4600

Miles: 2.1	Easy
Elevation change 200 ft.	

N

WEATHER

Spring: Good
Summer: May be too hot
Fall: Good
Winter: Good many days

REPORT

OK Trail

Arizona Cypress

Dawa Trail

Cockscomb Trail

Arizona Cypress

Dawa Trail

Cockscomb Trail

Arizona Cypress

Girdner Trail

Dry Creek Road

Vultee Arch Road

152

Girdner Trail

P

1.1 mi.

2

1.0 mi.
Two Fences Trail

T

2.0 mi.

Sedona

Stop
Light

Y

89A

3.2 mi.

1

MP 371

Driving Distance One Way, Miles: 5.2
Hiking Distance One Way, Miles: 2.1

Van Deren Cabin

General Information
Location Map C4
Wilson Mt. USGS Map
Coconino Forest Service Map

Driving Distance One Way: 7.7 miles *12.4 km* (Time 30 minutes)
Access Road: Most cars, Last 2.5 miles *4.0 km* medium dirt road
Hiking Distance One Way: 0.5 miles *0.8 km* (Time 30 minutes)
How Strenuous: Easy
Features: Historic cabin, Views

NUTSHELL: This is a short easy hike to a historic cabin.

DIRECTIONS:
From the Sedona Y (the intersection of Highways 179 and 89A) Go:
    Southwest on Highway 89A (toward Cottonwood) for 3.2 miles *5.1 km* (MP 371) and then turn right on the Dry Creek Road (stoplight) **(1)** and follow it to the 5.2 mile *8.3 km* point. Turn right on unpaved FR 152 (sign for Vultee Arch, etc.) **(2)**. Follow the road to the 7.7 miles *12.4 km* point, turn right into the signed Brins Mesa Trail parking lot **(3)**, and park there.

TRAILHEAD: None. Start walking from the parking lot.

DESCRIPTION: Walk back down the road (retracing the last 0.1 mile you drove) for 0.1 miles *0.16 km* and then turn right on an unmarked dirt road that meets the main road at an acute angle. The jeep tours drive the road regularly but we think it is too rough for cars. At 0.2 miles *0.3 km* the road fords Dry Creek. If the water is high you might want to wait for another day. When you cross the creek the road goes to the top of the bank on the other side. The road forks there. Take the left fork and follow it to its end. From there you will see the shiny metal roof of the cabin. Walk over to it.
    The old homestead was composed of several acres, but the Forest Service purchased the cabin site only, and has devoted it to public use. The remainder of the old ranch is private property being developed as a subdivision.
    The cabin was placed on the site by pioneer Earl Van Deren in the 1890s. The oldest part is to your left as you face the building when first walking up to it. After he built the cabin, Earl fell in love but his fiancée refused to marry him until he had a larger home for them to live in. He added the second unit and connected the two buildings with a roof, forming a breezeway. This expansion satisfied his fiancée, and they married.

Photo: It is fascinating to visit this old cabin and to try to imagine what it would have been like to live there decades ago, when Sedona was a village.

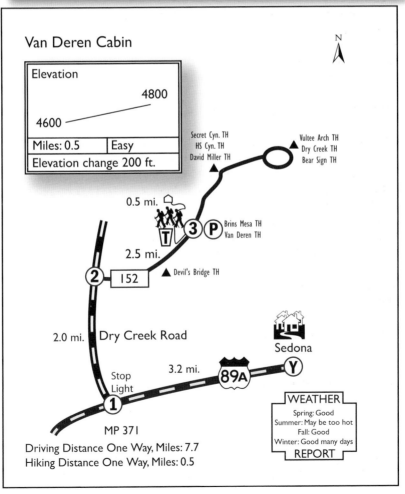

Van Deren Cabin

N

Elevation

4800

4600

Miles: 0.5	Easy
Elevation change 200 ft.	

Secret Cyn. TH
HS Cyn. TH
David Miller TH

Vultee Arch TH
Dry Creek TH
Bear Sign TH

0.5 mi.

3 P Brins Mesa TH
Van Deren TH

2.5 mi.

2 152 ▲ Devil's Bridge TH

2.0 mi. Dry Creek Road

Sedona

Stop
Light

3.2 mi. 89A Y

1

MP 371

Driving Distance One Way, Miles: 7.7
Hiking Distance One Way, Miles: 0.5

WEATHER

Spring: Good
Summer: May be too hot
Fall: Good
Winter: Good many days

REPORT

V-Bar-V Petroglyphs

General Information
Location Map G6
Casner Butte USGS Map
Coconino Forest Service Map

Driving Distance One Way: 17.4 miles *27.8 km* (Time 25 minutes)
Access Road: All vehicles, Short segment of good dirt road
Hiking Distance, Complete Loop: 1.1 miles *1.8 km* (Time 30 minutes)
How Strenuous: Easy
Features: Superb prehistoric rock art panels

NUTSHELL: Located on an old ranch in the Wet Beaver Creek country, this easy hike takes you to a wonderful protected rock art site.

DIRECTIONS:
From the Sedona Y (the intersection of Highways 179 and 89A) Go:
    South on Highway 179 (toward Phoenix) for 14.7 miles *23.5 km*, to the I-17 Interchange (1). Instead of going onto I-17, go underneath it and get onto the paved county road 618. You will pass the Beaver Creek Ranger Station and the bridge over Beaver Creek, where the paving ends. Just after the paving ends, you will reach a three-way fork at 17.4 miles *27.8 km,* where you will see a V—V Heritage Site (right) (2). Go through the gate and proceed to the parking lot. NOTICE: This site is gated and the hours of visitation are controlled. As we write this, it is open from 9:30 am to 3:30 pm, Friday to Monday. An entry fee is charged, of $3 per adult, although the sign says also that Red Rock passes are honored. Children under 17 are admitted free.

TRAILHEAD: At the Visitor Center.

DESCRIPTION: From the parking lot walk to the Visitor Center, pay your fee and ask for information. There is a toilet at the center.
    Follow the trail signs. You will immediately come to a chimney, all that remains of the 1930 ranch house. Notice the V—V inlaid into it with redrock. You then enjoy a short segment shaded by big trees, break out into a clearing and then come to the rock art site, a small area against red cliffs enclosed by an eight-foot high chain link fence. There is a gatekeeper's hut at the site, where a ranger is stationed to open and close the gate, protect the property and answer questions. Enter and enjoy.
    On the way back you will walk through open fields to the parking area.

Photo: The picture shows only a small portion of the rock art at this site.

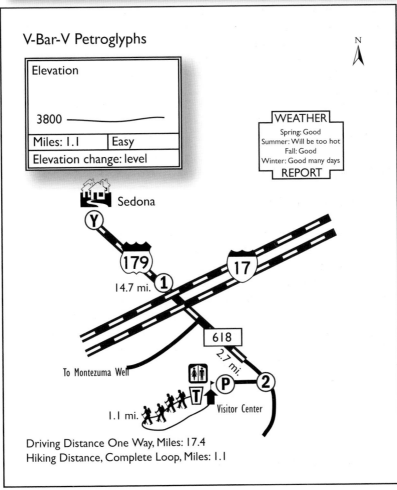

V-Bar-V Petroglyphs

N

Elevation	
3800 ———————	
Miles: 1.1	Easy
Elevation change: level	

WEATHER
Spring: Good
Summer: Will be too hot
Fall: Good
Winter: Good many days
REPORT

Sedona

Y

179 · 1 · 17

14.7 mi.

618

2.7 mi.

To Montezuma Well

P · T · 2

1.1 mi.

Visitor Center

Driving Distance One Way, Miles: 17.4
Hiking Distance, Complete Loop, Miles: 1.1

Vultee Arch Trail #22

General Information
Location Map C4
Loy Butte and Wilson Mt. USGS Maps
Coconino Forest Service Map

Driving Distance One Way: 9.6 miles *15.4 km* (Time 45 minutes)
Access Road: Last 4.4 miles *7.0 km* dirt road, but OK for most cars
Hiking Distance One Way: 1.6 miles *2.6 km* (Time 1 hour)
How Strenuous: Moderate
Features: Arch, Historic marker, Scenic canyon

NUTSHELL: This easy-to-reach hike located near Sedona takes you to a natural arch and a commemorative bronze plaque in a beautiful box canyon. **A personal favorite.**

DIRECTIONS:
From the Sedona Y (the junction of Highways 179 and 89A) Go:
Southwest on Highway 89A (toward Cottonwood) for 3.2 miles *5.1 km* (MP 371) to Dry Creek Road **(1)**. Turn right on Dry Creek Road and drive to the 5.2 mile *8.3 km* point **(2)**. Turn right on FR 152, the Vultee Arch Road, and follow it to its end at 9.6 miles *15.4 km.*

TRAILHEAD: At the three-panel map/bulletin board.

DESCRIPTION: The hiking trail is sandy and gives nice soft footing. The trail climbs gently as it progresses, passing through several life zones with interesting changes in the vegetation. At first you are in a forest of Arizona cypress. Then you pass through oak and pine and Douglas fir. The route is shaded the entire way, making it a good trail in hot weather.

The trail crosses a creek bed several times, so don't try to hike it when a lot of water is running. The creek is dry except for a few weeks in the spring or after a hard summer rain.

At 1.7 miles *2.7 km* you will reach a junction where the **Sterling Pass Trail** forks to the right.

Just beyond this you will break out into a clearing in a box canyon and the trail will climb onto redrock ledges. You will see Vultee Arch to your left. There is a trail leading to it that you can easily pick up. It is possible to walk right up to the arch and even to climb on top of it.

The historical bronze plaque is fastened to the face of the second tier of redrock ledges. It commemorates the airplane crash that killed aviation pioneer Gerald Vultee and his wife in 1938. They crashed on nearby East Pocket, when they were caught in a storm at night.

Photo: The Vultee Arch spans a wash and can be hard to see at times.

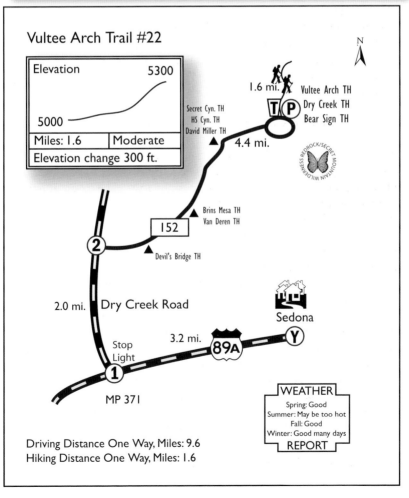

Vultee Arch Trail #22

Elevation
5300

5000

| Miles: 1.6 | Moderate |

Elevation change 300 ft.

N

1.6 mi.

Vultee Arch TH
Dry Creek TH
Bear Sign TH

T P

Secret Cyn. TH
HS Cyn. TH
David Miller TH

4.4 mi.

REDROCK/SECRET MOUNTAIN WILDERNESS

Brins Mesa TH
Van Deren TH

152

2

Devil's Bridge TH

Sedona

2.0 mi.   Dry Creek Road

Stop
Light

3.2 mi.   89A   Y

1

MP 371

Driving Distance One Way, Miles: 9.6
Hiking Distance One Way, Miles: 1.6

WEATHER
Spring: Good
Summer: May be too hot
Fall: Good
Winter: Good many days
REPORT

Weir Trail #85

General Information
Location Map G6
Apache Maid and Casner Butte USGS Maps
Coconino Forest Service Map

Driving Distance One Way: 17.0 miles *27.2 km* (Time 30 minutes)
Access Road: All cars, Last 0.1 mile *0.2 km* is a good gravel road
Hiking Distance One Way: 3.0 miles *4.8 km* (Time 2.25 hours)
How Strenuous: Moderate
Features: Permanent Stream, Steep-walled canyon, Redrock, Pools

NUTSHELL: You hike a historic cattle trail along the west bank of Wet Beaver Creek on the Bell Trail, then veer off through redrocks to the water.

DIRECTIONS:
From the Sedona Y (the intersection of Highways 179 and 89A) Go:
    South on Highway 179 (toward Phoenix) for 14.7 miles *23.5 km* (MP 298.9), to the I-17 intersection **(1)**. Go straight rather than getting on I-17. Follow paved FR 618 until you see a sign for Beaver Creek Ranger Station and trailheads at 16.9 miles *27.1 km* **(2)**. Turn left and drive to the new (opened in the spring of 2004) parking area at 17.0 miles *27.2 km*.

TRAILHEAD: At the parking lot. Follow the Bell Trail signs.

DESCRIPTION: You must hike the Bell Trail for 2.5 miles *4.0 km* to reach the Weir Trailhead. Cattle rancher Charles Bell built the main trail in 1932, to take cattle to the top of the Mogollon Rim in the spring and return them in the fall and it is an old jeep road up to the Weir Trail junction.
    At about 0.8 miles *1.3 km*, look for a large boulder on the left side of the trail. Facing away from you are a number of interesting petroglyphs.
    At 1.7 miles *2.7 km* you will find the **White Mesa Trail #86** to your left. You enter the wilderness here. At the 2.2 mile *3.5 km* point you will hit a fork where the **Apache Maid Trail #15** branches to the left and climbs Casner Butte. Continue hiking the Bell Trail.
    About 0.25 miles *0.4 km* beyond this fork you will find the junction with the Weir Trail. There is a sign. The Weir Trail goes to the right, down to the water. The trail is well marked and goes into a most attractive area where you get up close and personal with lovely redrock buttes. The trail winds down the face of them to the creek. There you find the weir, a low dam, at a gaging station, where water flow is measured. The place has beautiful big trees and redrocks, with a sandy beach and a pool. You can explore along the creek or go back up a bit and play around the redrocks.

Photo: This is the most interesting part of the Weir Trail, where it passes through redrock formations and goes down to the waters of Wet Beaver Creek.

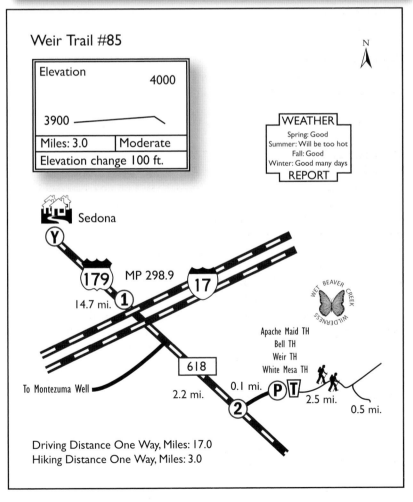

Weir Trail #85

Elevation	
	4000
3900	
Miles: 3.0	Moderate
Elevation change 100 ft.	

N

WEATHER
Spring: Good
Summer: Will be too hot
Fall: Good
Winter: Good many days
REPORT

Sedona

Y

179 MP 298.9 **17**

14.7 mi. **1**

WET BEAVER CREEK WILDERNESS

Apache Maid TH
Bell TH
Weir TH
White Mesa TH

618

To Montezuma Well

2.2 mi. 0.1 mi. **P T**

2 2.5 mi.

0.5 mi.

Driving Distance One Way, Miles: 17.0
Hiking Distance One Way, Miles: 3.0

West Clear Creek Trail #17

General Information
Location Map G6
Buckhorn Mtn., Walker Mtn. USGS Maps
Coconino Forest Service Map

Driving Distance One Way: 29.5 miles *47.2 km* (Time 1 hour)
Access Road: All cars, Last 12.3 miles *19.7 km* good dirt road
Hiking Distance One Way: 1.5 miles *2.4 km* (Time 45 minutes)
How Strenuous: Easy
Features: Historic ranch, Permanent creek, Beautiful redrocks

NUTSHELL: This easy trail takes you through an interesting old ranch to a lovely creek in a deep scenic canyon.

DIRECTIONS:
From the Sedona Y (the intersection of Highways 179 and 89A) Go:
   South on Highway 179 (toward Phoenix) for 14.7 miles *23.5 km*, to the I-17 Interchange **(1)**. Instead of going onto I-17, go underneath it onto paved road FR 618. The paving ends at the Beaver Creek Bridge. Stay on FR 618. At 26.5 miles *42.4 km* you will come to a road to the left (FR 215) to the West Clear Creek Campground **(2)**. Turn left on FR 215 and go to the 29.5 mile *47.2 km* point, all the way to the end, where the road is blocked by a steel pole fence. There is a parking area here.

TRAILHEAD: At the gate in the fence.

DESCRIPTION: This trail takes you across the old Bull Pen Ranch. Go through the gate and follow the signs. The trail passes through a lush riparian forest, then scrubland, and finally an open field.
   To your left as you walk the length of the field you see a rock house with cactus growing on its roof. Behind the rock house, on the north side of the canyon, there is a ledge of red sandstone adding a welcome touch of color to the landscape. The ranch site is truly beautiful.
   You walk to the end of the field and then the trail dips down to the creek. There you will find redrock ledges just above the water that seem to have been placed there by nature as places to sit and take the sun and watch the creek gurgle by.
   The trail continues, hugging the red cliffs and almost hidden by the vegetation. You will encounter old irrigation pipe, and if you pay attention, you can see that the trail follows the pipeline. It ends at another lovely pool at 1.5 miles *2.4 km.*

Photo: One of the many pleasant pools that greet you on this great trail.

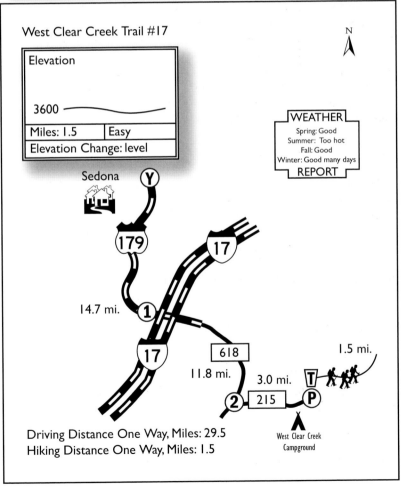

West Clear Creek Trail #17

N

Elevation	
3600	
Miles: 1.5	Easy
Elevation Change: level	

WEATHER
Spring: Good
Summer: Too hot
Fall: Good
Winter: Good many days
REPORT

Sedona **Y**

179 **17**

14.7 mi. **1**

17 618 1.5 mi.

11.8 mi. 3.0 mi. **T**

2 215 **P**

West Clear Creek
Campground

Driving Distance One Way, Miles: 29.5
Hiking Distance One Way, Miles: 1.5

West Fork Trail #108

General Information
Location Map B5
Dutton Hill and Munds Park USGS Maps
Coconino Forest Service Map

Driving Distance One Way: 10.5 miles *16.8 km* (Time 20 minutes)
Access Road: All cars, All paved
Hiking Distance One Way: 3.0 miles *4.8 km* (Time 90 minutes)
How Strenuous: Moderate
Features: Gorgeous canyon with stream

NUTSHELL: One of the best and most popular hikes in Arizona, a streamside trail in a magic canyon. **A personal favorite**.

DIRECTIONS:
From the Sedona Y (the intersection of Highways 179 and 89A) Go:
   North on Highway 89A (toward Flagstaff) for a distance of 10.5 miles *16.8 km* (MP 384.7) **(1).** You will see a road sign for the parking area, which requires a sharp turn to your left (W). An entry fee is required.

TRAILHEAD: At the parking lot.

DESCRIPTION: Cross over Oak Creek on the footbridge, climb up the opposite bank and turn left (S) on a wide sandy track. Soon you will draw abreast of houses across the creek. Just beyond the last house, you will walk through the ruins of Mayhew's Lodge. This point is at 0.3 miles *0.5 km.*
   The Dad Thomas family (**Thomas Point Trail**) built a home here, which was remodeled as a hunting and fishing lodge in the early 1900s. Carl Mayhew bought and enlarged it in 1925. Zane Grey used the location as the setting for his novel *The Call of the Canyon.* The Forest Service bought the lodge in 1969 only to have it burn in 1980.
   As you enter the West Fork canyon you are aware of its charm, with the gentle stream flowing through a lush habitat framed by tremendously high colorful canyon walls—a magic place. The trail follows the streambed, crossing back and forth over the water. At the crossings you will find stepping stones that allow you to get across, but count on getting your feet wet.
   The canyon is narrow, so you are often right next to the cliffs. The stream has undercut them in many places, creating interesting overhangs. You feel the majesty of the canyon on this hike, for the cliffs absolutely dwarf you. The canyon is 12.0 miles *19.2 km* long. The official trail stops at 3.0 miles *4.8 km,* a distance that allows you to see some of the finest parts. Don't try to make the full hike without special preparations.

Photo: The stream has undercut the redrock, creating a magnificent over-hang, just one of the beauties of this very special place.

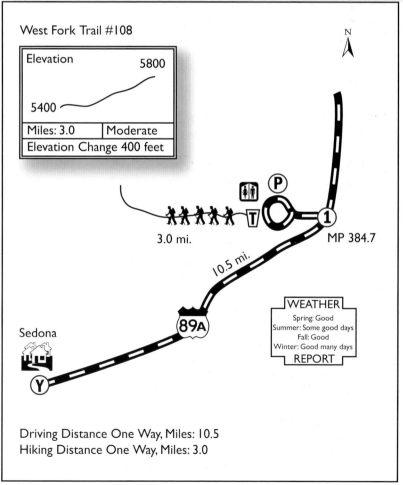

West Fork Trail #108

Elevation 5800

5400

Miles: 3.0 | Moderate
Elevation Change 400 feet

3.0 mi.

10.5 mi.

MP 384.7

Sedona

89A

WEATHER
Spring: Good
Summer: Some good days
Fall: Good
Winter: Good many days
REPORT

Driving Distance One Way, Miles: 10.5
Hiking Distance One Way, Miles: 3.0

White Mesa Trail #86

General Information
Location Map G6
Casner Butte USGS Map
Coconino Forest Service Map

Driving Distance One Way: 17.0 miles *27.2 km* (Time 30 minutes)
Access Road: All cars, Last 0.1 miles *0.2 km* is a good gravel road
Hiking Distance One Way: 2.4 miles *3.8 km* (Time 1.5 hours)
How Strenuous: Hard
Features: Permanent Stream, Rock Art, Views

NUTSHELL: This trail follows the Bell Trail along the banks of Wet Beaver Creek and then branches off to climb to the top of a mesa.

DIRECTIONS:
From the Sedona Y (the intersection of Highways 179 and 89A) Go:
South on Highway 179 (toward Phoenix) for 14.7 miles *23.5 km* (MP 298.9), to the I-17 intersection **(1)**. Go straight under the freeway rather than getting on it. Follow paved road FR 618 until you see a sign for Beaver Creek Ranger Station and trailheads at 16.9 miles *27.1 km* **(2)**. Turn left. Park in the new (opened in the spring of 2004) lot at 17.0 miles *27.2 km*.

TRAILHEAD: Several hiking trails here share a common trailhead that is well marked with signs at the parking area. (See the map).

DESCRIPTION: From the trailhead follow the **Bell Trail** along Wet Beaver Creek. The trail is an old road, broad and easy to walk. It was built by cattle rancher Charles Bell in 1932, as a means for taking his cattle to the top of the Mogollon Rim. The White Mesa trail is another historic cattle trail.
     At about 0.8 miles *1.3 km*, there is a large boulder on the left side of the trail with a number of interesting petroglyphs on the side facing north.
     The White Mesa Trail starts 1.7 miles *2.7 km* from the parking lot. There is a small sign and a log stand. The rocky trail goes up the south wall of Casner Canyon in a straight line, climbing 1,000 feet in 0.7 miles *1.2 km*. Along the way you are treated to good views and some shows of colorful redrock.
     The top of the mesa is covered by a thick layer of lava forming sheer cliffs. This trail takes advantage of a gap in the lava and emerges at the top. The trail ends abruptly at a cairn at a point 2.4 miles *3.8 km* from the parking lot.
     We suggest that you turn left and walk to the edge of the mesa overlooking Beaver Creek (about 0.2 miles *0.32 km*) for some excellent views of Wet Beaver Creek and the surrounding area.

Photo: Rocks and cactus are your companions as you make this steep climb.

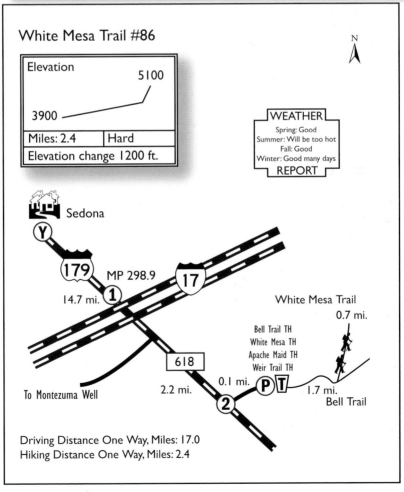

White Mesa Trail #86

N
↑

Elevation

5100

3900

| Miles: 2.4 | Hard |

Elevation change 1200 ft.

WEATHER
Spring: Good
Summer: Will be too hot
Fall: Good
Winter: Good many days
REPORT

Sedona

Y

179 MP 298.9 **17**

14.7 mi. **1**

White Mesa Trail

0.7 mi.

Bell Trail TH
White Mesa TH
Apache Maid TH
Weir Trail TH

618

0.1 mi. **P T**

To Montezuma Well

2.2 mi. **2**

1.7 mi.
Bell Trail

Driving Distance One Way, Miles: 17.0
Hiking Distance One Way, Miles: 2.4

Wilson Canyon Trail #49

General Information
Location Map D5
Munds Park USGS Map
Coconino Forest Service Map

Driving Distance One Way: 1.1 miles *1.8 km* (Time 5 minutes)
Access Road: All cars, All paved
Hiking Distance One Way: 1.5 miles *2.4 km* (Time 1 hour)
How Strenuous: Moderate
Features: Views, Near Sedona

NUTSHELL: Wilson Canyon is spanned by Midgley Bridge. You walk along the banks of the canyon and then climb out for magnificent views.

DIRECTIONS:
From the Sedona Y (the junction of Highways 179 and 89A) Go:
    North on Highway 89A (toward Flagstaff) for 1.1 miles *1.8 km* (MP 375.9). Go over Midgley Bridge **(1)** and turn left into the parking area **(P)**.

TRAILHEAD: At the back of the parking lot.

DESCRIPTION: This is a very popular spot and you may not find parking. If not, go up the road a bit. There are several wide shoulders for parking.
    Walk to the picnic tables at the end of the parking lot. There you'll find the Wilson Monument, a bronze plaque set in stone, a three-panel map/sign and beyond that two rusty signs. Take the one to Wilson Canyon #49.
    The Wilson Canyon hike is little more than a leisurely stroll at first, as you walk along the old highway alignment. Turn around and look at Midgley Bridge as you go and imagine what the highway would have been without it. At the end of the old highway the trail changes to a footpath and the canyon becomes shallow. You will cross the bed of the canyon twelve times, always walking along one bank or the other. Cairns in wire cages mark the way.
    At about 0.5 miles *0.8 km* you will see a footpath going uphill to your left. This is the end of the **Jim Thompson Trail.** Beyond this point you enter the Redrock-Secret Mountain Wilderness.
    Wilson Canyon is not deep but your views are confined to the banks of the canyon by the trees and shrubs. The canyon itself is quite attractive and delightful and the going is easy. You will begin to get some glimpses of very high towers and formations as you go. Near the end of the trail it lifts out of the canyon and goes to the top of a red knob. This is by far the hardest part of the trail but is well worth the effort, as you emerge in a box canyon against Wilson Mountain where you enjoy truly stunning views.

Photo: Dick is walking along the early part of the trail, which was an old road. It dips down into the scenic canyon from here.

Wilson Canyon Trail #49

N

Elevation	
4900	
4500	
Miles: 1.5	Moderate
Elevation change 400 ft.	

WEATHER
Spring: Good
Summer: May be too hot
Fall: Good
Winter: Good many days
REPORT

REDROCK/SECRET MOUNTAIN WILDERNESS

1.5 mi.

T

P

Sedona   1.1 mi.   89A   1   MP 375.9

Y   Midgley
Bridge

Driving Distance One Way, Miles: 1.1
Hiking Distance One Way, Miles: 1.5

Wilson Mountain North Trail #123

General Information
Location Map C5
Munds Park and Wilson Mt. USGS Maps
Coconino Forest Service Map

Driving Distance One Way: 5.3 miles *8.5 km* (Time 10 minutes)
Access Road: All cars, All paved
Hiking Distance One Way: 4.3 miles *6.9 km* (Time 4.0 hours)
How Strenuous: Hard
Features: Views

NUTSHELL: Located just north of Sedona, Wilson is the highest mountain in the area. This trail climbs Wilson's north face.

DIRECTIONS:
From the Sedona Y (the intersection of Highways 179 and 89A) Go:
    North on Highway 89A (toward Flagstaff) for a distance of 5.3 miles *8.5 km* (MP 379.5), then turn left into the Encinoso Picnic Area and park **(1)**.

TRAILHEAD: At the north end of the parking lot. There is a big sign.

DESCRIPTION: The trail climbs to the top of a small ridge at about 0.25 miles *0.4 km*, where you have a good vantage point to look across the canyon at the cliffs of the east wall, where the Encinoso Waterfall sometimes runs.
    From this ridge the trail climbs gently for another 0.75 miles *1.2 km* along a refreshing, wooded side canyon through a lovely mixed forest.
    At 1.0 miles *1.6 km* the serious work begins. Here the canyon pinches in and the trail begins a steep climb. You will ascend 1,300 feet in 0.5 miles *0.8 km*. If you want an easy hike, the 1.0 mile point is the place to stop.
    After this hard haul, you top out on a flat flank of Wilson called First Bench. You will have great views to the north from here. Across Oak Creek Canyon you will see a major tributary, Munds Canyon, which empties into Oak Creek at Indian Gardens.
    Keep walking south along First Bench. At the 1.8 mile *2.9 km* point, at the edge of First Bench, you will intersect the **Wilson Mt. South Trail** coming up from Midgley Bridge. The junction is well marked with cairns. Take a look off the rim; it's great! This is another good stopping place.
    From this trail junction, you can go to the top of the mountain. See **Wilson Mountain South** for details. You have to hike 1.0 miles *1.6 km* to the Tool Shed, at the top of the mountain, 800 feet, then hike a level trail 1.5 miles *2.4 km* to the North Rim viewpoint, a total of 4.3 miles *6.9 km* from Encinoso.

Photo: This photo was taken from a bench on this trail. You are looking across Oak Creek Canyon at Encinoso Falls. It seldom runs, but when it does, this trail takes you to the best place from which to view it.

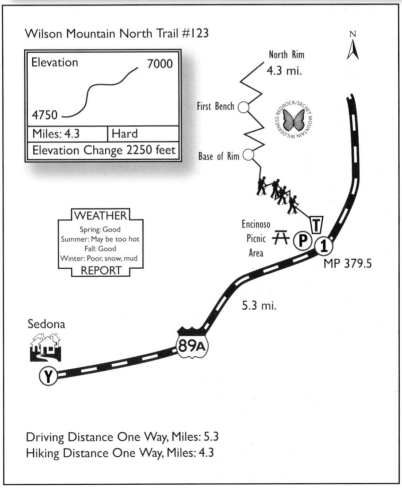

Wilson Mountain North Trail #123

N

Elevation 7000

4750

Miles: 4.3 | Hard

Elevation Change 2250 feet

North Rim
4.3 mi.

First Bench

Base of Rim

REDROCK/SECRET MOUNTAIN WILDERNESS

WEATHER
Spring: Good
Summer: May be too hot
Fall: Good
Winter: Poor, snow, mud
REPORT

Encinoso
Picnic
Area

P ① T

MP 379.5

5.3 mi.

Sedona

89A

Y

Driving Distance One Way, Miles: 5.3
Hiking Distance One Way, Miles: 4.3

Wilson Mountain South Trail #10

General Information
Location Map D5
Munds Park and Wilson Mt. USGS Maps
Coconino Forest Service Map

Driving Distance One Way: 1.1 miles *1.8 km* (Time 5 minutes)
Access Road: All cars, All paved
Hiking Distance One Way: 5.3 miles *8.5 km* (Time 4.5 hours)
How Strenuous: Hard
Features: Views

NUTSHELL: This popular hike starts at Midgley Bridge, north of Sedona, and goes up Wilson Mountain to the highest point in the area.

DIRECTIONS:
From the Sedona Y (the intersection of Highways 179 and 89A) Go:
   North on Highway 89A (toward Flagstaff) for a distance of 1.1 miles *1.8 km* (MP 375.9) **(1)**. Just across Midgley Bridge is the parking area (left).

TRAILHEAD: At the back of the parking lot. Look for the sign.

DESCRIPTION: We divide the trail into three parts:
   1. Midgley Bridge to First Bench, 2.8 miles *4.5 km*, a 1,600' climb;
   2. First Bench to Tool Shed, 1.0 miles *1.6 km*, an 800' climb;
   3. Tool Shed to North Rim, 1.5 miles *2.4 km*, fairly level.
   Midgley Bridge to First Bench: This is a steep climb from the start over a high desert landscape, with juniper, manzanita and cactus. As you rise, you reach an area with little shade where you switchback to the top. Finally you break over the top of First Bench, a long plateau running the length of the east side of the mountain. The views from here are very fine.
   First Bench to the Tool Shed: Take the path going left, toward the high cliffs. You will soon climb above First Bench into a heavy forest of pine and oak. This has a decidedly alpine feeling. After a 500-foot climb you will come onto an intermediate top, where the land is pretty level, then make a modest 300 foot climb to the Tool Shed, where fire-fighting tools are stored. The main trail goes ahead here, with a side trail to the left.
   Tool Shed to North Rim: This is a delightful walk through a cool forest on nearly level ground, very easy compared to the first two phases of the hike. You will be walking out to the mountain's north edge. When you come to a pond on the east side of the trail, you are almost at the end. Keep walking from here and you will soon come out onto a cliff face where you will find a soul-stirring view.

Photo: Wilson Mountain is the highest peak in the Sedona area and this tough trail takes you to the top for truly fine views.

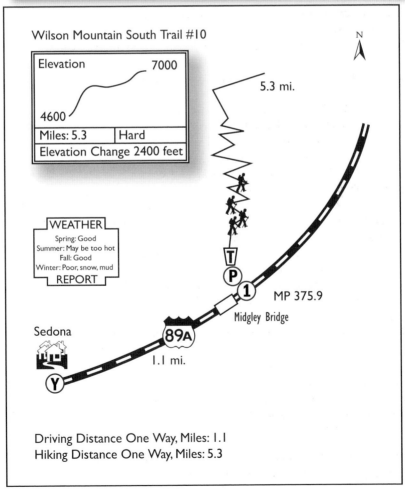

Wilson Mountain South Trail #10

N

Elevation   7000

4600

| Miles: 5.3 | Hard |
| Elevation Change 2400 feet ||

5.3 mi.

WEATHER
Spring: Good
Summer: May be too hot
Fall: Good
Winter: Poor, snow, mud
REPORT

T
P
1   MP 375.9

Midgley Bridge

Sedona

89A
1.1 mi.

Y

Driving Distance One Way, Miles: 1.1
Hiking Distance One Way, Miles: 5.3

Woods Canyon Trail #93

General Information
Location Map G5
Munds Mt. and Sedona USGS Maps
Coconino Forest Service Map

Driving Distance One Way: 8.7 miles *13.9 km* (Time 15 minutes)
Access Road: All cars, Paved except last 0.1 miles *0.16 km*
Hiking Distance One Way: 3.25 miles *5.2 km* (Time 3.5 hours)
How Strenuous: Moderate
Features: Views, Running water (sometimes), Riparian habitat

NUTSHELL: This trail follows Woods Canyon, through which Dry Beaver Creek flows.

DIRECTIONS:
From the Sedona Y (the intersection of Highways 179 and 89A) Go:
South on Highway 179 (toward Phoenix) for 8.6 miles *13.8 km* (MP 304.8) to an unmarked dirt road to your left **(1)**. Turn left on the road, go through the gate and drive down to the parking area.

TRAILHEAD: At the three-panel map/sign at the parking area.

DESCRIPTION: The trail follows old jeep roads at first, bringing you onto the floor of the canyon, where you will see that it is quite an impressive place, with massive high walls. The canyon habitat supports a lush growth of vegetation, including wildflowers in the spring. At 1.1 miles *1.8 km* you will find a trail register. Please sign it. At 2.0 miles *3.2 km* you will come to a fence. Just beyond the fence you will find a sign for the **Hot Loop Trail**, which branches off to the left, going uphill. The Woods Canyon trail goes straight, turning into a footpath.

The water channel is off to your right and you move ever closer to it as you hike, reaching the water's edge at about 3.0 miles *4.8 km*. We recommend going to about 3.25 miles *5.2 km* where the path goes onto a sloping redrock shelf above the water, a very attractive place to sit and enjoy Dry Beaver Creek. We recommend stopping here.

Woods Canyon goes 12.0 miles *19.2 km*, all the way to Interstate-17 at the Fox Ranch Exit where the freeway spans it.

The developed part of the trail dwindles at the 4.0 mile *6.4 km* point. The Forest Service rates the trail as 6.2 miles *9.9 km* long but the last part has difficult footing. To hike the entire length of the canyon is a very rough trip. It can be done, but only by very strong and very well prepared hikers with someone ready to "catch" them at the far end.

Photo: The early part of this trail, shown here, is wide and open, but it narrows as you enter the canyon, where the waters of Dry Beaver Creek sometimes run.

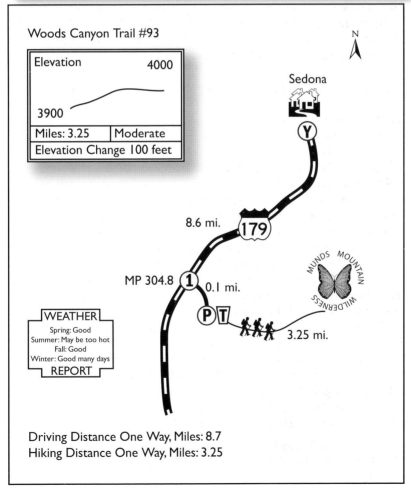

Woods Canyon Trail #93

N

Elevation   4000

3900

| Miles: 3.25 | Moderate |
| Elevation Change 100 feet | |

Sedona

Y

8.6 mi. 179

MP 304.8 1 0.1 mi.

MUNDS MOUNTAIN WILDERNESS

P T 3.25 mi.

Driving Distance One Way, Miles: 8.7
Hiking Distance One Way, Miles: 3.25

Additional Trail Photos

Photo: This viewing platform is found at the end of the Tavasci Marsh Trail at Dead Horse State Park, pages 88-89.

Photo: You can see almost all of the prominent Sedona land formations from the top of Overlook Point, pages 160-161.

Additional Trail Photos

Photo: There are fine views from the Eagle's Nest Trail at Red Rock State Park, pages 178-179.

Photo: Slide Rock, pages 196-197. This shot was taken from the highway, looking out over the creek, with the old apple packing shed as background.

Sedona Vortex Information

Many people claiming to be authorities have spoken about the Sedona Vortexes (or Vortices). Some of them make very specific claims about them, for example, that a particular Vortex is male, female, electric, magnetic, Yin, Yang, etc. These authorities don't always agree with each other about the Vortexes.

We think it is a mistake to go to a Vortex expecting to find a certain anticipated experience. If you do, you may set up a self-fulfillment trap, where you deceive yourself into thinking that you have found what you were told you would find, rather than having your own authentic experience. We recommend that you approach a Vortex openly, seeking no pre-determined result.

The Vortexes are not hard to reach. You could easily visit all of them in a single day if you wish. Approach each one as a reverent seeker, open to what is there for you. Be quiet and unobtrusive so that you do not disturb others who are visiting the sites.

Experiences at the Vortexes range from negative to neutral to cosmic. Each site is a place of beauty, worth visiting for aesthetic reasons; so your time will not be wasted even if you do not have a life-altering reaction. See the Index on page 256 for Vortex sites that we recommend.

Scenic Drives

Airport Hill. This is a very easy short drive. The road is paved all the way. It takes you past one of the Sedona Vortex spots to the top of the mesa where the Sedona Airport is located, an excellent viewpoint from which to see Sedona and some of its famous landmarks. When you get to the top, turn left and go toward the cross. You will find a fine lookout point there. There are hiking trails on Airport Mesa. See Overlook Point Trails on page 160.

Boynton Canyon. If your time is limited and you want to see some of the redrock back country, this is a nice short drive over paved roads. See Boynton Canyon Trail on page 44 for directions.

Honanki Ruins. You will drive 16.2 miles *25.9 km* through some beautiful backcountry, allowing you to get away from town and see some great rock formations. At the end of the trip you will be within an easy walk from the best Indian ruin in the area. See page 108.

Oak Creek Vista. By taking this drive you will travel the length of Oak Creek Canyon, a beautiful scenic area. At the end of the drive you will be at a high point from which you can see the canyon, take a nature walk, sample some Indian jewelry and learn about the area. See page 14 for directions.

Schnebly Hill Road. This is a favorite six mile drive that takes you through some breathtaking redrock country to the top of a hill from where you can enjoy sweeping views. The road is paved for the first mile. The rest is unpaved and can be rough. See the Munds Mt. Trail page 152 for directions.

Index